Mother Time

Mother Time

Women, Aging, and Ethics

Edited by
Margaret Urban Walker

ROWMAN & LITTLEFIELD PUBLISHERS, INC.
Lanham • Boulder • New York • Oxford

ROWMAN & LITTLEFIELD PUBLISHERS, INC.

Published in the United States of America
by Rowman & Littlefield Publishers, Inc.
4720 Boston Way, Lanham, Maryland 20706

12 Hid's Copse Road
Cumnor Hill, Oxford OX2 9JJ, England

British Library Cataloguing in Publication Information Available

Library of Congress Cataloging-in-Publication Data

Mother time : women, aging, and ethics / edited by Margaret Urban
   Walker.
      p.   cm.
   Includes bibliographical references and index.
   ISBN 0-8476-9260-4 (cloth : alk. paper)
   1. Aged women—Social conditions.   2. Aging—Moral and ethical
aspects.   I. Walker, Margaret Urban, 1948–   .
HQ1061.M67   1999
305.26—dc21   98-45361
                                                                   CIP

Printed in the United States of America

∞ ™ The paper used in this publication meets the minimum requirements of
American National Standard for Information Sciences—Permanence of Paper for
Printed Library Materials, ANSI Z39.48–1984.

For
my sister Linda
and
my brother Frank
remembering how we cared

Contents

Acknowledgments

This project was made possible by a grant to the Ethics Center of the University of South Florida from the Commission on Aging with Dignity. The Ethics Center of the University of South Florida provided the material and staff support for all phases of the project. A working conference that allowed contributors to generate and refine ideas was hosted by the Center on February 20–22, 1998. The conference was funded by the Pettus-Crowe Foundation, with additional support from the Florida Department of Elder Affairs. On behalf of the Ethics Center, I thank these sponsors for seeing the importance of seeding discussion on ethics, women, and aging. The views expressed in the chapters, of course, represent only those of individual authors.

In organizing the project and editing the volume for the Ethics Center, I was fortunate to have the assistance and counsel of colleagues and staff at the Center. Peter French, director of the Center, initiated the project idea, followed its progress with keen interest, and remained enthusiastic in his support for it throughout. Peggy DesAutels, assistant director of the Center, provided advice, encouragement, and her characteristic good judgment throughout the project's development; she also served as a facilitator for sessions at the contributor's conference. Robin Fiore was indispensable at several key points in helping me move the project along; with Peggy, she was instrumental in designing a novel and successful conference format. Kathy Agne, the Center's office manager, was tireless and exact in working out all travel and local conference arrangements with participants. She brought generosity and good cheer to all phases of the project and conference, from providing Florida oranges from her own backyard tree for our guests, to preparing the final manuscript for publication with energy and care. Asuncion St. Clair efficiently organized the original invitations to contributors.

I am grateful for the complete support and enthusiasm of Maureen MacGrogan; one blessing of a scholar's life is having a good friend who's a great editor. Very special thanks go to Lynn Gemmell, our production editor, for steering us through a high-speed production process with a steady hand and a clear head.

Finally, I want to thank the contributors to this volume, who rose on short notice to a challenge to tread on what was for most of them new ground. It has been a pleasure to be instructed by their work. I have been rewarded not only by what they have done, but by the cooperation and camaraderie they have displayed throughout.

Margaret Walker
St. Petersburg
May 1998

Introduction

Margaret Urban Walker

*A*m I old? Am I "older"? When am I old, and how can I tell? Who determines this? How does my growing older affect my experience of myself? How does the evidence of my aging affect others' experiences of me? If I ask these questions, I ask about the reality and experience of aging. If I ask whether it makes any difference whether the person asking these questions is female rather than male, I broach the topic of gender and aging. And if I ask how the reality and the experience of aging affect understandings—women's own and others'—of women's selves and their moral agency, of their responsibilities to themselves and to others, and of others' responsibilities to them, I enter fairly novel territory. It is this largely unfamiliar terrain into which the authors in this volume were invited. Under significant constraint of time, they were asked to make initial and exploratory journeys into "ethical issues in women's aging."

The very notion that women's aging presents distinctly moral problems, both for women and about them, is not obvious. What is striking is how little this nexus of topics—women, aging, and ethics—has so far been explored. There are large literatures on aging in social science, gerontology, and medicine. In the past two decades empirical research specifically on women's aging has been growing in tandem with an elderly population in our society that is ever more disproportionately female at the close of the twentieth century. A small literature on ethics and aging has emerged in the past twenty years as well. It includes humanistic, cultural, and critical studies that explore the history, meaning, and societal construction and valuation of aging, as well as medical, legal, and ethical issues about health care and the end of life. Yet this ethical work has not much addressed situations and experiences of women, or the ways that gender in our society distinctively shapes the reality, experience, and meaning of aging.

Our project was to begin an exploration of assumptions, practices, and

1

policies that affect women's experiences in aging in morally significant ways. In an ethical investigation of women's aging, we need to identify ways aging affects women's moral standing in later life. A person's moral standing encompasses the respect, recognition, and concern that person elicits from others in her community, the responsibilities exacted from her and owed to her, and her own sense of value, selfhood, and responsibility. Risks to moral standing include indignity, harm, exploitation, neglect, or diminishment of self-respect, social participation, and a sense of one's value as a human being, a contributor to a community, or a citizen. Research on gender, race, economic standing, and disability has shown that obstacles for people disadvantaged on these bases are not only social and political but moral ones. Inferior or marginal social positions invariably entail and are expressed through diminished moral recognition and subordinate moral status. So it is, many of us argue in this volume, with aging, and with women's aging even more so. We need more work on the gendered effects of aging on moral standing for both men and women, and on interactions of aging with other factors that define social privilege or devaluation, putting women (and perhaps certain populations of men) at additional or distinct moral risk. At the same time, we sought to explore women's contributions to society, their capabilities in relationships, and the definitions of meaning and value through which they express their membership in communities, their citizenship, and their moral agency. We need to appreciate women's own resources for maintaining, repairing, or transforming agency and preserving dignity as aging changes women's experiences of their social places and moral identities.

Three working assumptions guided this project. First: Aging is not being sick or dying. Without denying the realities of illness, disability, and dependency that are common in advanced old age, and that many of us discuss below, ethical attention to aging must take a broader view than preoccupation with health care delivery and end-of-life choices. It takes a long time to grow old, and what one is doing during that long time in later life is aging. Aging is living through the process of physical change, shifting cultural expectations, and social and personal adjustments that later life brings. Attention to illness, disability, dependency, or incapacity in aging must be situated within that broader cultural and personal experience. Many challenges and adjustments that people confront in later life do not concern disease and disability. They concern changes in roles, self-understanding, appearance, expectations, values, economic resources, or social opportunities. Where aging does confront us with losses or changes in health or function, it is important to identify how these challenges are negotiated, and how they may be eased or aggravated, in a cultural context shaped by gender, class, race, and a presumption of "normal" abilities.

Second: There is every reason to assume that gendered roles, expectations, standards of appearance, ideals of self, and conceptions of responsibility play a large role in structuring women's diverse life experiences in aging. We know, after several decades of feminist scholarship, how pervasively gender shapes all aspects of life in our society. Even so, the burgeoning body of work in recent decades in women's studies and feminist theory has paid little attention to older women and women's aging. If we are tempted to think that gender matters less as women age, this might well be the dubious product of a cultural prejudice itself rooted in some of our society's gender norms: that since "womanliness" or "femininity" matters only in relatively young (that is, heterosexually "desirable" and reproductively capable) women, we can stop taking gender seriously as women age. This mistaken idea recycles a common negative stereotype of the "genderless" (read: sexless or neuter) older woman. It also embodies a deeply mistaken assumption about gender. Gender is by no means exclusively about sexual and reproductive matters. It encompasses the whole set of symbolic representations, material conditions, and social practices that define sexual divisions of labor, opportunity, recognition, responsibility, and reward.

Third: An explicitly ethical discourse about what aging means for women is important not only for women but for ethics. We might suspect that in a society where gender roles continue to shape many facets of men's and women's lives differently, representations of moral ideals, values, and responsibilities in ethics that include perspectives and life experiences of both men and women will differ from those that do not. A large body of work in feminist ethics has confirmed this. Ethical conceptions historically prominent and still dominant in our society and academic literatures have been almost entirely a product of men who are also otherwise privileged by race, ethnicity, class, and education. The conceptions they have authored often fail to reflect values and responsibilities involved in roles, tasks, and domains of life assigned to or associated with women. Moreover, if the "typical" or presumably "normal" moral agent in these discussions is not usually imagined as female, "he" is also not pictured as a child, an economically or educationally disadvantaged person, or a member of an historically devalued racial, ethnic, sexual, age, or other social group whose members have suffered discrimination, exclusion, or violence. And he is not usually thought of as someone who is ill, frail, or disabled. Work in feminist ethics has magnified the centrality of relations of dependence and interdependence, intimacy, friendship, trust, nurturance, care, and responsibility in human life. It has also tended to question the preeminence, or contest the prevailing interpretations, of publicly dominant moral and political ideals of autonomy, equality, impartiality, and rights. Many of our chapters try to show that when we do critical work in ethics to create a fuller picture of the ethical dimensions of women's experience in aging, we also reveal some things about the limits of some social, political, and moral ideals, and about alternative ways to interpret and apply them.

It will be obvious to readers that the contributors to this volume do not agree among themselves on a variety of questions that are raised herein, for example, on the value of autonomy as a central moral and social ideal, or on the degree to which an understanding of aging-as-decline is socially constructed. It will be obvious as well that the questions raised here are only a few of those that might be taken up. This collection does not pretend to represent all options for ethical thought within this barely defined field, or to touch many of the hugely varied experiences of women as they age with different burdens, resources, opportunities, and views of life. Our project here is intended as a sampler, an experiment, and an incitement to further, larger, and different discussions. We hope these chapters cause readers to think about, and inevitably to think beyond, what we have discussed here, and so to think about women's aging from an ethical perspective.

· *Part One* ·

Looks

· *1* ·

There Are No Old Venuses: Older Women's Responses to Their Aging Bodies

Frida Kerner Furman

*S*everal years ago I entered Julie's International Salon to get a haircut, little knowing that I would end up writing a book about the shop and its women patrons. Thus was born *Facing the Mirror: Older Women and Beauty Shop Culture.*[1] Why would a feminist social ethicist conduct an ethnographic study of a neighborhood beauty shop? I did not set out to do this study, but I was immediately attracted to the lively community that staff and customers have developed among themselves at Julie's. The clientele, made up mostly of older Jewish women, finds a safe moral space in this setting to discuss ailments, express affection and support, share lived experiences, and encourage each other along. A middle-aged Jewish feminist, I was challenged to confront the age-segregated nature of our society as I recognized my ignorance about older women, other than my close elderly relatives.

I decided that a beauty shop, with all its culturally trivialized connotations, was a worthy subject of ethical study, and so were the older women who regularly inhabit it during their weekly standing appointments but whose voices are virtually never heard in the public sphere. My decision initially was met with skepticism and stereotyping on the part of some colleagues, indicating the powerful extent to which even academics internalize cultural assumptions: the chair of a university grant committee wanted me to convince committee members that the subject matter of my study wasn't trivial; a sociologist surmised that older women's "blue hair" undoubtedly reflected a "time warp"; an academic friend felt I would find the women's conversations to be terribly boring. In the long run, I was awarded the grant, and the study came to address women's engagement in caring work, both within and outside the salon, but most centrally, women's concerns with their bodies, concerns tied to cultural constructions of femininity and aging. In this chapter I propose that women's responses to

7

their aging bodies are not always of a piece: shame and inadequacy frequently coexist with resistance to cultural ideals.

Listening and Observing at Julie's International Salon

The twenty women I interviewed in depth are white, mostly Jewish, and consider themselves middle class. They are between 65 and 85 years old and, save for one, are U.S.-born. I have every indication that they are heterosexual. Half of them are married, the other half widowed (only one participant was divorced in her youth and remains unmarried). Half completed high school; one-fourth, college; the rest never finished high school, as economic necessity demanded they get jobs to help their families.

Julie's International Salon is an "old-fashioned" beauty parlor, populated exclusively by female staff and customers. The shop's unpretentious style and frequently unkempt looks encourage sociability just as they level socioeconomic distinctions. Social interaction is marked by physical gestures of affection, group sociability, and an uninhibited display of humor. During the lengthy period of participant observation I conducted for this study, I witnessed on several occasions a "social drama," to use Victor Turner's term,[2] which remains stubbornly imprinted in my mind. While spending time at Julie's trying to understand the experiences of its older customers, I observed the behaviors of a woman I call Sheila and those around her.

> Sheila does not particularly call attention to herself since in most ways she looks like many of the other women: light brown hair, seventy-something, Jewish, average height and weight, reserved. One thing does stand out, though. She has very little hair; so little, in fact, that her light scalp makes itself conspicuous: it is largely bare, sprouting a few strands of hair here and there.
>
> On more than one occasion, I find myself fascinated, almost unable to withdraw my glance from the process of beautification involving this customer of Julie's International Salon. After being shampooed, Sheila sits at her beautician's station, where she has her hair rolled into a few curlers. Then she settles under an old-fashioned dryer in the back of the shop until returning to her hairdresser's station, magazine in hand. There she sits, uttering not a word, eyes fixed on the printed page. By now her beautician is working in silence at her side, completely engrossed in "combing out" a wiglet of the same hair color, which, perched on a plastic model, has also been set in rollers. The usual communication between beautician and customer is suspended during this time—no amiable chatter, no eye contact via the facing mirror. Other customers appear to ignore these proceedings. Once the wig is placed on Sheila's head and

the beautician begins to integrate her hair with the wig's, everything changes. Like magic, the magazine is set down, and the reserve between customer and hairdresser dissolves as they become engaged in friendly conversation, laughter, and eye contact. Normalcy, it seems, has been restored.

Turner believed that a social drama entails a temporary breach in the expected, normalized order of social relations, often enacted in symbolic terms; the drama is eventually resolved when the alienated social actors are reintegrated into the social structure. Such dramas allow us to investigate sociocultural norms and relations as they are embedded in actual social processes. I use this dynamic episode to enter a discussion of older women's perspectives on their aging bodies, which later in the chapter will rely far more on their reflections as opposed to their actions.

Older Women's Bodies: Discourses of Shame and Resistance

Sheila, her beautician, and other customers implicitly agree to leave unacknowledged the reality of her hair loss by suspending normal social exchange while that reality is visually inescapable. Sheila and her hairdresser engage in "civil inattention"[3] as a way of circumventing a painful truth: Sheila is no longer culturally perceived as a whole woman when her actual head, with its visible scalp, is fully exposed. While hair loss may be commonplace among men, whatever injuries to self-esteem that may carry for the individual man, hair loss for a woman signals a powerful transgression against the cultural norms of femininity.

Anthropological studies suggest that across time and cultures, the female head has been eroticized by the male gaze. Women's hair, in particular, has come to be seen as a mark of fertility or generativity—in short, of sexuality.[4] In our society, as women age, their gray hair signals the diminution if not the loss of sexual appeal, a central measure of women's social value. That may explain the popularity of hair coloring for graying women at Julie's and countless other hair salons. Hair loss is harder to conceal, and hence its threat to feminine identity is considered more serious. While I interview Shelley, 82, for example, she tells me, soto voce, that she has a "problem" with her hair: there is a balding spot at the back of her head. Her beautician's job is to hide it as well as possible.

As an outsider to Julie's International Salon, the drama around Sheila is fascinating to me, including the fact that customers seem to simply ignore the whole proceedings; or perhaps they self-consciously look away. When

Sheila's scalp is revealed in its virtual nakedness, she may be perceived by onlookers as a threat in several ways. Other older women may imagine that some day their "problem" with hair loss may become the disaster now inscribed on Sheila's head: almost no hair whatsoever. Looking away may be a way that some women protect themselves from a possible future of unredeemed feminine failure due to old age. Women might see themselves in a continuum with Sheila and hence distance themselves from her in order to see themselves as still young enough to "pass" as feminine subjects. Alternatively, Sheila may well perceive herself and be perceived by others as representing a difference *in kind* vis-à-vis her hair loss: this is not hair loss; this is baldness. As such, she becomes an Other. Sheila's almost bald head may connote the ravages of cancer treatments. Or it may be reminiscent, especially for Jewish spectators, of the coercive practices of the Nazi concentration camps, where all inmates had their heads shaved. I wonder what psychological links might be drawn between that form of universal depersonalization and of female defeminization—used to disrupt normal personal identity—and the "natural" loss of hair as a result of aging or disease. In all cases the individual woman is deprived of ordinariness, the ability to pass as just another woman. And she becomes stigmatized.

A question worth pondering is whether the stigma culturally applied to women like Sheila also applies to other older women by virtue of their age, as they lose the ability to conform to dominant standards of femininity. Such stigma results not from changes in the body as such, but from social constructions that read the older female body in negative ways. Parallel observations may be drawn from work in disability studies, which can usefully extend feminist theory when interpreting the experiences and representations of older women.

Feminist analysis of femininity and its oppressive norms for women has been useful in deconstructing power relations that maintain women's subordination. Women's failures to meet feminine body ideals cause harm to women throughout the life cycle, but perhaps most markedly in older age. For as women age, many can no longer represent in their bodies—and not only in the hair of their heads—some important feminine qualities, such as sexual attractiveness, youth, and slenderness. Such losses often result in women's experience of shame, which denotes their perceived failure in meeting "disciplinary practices of femininity."[5] In addition, I would suggest, such shame reflects a transgression of internalized cultural standards of bodily acceptability, which Susan Wendell calls "disciplinary practices of physical normality"[6]—including health, appearance, and performance.

When I observed Sheila, I had a hard time looking away. As David

Mitchell and Sharon Snyder point out, responses to physical difference frequently involve a binary process of fascination and repulsion.[7] This is consistent with the dualistic tendency in the West, both ancient and modern, of thinking in dichotomous ways—body/soul, reason/emotion—and of the current cultural desire, according to Lennard Davis, to "split bodies into two immutable categories—whole and incomplete, abled and disabled, normal and abnormal, functional and dysfunctional. . . . In this same primitive vein, culture tends to split bodies into good and bad parts. There are cultural norms considered good and others considered bad . . . not masculine or feminine enough, not enough or too much hair on the head or other parts of the body. . . ."[8] To complement the "bad" inventory, I would add: not young-looking enough, that is, looking old, especially if one is a woman; for youth and beauty go hand in hand in our cultural construction of femininity.

From the perspective of those who embody dominant cultural norms, the old represent a disruption of the visual field.[9] Like others who are classed as abnormal or disabled, the old come to be seen and evaluated as less-than. This may be why a number of women I talk to at Julie's claim to be "middle-aged" or "older," not "old," and why so many long to continue looking younger than their years as long as possible. Most of these women are active and vital; their impairment is socially constructed: it consists of their incapacity to look young and to be considered attractive—and hence their inability to be seen and valued.

Sheila is undoubtedly aware of other people's stares, of the implicit judgment that comes from being watched and evaluated from the "empowered position of the norm,"[10] from the perspective of the nonbald women at Julie's who still retain their hair and thus some measure of feminine acceptability. I see her responding in a couple of ways. On the one hand, Sheila expresses shame when she averts her glance from beautician and customers, fixes her gaze on her magazine, and avoids conversation while her scalp is exposed. Others endorse her shame via the universal silence that accompanies her beautification/"normalization" ritual.[11] When her shame is repaired by her wig. Sheila engages in typical salon social interchange; she is reintegrated into salon life and becomes, once again, one of the "beauty shop friends." On the other hand, Sheila must be seen as more than a victim of cultural conventions and hegemonic practices. She also exercises agency by deflecting her gaze and hence signaling appropriate behavior to those around her. She controls social exchange in a way that may feel safe and self-protective for her, regardless of how others may wish to relate to her.

Perhaps older women live in "double consciousness," to use W. E. B. Du Bois's notion that an oppressed group sees reality both through internalized perspectives of the dominant culture and through an alternative vision of its own.[12] While older women as a group cannot be considered oppressed in the same ways as the African Americans who gave rise to Du Bois's insight, I believe that they constitute a marginalized group frequently made invisible through the tools of cultural imperialism.[13] These include being subjected not only to the *male* gaze, but also to the gaze of *youth*, for as a society we increasingly normalize youth as we stigmatize old age. Some Jewish women—those who are thought to "look Jewish"[14]—are subjected to the gaze of the *dominant culture*, as well, which still evaluates "ethnic looks" from the perspective of nonethnic whiteness. Older women also are seen, and see themselves, from the perspective of *physical normality*, those body ideals generated and maintained by the nondisabled that include norms of appearance but also of physical and mental health, energy, strength, mobility, and proper control.[15]

Responses to an Aging Body: Shame

Sheila reveals shame because she has so little hair. Her head represents her failure to meet multiple social expectations—that she look feminine, that she look young, that she look "normal." Some women I interviewed report feeling shame about their weight, others about facial lines. Marny, a tall, elegant woman of 64, candidly expresses her feelings in response to her weight gain: "I feel shame and disgust, no doubt about it. . . . I never really had a weight problem until this old age business of being fat. That kills me. I feel considerably overweight." As she compares her current looks with a younger picture of herself, Marny says, "I wouldn't consider myself good-looking any more, and that has to do with my age; I think I look nice-looking. Good-looking is really attractive, and that's why I said, 'nice-looking.' " In this reading, older women like herself cannot be "really attractive." Marny struggles semantically as she measures her appearance against an internalized scale of female beauty.

Sylvia's self-esteem is injured because she sees herself as both fat and unattractively lined. "The face, the face I'm ashamed [of]," she declares in her accented English. "Yes, I'm ashamed, I know. I'm ashamed of my face. Yes." I show her a Polaroid photo I have taken of her and ask her what she sees. "Old, old, okay? It bothers me!" she exclaims. "I look a lot older than my grandmother [did at my age—77], okay? And she did not look that old, okay?" She tries to understand why this is: Is it the stress involved in caring for her ailing husband that has caused the lines? Is it genes? She tries to gain some sort of control over a situation about which she feels helpless and pained. At another time she tells me she does not like herself in older age because "I don't look good. I'm too small to be fat."

Evelyn, 77, anguishes over the changes she notes upon her face: "I can't stand the person that I see when I look [at myself]," she says, as she catalogues a nose that appears to have grown larger, eyes that seem to have become smaller, skin that is now wrinkled. In addition, some years ago, she developed Bell's palsy. This condition affects the nerves on the right side of her face, slightly pulling up her lip on that side, altering the aperture of the eye by a small amount; at least that's how it looks to this observer. She feels self-conscious and ashamed about her face now. "I look in the mirror and Lord, if there's a God in heaven, he sure punished me. He gave me my share of distortion." From Evelyn's perspective, she has failed in two ways—in regards to both femininity and body normality. The "distortion" in her face prevents her from living in her body unselfconsciously; rather, it becomes her defining characteristic, subject not only to aesthetic but also to moral judgment. As Madonne Miner argues, "Female bodies, like bodies of color, homosexual bodies, *and* disabled bodies, are positioned culturally so as not to forget their embodiment,"[16] a view echoed by Iris Marion Young: "When the dominant culture defines some groups as different, as the Other, the members of those groups are imprisoned in their bodies."[17] Evelyn's response to her face is that of utter shame and humiliation, to the point that often she does not want to leave her house.

Sadie's strategy in coping with physical changes is to deny them. At age 80 she looks at a photo when she was 32 or 33. "I don't think I look too different. I really don't because my features are about the same. . . . I don't think I've changed that much. I don't think I look much older."

The poet and writer Nancy Mairs confides, "I was never a beautiful woman, and for that reason I've spent most of my life (together with probably at least 95 percent of the female population of the United States) suffering from the shame of falling short of an unattainable standard." Now that she has multiple sclerosis, Mairs says, "I have an additional reason to feel shame for my body, less explicitly connected with its sexuality: it is a crippled body . . . measured by the standards of physical desirability erected for every body in our world."[18] Mairs feels shame, she tells the reader, because of what she is—female and disabled—and not because of something she has done or could have done,[19] a perspective on shame supported by Sandra Bartky: "Shame involves the distressed apprehension of oneself as a lesser creature. . . . [It] is called forth by the apprehension of some serious flaw in the self."[20]

To listen even casually to women's conversations about their bodies at Julie's means to hear self-deprecatory comments such as these: "I think I look like a pig. I've been eating a lot this week," says Svetlana. "I look at myself in the mirror and I see a witch," retorts Blanche. In a similar vein, when Beatrice looks at a Polaroid photo I have just taken of her, she exclaims in distress, "I look like a witch!" How far must the feminine consciousness travel from the perception that one *looks* like a pig or like a witch to the conviction that one *is* a pig or a witch?

Sylvia tells me, "When a woman gets old, she hates herself." Sylvia is the only study participant with such a categorically negative attitude. Yet it communicates the loss of value many older women experience; it exposes the naked truth that in our society "there are no old Venuses."[21] Beauty, and hence social worth and approval, are reserved for the young.

Of course, as Mairs suggests, women's negative judgments of their bodies begin much earlier in life as they measure their own inadequacies against cultural ideals. Some study participants are aware of the sources of their feminine ideals: fashion magazines, movie stars, fashion designers. Lucy, for example, tells me, "In my eyes I have to look as close to perfect as I can, or as close to perfect as I see perfection, which may not be as you see it. . . . I know what's going to look good and I know what isn't." Lucy's images are informed by twenty years of selling Anne Klein fashions.

Body size has been a problem for several women through most of their lives; they have always seen themselves as too large or too tall. In this way they reveal the cultural tendency to split the body into good and bad parts, alluded to earlier; for women the emphasis all too often is to emphasize the bad. Alice agonized about her size even as a child: "I always wanted to be tiny." Marny says, "I remember thinking that I hoped [my daughters] wouldn't be as tall as me or taller, and I hope they don't have kinky hair. And I got my wishes." When saleswomen admire her height and her capacity to "carry" clothes, she complains, "I don't want to be tall. I want to be small." Reva tells me, "I always felt too big, and when I was in school, no matter how smart I was, I always had to sit in the back because they couldn't see." In time she was able to turn her sense of inadequacy into a strength, however: "But I have found: walk tall. There is a presence about you. I had some sort of a confidence maybe because I was a big woman. . . . I had that commanding air about me." By reinterpreting the meaning of her height, Reva begins to combat received cultural meanings; she engages in the process of resistance, of reclaiming her own agency.

Responses to an Aging Body: Resistance

Women in this study resist in various ways cultural body norms, both regarding femininity and normality. Two women I interview engage in resistance through a critical analysis of cultural ideals for the female body. Merle, for example, recognizes the coercive nature of the norm of thinness as she comments on cultural expectations: "I was always a slim person. I'm heavier now than in my younger times. But you are not [seen as] a good-looking person unless you're thin, like a coat hanger." Martha advances a critique of the advertising industry, which she believes is setting the standards of

> what is considered to be attractive, and thin seems to be the "in" thing. This is really abnormal. Most people are a variety of different weights and built differently. Some are big-boned, and some are small, and so on. But if you can't fit into that size four or six or even two. . . . But those are the standards we seem to have now. But they're artificial. Nobody really *looks* that way.

Armed with this awareness, Martha is more readily able to accept her body and its changes in ways that escape other older women, who have internalized more deeply cultural representations that idealize feminine beauty in a body perpetually thin and young.

The acceptance of an older body—heavier, slower, sometimes sagging, and frequently sporting a lined face and graying hair—is not automatic. Rather, it is achieved through processes of resistance against the dominant culture that denigrates women's older bodies as it makes them invisible. Some women agree that the older body is unattractive and inadequate; they attempt to look younger through various interventions, such as coloring their hair. Whether this act is capitulation or resistance is not always clear, however. A woman I call Fay colors her hair regularly. Though now retired, this practice began while she worked in the business world, the competitive nature of which "demands that women look their best." Her work entailed a lot of contact with the public, "who feel confident if I feel confident." It was clothes and grooming, including regular hair dyes, that gave her this confidence. From her vantage point, by engaging in such feminine practices she claimed some authority for herself. Such self-conscious understanding and manipulation of the system to advance her own interests do constitute a type of agency, as they lead to Fay's success. In the long run, however, the system is left unchanged by this sort of individualistic instrumentalism.

Some women accept their changed bodies with grace, others with some resignation. Anna declares with feeling, "Whatever you see is me." Sara says, "I realized that I don't look the way I used to look, and that can't be helped. That cannot be helped." Dori concedes that as she's grown older she's gotten better at accepting limitations: "Your attitude changes. You don't expect things to be done rapidly as they used to be, from your emotions to your movements."

Martha has come to accept her aging face: "Well, I'm showing time, showing physical changes. . . . I don't really like it, but I don't really feel as if it's the worst thing in the world. It's just a natural process." Significantly, she adds, "I have lines in my face, yes. I think they are character lines. I don't really think they're necessarily detractors." Calling her wrinkles "character lines" undermines a negative reading of them. She thereby resists a discourse that would render her unattractive in relation to her face. Lucy discusses her lines in a similar manner: "I earned every one of them." Ideally she would love to get rid of them but recognizes that age should show somewhere in the body, so she advises acceptance: "Hey, this is what it is." Reva, for her part, refers to her wrinkles as "my stripes, my service stripes," adding another image that marks wrinkles as signs of accomplishment, contesting their more frequent association with decrepitude or decline.

A decisive gesture of resistance against normalizing practices of femininity is the universal rejection of cosmetic surgery by the customers of Julie's International Salon. For some women, fear is one concern preventing them from putting themselves under the surgeon's knife. But often their refusal goes beyond fear. Sadie, for example, is adamant when she declares, "I think these women are nuts. What they are doing to their bodies and faces . . . I don't want to touch my face. . . . You can't take your skin and just play around with it. It wouldn't be healthy for the body or my face. . . . Why monkey around with your own body?" Sadie rejects cosmetic surgery because it threatens her embodied personal integrity. A similar sentiment is expressed by Teri, who says, "Even if I could afford it, I wouldn't spend my money for that. This is life. This is the way it's supposed to be and you're just going against your being. . . . Here I am, take me or leave me. What you see is what you get!" Concerned about their bodily well-being, these and other women opt to "look their age" rather than to regain their more youthful, feminine looks via surgery. This refusal could serve as a collective strategy by speaking to the power of women as consumers to influence market conditions.[22]

I had occasion to observe a number of collective efforts of resistance during my involvement in participant observation at Julie's. These are often expressed through seemingly self-deprecating humor, as when women laugh together at their double chins—"turkey necks," as they often call them—or at their seemingly advanced stages of pregnancy, judging by the size of their bellies. In my view these moments of collective mirth contest the social unacceptability of women's aging, the loss of youthful bodies and feminine attractiveness, by bonding women around the inevitability of aging. This form of humor pokes fun at our society's unrealistic expectations that women remain forever the icons of youthful beauty and sexuality.

Resistance presents itself in yet another manner, namely, in the articulation of alternative values to those espoused by the norms of femininity. Clara gives us a particularly moving rendition of choosing inner personal qualities over external appearance as a measure of human worth.

> Well, personally, I think anyone who becomes a fanatic about her looks has lost a great deal of other things on the way. Instead of a model, a doll, a little robot, a perfect little woman, she's lost sight of the fact that first she's a human being, and a woman, and a person. And what has she given to the world? . . . Who's going to look at her? Does she care? . . . Would you care? . . . At this point in my life, I'm relaxing and it's fine, no big deal. I wear a size fourteen, instead of a ten. I don't really care anymore. Really. With age comes—you're slowing down, you're taking life easier. You have to slow down because your body doesn't let you accelerate the way it did before. . . . Gradually, gradually, you slow down. Your body slows down. And who really cares? But give me the person that I can talk to. That's the person, I don't care if your nose is long or short. Give me the person. That's the important part.

Clara's narrative sides with women's inner life, dignity, and agency, in clear opposition to dominant, middle-class cultural feminine ideals. Other study participants agree. Martha believes that there are advantages to becoming older.

> Oh, definitely . . . I think you do get a perspective you haven't had previously. There are things that are important in one period of life [that] are no longer important. And there is a freedom you have. You don't have that many obligations. . . . You can, probably for once in your life, decide what you want. . . . You can make your own decisions and you can either make yourself happy or you can make yourself upset. But you do have choices. . . . And getting back to the issue of attractiveness . . . even that doesn't become as important, in terms of other people. I find that a lot of the older people who show a lot of the age, they keep

going through things. They're having trouble with their eyes, and their cataracts removed, and so on. And they're losing a great amount of weight because of illness and so on. But they're loved for themselves. People are very accepting. They are their friend. And they're not measuring, you know, whether or not you're beautiful or you have beautiful clothes. It doesn't matter.

Martha's lived experience, her own struggles with illness and limitation, and her observation of those around her, present her with a way, alternative to those of the dominant culture, of seeing and evaluating the old. She feels love, not disdain, for those in ripe old age who perhaps have grown dependent, may look old, but remain radiant in their individuality and personal integrity. Martha herself is not free of internalized body ideals. She wishes she were thinner and is pleased that her facial lines are not overly pronounced. But her life among her same-age peers has given her a countervailing perspective on who the old are, one that rejects surface readings of the body and appreciates the inner being. In short, she views her reality with a kind of double vision.

Lucy feels she's gotten better with age "in every way. . . . I think you grow as you get older." "*Everything* gets better as you get older?" I ask her, a bit incredulous. "Sure, because I have to tell you, if it isn't, you are in deep shit." Later on we talk about how attitude affects our vantage point. "Isn't everything attitude? You know, a cup is half empty or half full; it's one or the other. Why does it have to be half empty? Why not half full?" This kind of acceptance of things as they are is characteristic of Lucy. For example, health is "not a major problem," she tells me, "because it's an 'is' and I can't control it." I ask her if there are some negative things associated with getting older, in addition to the positive things she has already noted. "What? What's negative?" she asks a bit impatiently. "Well, I don't know what your health situation is," I tell her, "but I suppose I mean aches and pains and illness." She puts me in my place when she asks, rather rhetorically, "Are you trying to tell me that you don't have any aches and pains?" "I do," I reply earnestly, "but I think it gets worse and increases as one gets older." "That's not the issue," she retorts. "The issue is you have them when you're younger, as well as when you're older. Except that when you're older you realize you had them when you were younger."

I find Lucy's perspective to be interesting and provocative. It opens up a fresh angle of vision into the situation. Lucy is de facto *normalizing* old age by contesting its radical difference from youth or middle age. In doing this she is rejecting the dominant culture's attempt to segment the life trajectory into discreet stages, each characterized by unique experiences. I believe in doing this she questions the assumption that there is any significant difference between adulthood and old age. She is wanting to move old age from margin to center, to destabilize the notion that older people are Others by virtue of ill health, or that old age is a decline from something more important.[23] In fact, she elevates old age by arguing that, in fact, everything gets *better* in older age.

While Lucy's is decidedly a minority view among the customers of Julie's International Salon, she points the way to an oppositional stance against oppressive cultural norms. Clara and Martha, in their own ways, have engaged in parallel stances. All three ground their views on their own experiences of older age, and their reflections upon those experiences. It is these experiences, shared sometimes with older people, that provide them with an alternative vision from the dominant culture's, which, as we have seen, frequently silences older women through shame.

Listening to Older Women Speak Out

David Maitland argues that as people grow older, they come to form part of a counterculture, one that passes judgment on sociocultural values, given their detachment from dominant cultural attitudes.[24] Given my experience at Julie's International Salon, I don't think older people as a whole are detached in this manner, and certainly not from all dominant values. But I believe older people have the capacity for this "vocation," as Maitland calls it. I am not convinced their capacity to critique devolves from "detachment"; rather, it comes from experience, reflection, and perspective developed over a long life. In like manner, Susan Wendell suggests that it is the *experience* of disability that places people with disabilities "in a better position to notice and criticize cultural myths about the body and mind."[25] A critical question becomes how to make the personal the political in this regard, how to bring to life Maitland's counterculture to combat older women's shame and unsettle the dominant culture's adulation of youth and youthful sexuality as central measures of women's worth. It may involve strategies for regarding the older woman as an "outsider within" the dominant culture, to use Patricia Hill Collins's term.[26]

"Speaking out loud," writes Nancy Mairs, "is an antidote to shame. . . . I can subvert its power, I've found, by acknowledging who I am, shame and all, and, in doing so, raising what was hidden, dark, secret about my life into the plain light of shared human experience."[27] Mairs has done these things by writing and speaking about being a woman living with multiple sclerosis. Poet and essayist Audre Lorde wrote, "My work is to inhabit the silences with which I have lived and fill them with myself until they have the sounds of brightest day and the loudest thunder. . . . I am learning to speak my pieces, to inject into the living world my convictions of what is necessary and what I think is important without concern (of the enervating kind) for whether or not it is understood, tolerated, correct or heard before."[28] She wrote these words after undergoing a mastectomy as a way to deal with that trauma, but also to call into question the dominant ideals of femininity that place greater importance on a woman's appearance than on her physical health or inner experience.

It has been encouraging to see publications of older women's writings in recent years, which of course are an important avenue for making their voices heard.[29] For my part I have chosen to listen to the voices of ordinary older women, those who neither write nor publish but whose experiences of shame and gestures of resistance can serve as warnings and models, respectively, concerning the work of criticism and empowerment still before us. "Speaking out assumes prerogative," says legal theorist Margaret Montoya. "Speaking out is an exercise of privilege. Speaking out takes practice."[30] Montoya calls the disempowered to speak out as a way of inserting themselves into social power. I see my work as an occasion for ordinary older women, who are typically absent from public discourse, to speak out and to be listened to, for their insights to illumine our own, and for their experiences to teach us something about their lives, the social world as they see it, and the constraints and possibilities shaping their moral agency. Listening to older women as they speak out has provided me with an opportunity for cultural criticism and social ethical analysis. Who says a beauty shop is a morally trivial space?

Notes

1. Frida Kerner Furman, *Facing the Mirror: Older Women and Beauty Shop Culture* (New York: Routledge, 1997).

2. Victor Turner, *Dramas, Fields, and Metaphors: Symbolic Action in Human Society* (Ithaca: Cornell University Press, 1974), ch. 1.

3. Erving Goffman, *Behavior in Public Places* (New York: Free Press, 1963).

4. See, for example, Howard Eilberg-Schwartz and Wendy Doniger, eds., *Off with Her Head! The Denial of Women's Identity in Myth, Religion, and Culture* (Berkeley: University of California Press, 1995).

5. Sandra Lee Bartky, *Femininity and Domination: Studies in the Phenomenology of Oppression* (New York: Routledge, 1990), ch. 5.

6. Susan Wendell, *The Rejected Body: Feminist Philosophical Reflections on Disability* (New York: Routledge, 1996), ch. 4.

7. David T. Mitchell and Sharon L. Snyder, "Introduction: Disability Studies and the Double Bind of Representation," in *The Body and Physical Difference: Discourses on Disability*, ed. David T. Mitchell and Sharon L. Snyder (Ann Arbor: University of Michigan Press, 1997), 15.

8. Lennard J. Davis, "Nude Venuses, Medusa's Body, and Phantom Limbs: Disability and Visuality," in *The Body and Physical Difference: Discourses on Disability*, ed. David T. Mitchell and Sharon L. Snyder (Ann Arbor: University of Michigan Press, 1997), 53. For a discussion of the development of the concept of normality in the West in the past 150 years, see Ian Hacking, "Normal People," in *Modes of Thought: Explorations in Culture and Cognition*, ed. David R. Olson and Nancy Torrance (Cambridge: Cambridge University Press, 1996), 59–71.

9. Davis, "Nude Venuses," 53.

10. Davis, "Nude Venuses," 53.

11. On normalization, see Susan Bordo, *Unbearable Weight: Feminism, Western Culture, and the Body* (Berkeley: University of California Press, 1993).

12. W. E. B. Du Bois, *The Souls of Black Folk* (New York: Penguin Books, 1989), ch. 1.

13. See Iris Marion Young, *Justice and the Politics of Difference* (Princeton: Princeton University Press, 1990), 58–61.

14. On "Jewish looks," see Furman, *Facing the Mirror*, 75–85.

15. Wendell, *The Rejected Body*, 86.

16. Madonne Miner, "Making up the Stories as We Go Along," in *The Body and Physical Difference: Discourses on Disability*, ed. David T. Mitchell and Sharon L. Snyder (Ann Arbor: University of Michigan Press, 1997), 292–93.

17. Young, *Justice and the Politics of Difference*, 123.

18. Nancy Mairs, *Carnal Acts: Essays* (New York: HarperCollins, 1990), 87, 86.

19. Mairs, *Carnal Acts*, 91.

20. Bartky, *Femininity and Domination*, 87.

21. Davis, "Nude Venuses," 58.

22. Kathryn Pauly Morgan, "Women and the Knife: Cosmetic Surgery and the Colonization of Women's Bodies," *Hypatia* 6, no. 3 (Fall 1991): 42.

23. For an extended discussion of the last assumption, see Margaret Morganroth Gullette, *Declining to Decline: Cultural Combat and the Politics of the Midlife* (Charlottesville: University Press of Virginia, 1997).

24. David Maitland, *Aging As Counterculture: A Vocation for the Later Years* (New York: Pilgrim Press, 1991).

25. Wendell, *The Rejected Body*, 69.

26. Patricia Hill Collins, "Learning from the Outsider Within: The Sociological Significance of Black Feminist Thought," *Social Problems* 33, no. 6 (1986): 14–32.

27. Mairs, *Carnal Acts*, 91, 92.

28. Audre Lorde, *The Cancer Journals* (San Francisco: Aunt Lute Books, 1980), 40, 48.

29. See, for example, Jo Alexander, Lisa Domitrovich, Margarita Donnelly, and Cheryl McLean, eds., *Women and Aging: An Anthology by Women* (Corvallis, Oreg.: Calyx Books, 1986); Janet Ford and Ruth Sinclair, *Sixty Years On: Women Talk about Old Age* (London: Women's Press, 1987); Sandra Haldeman Martz, ed., *When I Am an Old Woman I Shall Wear Purple* (Watsonville, Calif.: Papier-Mache Press, 1991); Peggy Downes, Patricia Faul, Virginia Mudd, and Ilene Tuttle, eds., *The New Older Woman: A Dialogue for the Coming Century* (Berkeley, Calif.: Celestial Arts, 1996); Marilyn Pearsall, ed., *The Other within Us: Feminist Explorations of Women and Aging* (Boulder, Colo.: Westview Press, 1997).

30. Margaret E. Montoya, "*Máscaras, Trenzas, y Greñas*: Un/masking the Self While Un/braiding Latina Stories and Legal Discourse," in *Beyond Portia: Women, Law, and Literature in the United States*, ed. Jacqueline St. Joan and Annette Bennington McElhiney (Boston: Northeastern University Press, 1997), 284.

· 2 ·

Miroir, Mémoire, Mirage:
Appearance, Aging, and Women

Diana Tietjens Meyers

There is nothing lovely about the sight of me. I have been taught that firm and unlined is beautiful. Shall I try to learn to love what I am left with? I wonder. It would be easier to resolve never again to look into a full-length mirror.

—Doris Grumbach, 77

Straddled hands and knees over the silvered glass I caught sight of my face. Stopped shocked. I watched the crawling creature warily. . . . This was not me.

—Janet Burroway, 211

The trick has always been to look only selectively into the mirror. To see the bright eyes, the shining hair, the whispered print of the blouse falling open to reveal soft tanned cleavage, the shapely curve of a taut muscular calf.

—Pam Houston, 151[1]

*A*ctually, it's far from easy to resolve never to look in a mirror. Reflecting surfaces are everywhere—in our homes, on the streets, in stores, restaurants, and theaters. Presumably, decorators install mirrors not only because they create illusions of greater space but also because many people enjoy glimpsing themselves or feel the need to glimpse themselves at frequent intervals. Mirror junkies find that anxiety—am I still there? do I look okay?—readily gives way to relief, if not satisfaction—there I am again, not too bad. Women, the history of Euro-American art demonstrates, have a special symbolic relation to mirrors.

In this chapter, I shall be concerned with an experience familiar to

23

many aging women—meeting a stranger in the mirror. Instead of encountering the face one has identified with, however ambivalently, one confronts an alien image. This face is disconnected from one's sense of self—it's not the face with which one entered long-standing, treasured interpersonal relationships and embarked on valued, enduring projects; it doesn't reflect one's continuing zest for life. Worse, it is an object of scorn and a constant reminder of mortality. With this "death mask vivant" permanently sealed in place, women feel shortchanged and stuck. Social possibilities dry up. Economic opportunities are cut off. Self-esteem plummets.

My question is how women can live with this reflected phantasm. And I don't mean grieving and enduring—soldiering on. I mean "live" in the richest sense of the term—appreciating, enjoying, even loving this time-altered visage. How can we salvage our face-esteem? How can we embrace the stranger in the mirror?

In pursuing these questions, I develop three main lines of thought. First, I present some strategies used by women who have undergone cosmetic surgery to reconnect with their radically transformed faces, and I explore parallel strategies that aging women might adopt. Second, I critique three assumptions about the self, the expressivity of faces, and the nature of beauty that undergird the strategies I present in the first section. After showing how these commonplace assumptions conspire against aging women, I propose some ways in which they could be modified to accommodate women's lifelong needs. Finally, I take up the symbolic association between death and the changes women's faces undergo as they age. It is important, I urge, for feminists to challenge this misogynist symbolism.

Miss Lonelyhearts' Guide to Identifying with the Stranger in the Mirror

In trying to think about how aging women might assimilate their changing appearance, I thought I might find some clues in the cosmetic surgery literature. Many aging women find it impossible to identify with the face they see in the mirror. Similarly, people who undergo cosmetic surgery on their faces emerge from their bandages and find a stranger returning their gaze from the mirror. Pursuing this avenue of inquiry, I examined Kathy Davis's account of the experience of a woman, Diana, who became the target of merciless teasing and harassment because of her protruding teeth and who submitted to a major surgical procedure and endured a long, severely painful recovery to correct this problem. Apparently, the operation changed Diana's face so dramatically that some colleagues at the school where she taught did not recognize her afterwards.

I was struck by a number of parallels between Diana's testimony and some of the excerpts from interviews with the aging clients of a beauty parlor that Frida Furman reports in her book, *Facing the Mirror*. First, these women condemn their appearance in hyperbolic terms. For example, Diana and one of Furman's subjects, Evelyn, invoke metaphors of congenital disability to symbolize their assessment of their appearance:

Diana: "I looked retarded" (Davis 1995, 100).

Evelyn: "I look like a birth defect" (Furman 1997, 95).

Whatever we may think about the ableist prejudices that undergird these tropes, these two women clearly mean to convey an absolute horror at their own appearance, a horror that I find poignant. A second similarity between Diana and Furman's subjects is their synecdochic psychology—their tendency to fixate on a single flaw and to condense the whole monstrous problem into that flaw (Furman 1997, 57; Davis 1995, 99–100). By localizing all of their disaffection with their appearance in a single facial feature, they shrink their problem to manageable proportions, but they vastly exaggerate the hideousness of that feature. Third, women who have had cosmetic surgery, as well as aging women, affirm continuity through physical change by appealing to an inner, unchanged, attractive self. Diana declares that her postoperative self is the same as her childhood self—a self that was "petted and hugged" (Davis 1995, 107). Similarly, when asked to respond to a recently taken photograph of herself, one of Furman's subjects, Clara, declares, "I see an old lady. . . . [But] I just brush it off. It isn't me. Because the me is inside, here [pointing to her chest]. And I'm still younger than springtime" (Furman 1997, 105). Through cosmetic surgery, Diana regains a face that fits her inner nature. Through passing time, Clara loses the face that fit her inner nature. But both are convinced that they have a core self that persists and that is well- or ill-represented by their outward appearance.

Davis's study of women who choose cosmetic surgery and Furman's study of elderly women converge on several themes: (1) the enormity of the perceived appearance problem, (2) the containment of dissatisfaction by concentrating it on one "ghastly" flaw, (3) the affirmation of an ongoing core self that is not disavowed, and (4) the complaint that an unattractive face conceals a likable self. In light of these overlapping approaches to self-understanding, I wondered whether Diana's strategies for coming to terms with and coming to identify with her surgically reconstructed, initially alien face might provide clues about strategies that could be deployed to acclimate oneself to a face gone strange as a result of aging. Diana's three principal strategies are externalizing identity continuity, affirming the congruence between her strange face and her authentic identity, and selective self-alienation. As I present these strategies, I consider how they might be adapted to aging women's situation. Then I point out how pioneering aging theorist Margaret Morganroth Gullette uses these very strategies to come to terms with her own aging appearance.

To offset her difficulty recognizing the face in the mirror as her own, Diana cites two kinds of constancy—her personality and her friendships—and she explains the latter in terms of the former. People, she says, always liked or disliked her for her personality, not for her appearance, and so her improved appearance hasn't made any difference to her close interpersonal ties (Davis 1995, 111). Telling herself that she has changed only superficially, Diana finds her surgically reconstructed face less disorienting.

Many of Furman's subjects also insist that their inner self persists despite the changes their bodies have undergone. But, as people age, the continuity of their relationships becomes increasingly tenuous (for insightful and moving discussion of this problem, see Sandra Lee Bartky's chapter 4 in this volume). Friends and family members may relocate, or one may move away oneself. The older one gets, the more likely it is that friends and family members will die. Age segregation in residences, lifestyles, and attitudes commonly blocks the formation of lasting, intimate intergenerational relationships. Consequently, many aging women won't find it easy to minimize the importance of their changed appearance by projecting their sense of inner continuity and self-worth onto a stable and valued social network. Nevertheless, one can imagine how women might collectively undertake to break down socially constructed barriers to using this strategy and how individuals might improvise ways to avail themselves of it (for helpful suggestions, see chapter 14 by Robin Fiore in this volume).

Diana's second strategy, which is another variant of the idea that one's inner self secures continuity, is to affirm a better fit between her true, enduring self—the self that used to be "petted and hugged"—and her surgically altered appearance (Davis 1995, 107). She can feel comfortable with her unfamiliar visage because she is convinced that the face she sees in the mirror more accurately represents who she really is—a person who deserves to be "petted and hugged." Her new face is very different, yet it is more truly her.

Interestingly, aging women could not identify with their wrinkled, sagging faces on the grounds that there is now a better match between their identity and their appearance without shaking up quite a few seemingly firm assumptions about physical appearance and the self. If the true self is a constant self, as Diana assumes it is, and if one's identity is most accurately reflected in one's aged face, as Diana claims her identity is most accurately reflected in her postoperative face, one's true self has never been and would not now be well represented by an unlined, tautly contoured, dewy face. Either one's enduring, authentic self is well represented by a youthful face, or it is well represented by an aging face. The same character and personality could not be well represented by such different appearances.

Now, supposing that one's true self is well represented by one's aging face and also that one has a good character and an agreeable personality, it follows that our standards of female physical attractiveness and our conventions of representation vis-à-vis correlations between inner states and facial features are seriously off base. If appropriated by older women, Diana's second strategy would have the curious consequence that admirable, congenial young women should yearn for the day when gravity and wear and tear finally leave their marks. Perhaps they would be well advised to undergo cosmetic surgery of the sort Kathryn Morgan recommends (1991). That is, if young women want their associates to be able to read their virtues off their faces, they should have wrinkles carved across their foreheads, bags implanted under their eyes, jowls attached to their jaw lines, and brownish blemishes splattered here and there. Adapting Diana's second strategy to aging women's needs has disquieting implications: Either we must give up the constancy of the self—we could, for instance, enshrine unpredictable, surprising variability as a desideratum, or we could partition life into different stages correlated with different virtues—or else we must give up our conventions of representing virtues and values, replacing them with heterodox standards of beauty.

Diana's second strategy seems unexceptionable until one draws out its implications for older women, but her third strategy is quite astonishing ab initio. Revisiting her history of humiliations, she excuses her harassers, saying she's just like them and it's normal to find ugliness repellent (Davis 1995, 110). Through a stunning reversal that amounts to selective self-alienation, Diana identifies with her tormenters' attitudes and behavior, and she disidentifies with part of her past—that is, the face they taunted and her suffering at their hands. Putting the past behind her and letting bygones be bygones, she strengthens her identification with her "new, improved," yet strange appearance. Diana's capitulation to self-hatred and her refusal to critique the cultural norms that foster the cruelty she endured are troubling. But I shall set these matters aside because adapting this strategy to the circumstances of aging women would not involve such problems.

Still, it's far from obvious how to adapt this strategy to the circumstances of aging women without becoming ensnared in yet another twisted logic. To embrace their present appearance, which by conventional standards is unattractive, by disidentifying with part of their past would be to repudiate the face that others thought pretty as well as their earlier pleasure at being admired for their looks. Whereas Diana embraces orthodox beauty norms and identifies with those who uphold them, elderly women would have to reject the equation of youth and beauty and create an alternative community of more discerning viewers who presumably would have a better grasp of the true nature of beauty.

Renowned portraitist Alice Neel deploys Diana's strategy of selective self-alienation. Asked why she never painted a self-portrait until she was eighty years old, Neel explains:

> I always despised myself. . . . I hate the way I looked. . . . I was a very pretty girl and I liked to use that with the boys, but I wasn't like me. My spirit looked nothing like my body. (Castle 1983, 40)[2]

Neel eschews orthodox beauty norms and valorizes her octogenarian looks. It is clear, too, that her self-portrait draws admiration. Still, this strategy gives me pause, for, premised as it is on embracing a univocal conception of beauty rather than on appreciating various forms of physical attractiveness, it would require sacrificing the narcissistic needs of younger women to those of older women. Thus, Neel's remarks sound a note of contempt for the pretty young woman whom men found alluring.

I doubt, moreover, that altogether abandoning ideals of beauty that accommodate youth is practically feasible or aesthetically credible. Neel's rendering of her face reveals skepticism, boldness, and defiance tempered by familiarity with woe. She holds the tools of her trade, a paintbrush and a rag, in her hands. Although seated on a couch, she is in the midst of her work—contemplating her subject, that is, herself seen in a mirror. She gives an unabashed description of her aged body—her hunched shoulders, pendulous breasts, bulbous belly, lumpy legs. Yet her body is not without tensility, for she looks as if she is about to rise and return to her canvas. Neel's image of her eighty-year-old self is undeniably inspiring. Nevertheless, it would be a pity to spurn an image like Joan Semmel's self-portrait, "Me Without Mirrors" (collection of the artist 1974), which depicts her supple, curvaceous, youthful body caught in a moment of self-cradling and self-caressing as she towels herself off.

In many respects, Margaret Morganroth Gullette's approach to the stranger in the aging woman's mirror recapitulates the strategies I have derived from Diana's testimony. Gullette urges us to reject the progress/ decline dichotomy and the autobiographical templates that cast life stories either as tales of progress or as tales of decline (Gullette 1997, 11). Rather, we should figure out how social forces conspire to enlist us in narratives that equate advancing age with decline, and we should develop "complex idiosyncratic narrative[s] of age identity" (Gullette 1997, 15, 18). With respect to the miseries of disidentification with an aging face, Gullette suggests that we remind ourselves of how unhappy we were with our youthful faces when we were younger, how vital our personal and professional midlives actually are, and how some forms of physical beauty have been sadly neglected (Gullette 1997, 58, 60, 64–65). "[Y]our story must be a *becoming*," she counsels (Gullette 1997, 61). But she stresses that a story of becoming is not the same thing as a progress story. Trying to counterbalance aged-face despair with a cheery progress narrative merely sets an emotional seesaw in motion—"You're beautiful. No you're not. Yes, you are. . . ." To escape from this syndrome, one must recognize that one's dissatisfaction with one's appearance stems from the poisonous ageist propaganda one has internalized, and one must reconnect with one's distinctive life story and unique subjectivity (Gullette 1997, 68).

Gullette's view rests on an uneasy admixture of social construction-ism—which is particularly in evidence in her dismissive account of women's choices to undergo cosmetic surgery (Gullette 1997, 70)—and classical individualism—which comes out in her optimism about women's ability to "decide what aging means to *me* at midlife, beyond decline ideology" (Gullette 1997, 12). However, I shall not pursue this difficulty. What I shall probe instead is Gullette's notion of a becoming, as opposed to a decline or progress, narrative, and her endorsement of a more "democratic" conception of beauty.

A becoming narrative tells a story of acceptable, assimilable change—I may not be getting better and better, but I'm not getting worse and worse, and I *am* okay. Yet, the face-narrative Gullette presents is in fact decidedly upbeat. She reports success in getting her career on track, in finally dedicating herself to work she really wants to do (Gullette 1997, 60). Also, she tells of debunking the fantasy of youthful self-approval and, with the help of this more realistic view of her past, gaining emotional equilibrium (Gullette 1997, 57–58). Surely, these are distinct advances. Indeed, if we weren't self-consciously striving to overcome binary oppositions, we'd call them progress. When Gullette focuses specifically on her feelings about her midlife appearance, she adapts and blends Diana's strategies. She repudiates the pleasure she once took in being noticed as a young female, and she harshly indicts her youthful "beauty" and her former looks, which she characterizes as "blurry as to identity, banally pretty, uncertain, even frightened; and when not frightened, foolish" (Gullette 1997, 62). In the past, her appearance didn't fit her inner self, but now it does. Her midlife self-presentation is more in keeping with her work and her feminist values—it strikes "a better balance between representing femaleness and 'me-ness' " (Gullette 1997, 63).

In one way, we would expect Gullette's thinking to depart from Diana's strategies, for she advocates a less exclusionary view of beauty. Yet, what Gullette actually does is to extol midlife beauty—she has learned to appreciate big, soft bodies and "interesting" faces with "well-defined features marked by intelligence and experience"—and to censure youthful beauty—slender, gym-trained bodies are "junior Cyborgs," and young faces are confined to a narrow repertoire of expressions (Gullette 1997, 64–65).[3] By admiring isolated facial features and by not demanding that the whole face approximate an ideal, she finds more women of her age cohort beautiful (Gullette 1997, 63). On her view, however, the young are denied admission to the temple of beauty. Although her conception of beauty inverts beauty orthodoxy, it does not proliferate types of beauty.

The Self, Representation, and Beauty— A Trio of Dubious Postulates

Reconfigured for use by aging women, Diana's strategies for deflecting her attention from the strangeness of her face and for identifying with her transformed face raise fundamental questions about the self, representation, and beauty. The Diana-derivative strategies presuppose (1) that people have stable, authentic identities—I shall call this the identity constancy postulate; (2) that people's inner nature can be deciphered from their outward appearance—I shall call this the facial legibility postulate; and (3) that an attractive inner nature is embodied in an attractive face—I shall call this the goodness-goes-with-beauty postulate. These assumptions may seem unimpeachable until one notices the binds they get us into when we adapt Diana's strategies to the needs of aging women.

To compensate for the unfamiliarity of one's face, it seems sensible to reassure oneself of the stability and worth of one's self by projecting it onto stable and worthwhile relationships or projects. However, this strategy is less viable for aging women, whose relationships are frequently derailed, curtailed, or terminated and whose health or other circumstances may interfere with their ability to sustain other pursuits. The complementary strategies of affirming a better fit between one's aging face and one's true self while disavowing one's youthful appearance involve disparaging the narcissistic pleasures of youth, dismissing the standards of attractiveness that undergird them, and replacing these conventional beauty ideals with counterideals of midlife beauty. This is a tall order. Not only does it seem psychologically perverse, but also it merely substitutes one exclusionary ideal for another. One must wonder, too, whether this counterideal will work for all aging women—octogenarians as well as fifty-year-olds; Latinas, Asian Americans, African Americans, and Native Americans, as well as Euro-Americans; and so on.

The identity constancy postulate gives rise to three dilemmas. First, this assumption undermines the ability of aging (and many other) women to see a correspondence between their inner self and their interpersonal relationships or their vocational or other projects. Thus, they cannot manage their anxiety about their changed and changing appearance by focusing their attention on their unchanged and unchanging commitments or activities. Second, assuming a normal American lifespan, this assumption entails that one's appearance will fail to coincide with one's inner nature for at least part of one's life. If the true self is invariant (at least throughout one's adult lifetime), and if the face is a window onto the soul, a changing face cannot aptly represent this constant inner nature. If one's face misrepresents one's true self when one is young, passing years may eventually bring one's appearance into alignment with one's inner nature. However, if one's face accurately reflects one's true self when one is young, passing years will inevitably leave one's appearance out of whack with one's inner nature. In either case, one is doomed to spend a significant part of one's life distraught by the mismatch between one's inner nature and one's outer appearance—a living violation of the facial legibility postulate. Third, in conjunction with the goodness-goes-with-beauty postulate, the identity constancy postulate underwrites exclusionary beauty ideals. If an attractive, unchanging inner nature is most aptly represented by a certain type of conventionally pretty face, a youthful face and an aging face cannot both be attractive. Attractiveness at one stage of life ensures unattractiveness at another, and women are doomed to spend a significant part of their lives in despair over their ugliness or toiling to overcome it (and probably both).

I believe that for purposes of understanding identity and agency, a looser conception of the self would not only suffice, it would be better. Born into and formed by misogynist, heterosexist, racist, ethnocentric, ableist, and classist societies as we are, we need to understand the true self as an evolving self if we are to overcome internalized markers of domination and subordination and if we are to resist unjust social structures and practices without sacrificing authenticity (for extended discussion, see Meyers 1989 and Meyers forthcoming). I would add, moreover, that few of us have invariant identities, and yet many of us don't feel hopelessly adrift. We exert a good deal of control over our lives, and our lives make a tolerable amount of sense to us. For purposes of self-knowledge and self-direction, then, assorted, intermittent, unfolding identity continuities suffice. We don't have identity constancy, and we don't need to conform to the identity constancy postulate.

Aging women needn't be saddled with the deleterious consequences of this overly exiguous postulate. A looser conception of the self will allow older women to see continuities in their style of interacting and living and in their values even in the midst of unsettling social losses and personal turmoil. Moreover, a looser conception that allows for the possibility that the virtues of youth may differ somewhat from the virtues of age would not preclude the possibility that a youthful face and an aged face could befit one's true self during different periods of one's life (for discussion of the virtues of age, see chapter 3 by Sara Ruddick in this volume). Thus, the trauma of feeling that there is an irremediable disparity between who one is and who one appears to be could be alleviated.

Still, loosening up our conception of the self won't fully address the problem of exclusionary beauty ideals, for these seem to have a life of their own and show little sign of succumbing to critique. One may accept that one's older self differs from one's younger self and that the same face could hardly speak for both. Yet, there's a strong tendency to lapse into thinking that one's older face (and perhaps one's older self, too) is less attractive, or else to defensively denigrate one's younger face (along with one's younger self). To address this bind, it is necessary to consider the question of representation—the facial legibility postulate.

The facial legibility postulate is not simply false, of course. We must and routinely do read emotions, desires, and motives off facial expressions. Occasionally, a person is saying one thing, but her face betrays her and exposes her deception. For this to happen, facial expressions must be revealing. Also, we seldom have trouble identifying emotions like sadness, anger, joy, or embarrassment on the basis of facial expressions. Indeed, facial expressions are called "expressions" because they normally express what people are feeling.

Nevertheless, it is important to recognize the limits of facial legibility.

I doubt, for example, that people can reliably differentiate a face contorted by rage from a face contorted by agony without knowing anything about the context. Also, it seems clear that interpretations based solely on facial expressions are quite crude. We may be able to tell that a person isn't happy simply by looking, but we can't tell whether a person is experiencing grief or despair simply by looking. Without contextualization, people's facial expressions do not enable us to divine much about the cavalcade of their passing subjective states, and, if we try to decode people's episodic inner states without the benefit of relevant contextual information, we are liable to go astray, possibly to run amuck.

However, worse mischief stems from the remarkably persistent, though peculiar belief that the way a person looks reveals something deep about who she is. This conviction is peculiar because it is counterbalanced by the belief that the face can mask a person's true nature and also because it is awfully mysterious how a person's character and personality are manifest on her face. Certainly, there is no natural or necessary correspondence between states of the soul and features of the face or their configuration. One can have the face of an angel and the soul of a Nazi. Moreover, ostensible correlations between facial features or types of face and character or personality traits often track derogatory or honorific stereotypes far better than they track inner realities—for example, the Jew's big nose supposedly signaling his greed or deviousness or a creamy complexion supposedly signaling purity of heart. The facial legibility postulate is suspect, then, for it memorializes a history of social stratification and bigotry.

Still, Diana thinks her reconstructed face fits her inner nature better, and Gullette thinks her midlife face fits hers better. Why do they think so? And why do they think it matters? Are these people captivated by some noxious fairy tale?

There seem to be several factors working here. First, because our culture furnishes a stock of face prototypes—for example, the innocent face, the world-weary face, the honest face, the priggish face, the shrewd face—we have a facial vocabulary and therefore the possibility of scrutinizing our own features and questioning their fit with what we know about ourselves. Second, presenting a face that does not fit one's character and personality carries a whiff of inauthenticity. So, one may feel derelict in some unspoken duty if one concludes that one's face is misleading. Also, since others form preconceptions about us based on their prototype-driven reading of our faces, we may want a good match in order to minimize misunderstanding and false expectations based on over- or underestimations of our character and personality. Third, the good fit we want may be less tied to specific traits of character or personality and more tied to an overall assessment of them. The idea might be that, if one thinks one has a decent character and an agreeable personality, one wants this self-esteem to be manifest in one's appearance—one wants to look as attractive as one feels one is inside. This doesn't seem to be about authenticity, however, since, so far as I know, people with odious characters and abrasive personalities never regret not having faces to match. Rather, people whose faces are considered ugly worry that few people will look beyond their appearance and notice their fine qualities, and consequently they fear social ostracism.

Two themes emerge from these observations, and they may pull in opposite directions. Insofar as people identify authenticity with the wholeness or unity of the self, a disparity between one's inner nature and one's outward appearance is inauthentic. An authentic individual's character and personality must be embodied in her face. So a person who values authenticity will want her face to fit her inner nature. Second, one's face is a social asset or liability. Since people prefer an asset, they may not care whether the asset accurately represents their inner nature or their feelings about themselves. Also, since some people have self-esteem although they lack decent characters or agreeable personalities, they may think that an attractive face accurately represents how they feel about themselves, and this match may overshadow any mismatch between their face and their character or personality traits.

I hope I've said enough by now to convince you that this is all smoke and mirrors. If we want to know who someone is, as opposed to how someone is feeling at the moment, we'd better listen to what they say and notice how they act in a variety of situations. Facial prototypes are poor indicators of enduring character and personality. The facial legibility postulate must be circumscribed—within limits, it applies to subjective episodes, but it does not apply to enduring traits at all. Ideally, then, we should strike the vocabulary of facial prototypes from our cognitive repertoire. This isn't likely to happen, though, for these prototypes are deeply ingrained in each of us and continue to be culturally reinforced through the history of art as well as through commercial and entertainment imagery. So, it might be wise to shave down our ambitions and consider whether anything can be done to shake the goodness-goes-with-beauty postulate—the broad equivalency between inward goodness and outward attractiveness together with the contrary equivalency between inward wickedness and outward ugliness.

A moment's reflection discloses the utter fatuousness of the presumption that an estimable character and personality will be embodied in a beautiful, or even an attractive, face. Yet, there is ample evidence that people commonly slide from seeing an attractive appearance to regarding the individual so perceived as more congenial, more intelligent, more competent, and more likely to be successful (Bersheid and Walster 1974, 168–71; Cash 1990, 54–56).[4] It is also worth noting that critical reflection does nothing to expunge the positive correlation between beauty and erotic appeal. And erotic response undoubtedly colors our perception of character and personality. Evidently, perceiving physical beauty primes people to notice good qualities, to place a positive construction on average ones, and to overlook mediocre or bad qualities. Despite the overwhelming evidence to the contrary, people persist in presuming that the Good and the Beautiful go hand in hand.

Nevertheless, I think it is possible to install some cognitive and emotional ballast to offset the pernicious tendencies that the goodness-goes-with-beauty postulate underwrites. To disabuse ourselves of the various associations between facial appearance and traits of character and personality, mental exercises in radical materialism might be salutary. Try to look at faces and concentrate on their biological functions—see eyes and noses as organs, mouths as orifices, skin as a protective sheath. Once you've reached the point where you're looking at a mere organism, allow yourself to endow it with non-physiological meanings and notice how arbitrary, and even bizarre, these physiognomic attributions are. It's eerie, but try this cleansing ascetic discipline on yourself.

Of course, we wouldn't want to do without aesthetic pleasure. So we also need a discipline to refurbish our aesthetic sensibilities. It helps to bear in mind that beauty is not an inborn property and that ideals of beauty are culture bound and historized. Thus, it is useful to dwell on stories like Hanan al-Shaykh's recollection of being despised for being too skinny in a culture that valorizes fleshy voluptuousness (al-Shaykh 1994) and renaissance images like Titian's zoftig Venuses. Although we are trained to find this or that beautiful, we can study other conceptions of beauty and learn to recognize and relish beauty on those terms. This discipline would undercut the tendency to rush to dismiss people—ourselves included—who are unusual looking or who are ordinarily deemed ugly.

These exercises in the disenchantment and reenchantment of the face might help us suspend judgment about people until we've interacted with them for awhile and gotten to know them a bit. If one forms a favorable opinion of someone, one's positive response to their character and personality would then influence one's perception of their physical qualities. We idealize those we love. Mothers are notorious for thinking their sons far more handsome than most of their sons' prospective mates do. Nor are mothers alone in this harmless aggrandizement. Few of us have gorgeous partners, but our love magnifies their allure. If we could form emotional attachments with minimal static from our first impressions of people's faces, we would discover more forms of beauty. Pam Houston (see epigraph) and Gullette (1997, 63) suggest another way to diversify our conception of beauty. When encountering a person, focus on a single (conventionally) good feature and then let your appreciation of that feature infuse the composite. Maybe we routinely do this without realizing it. After all, few of us demand that our friends measure up to exacting criteria of beauty. Heightened consciousness of how latitudinarian our aesthetic standards really are might serve as an antidote to overzealous self-criticism and self-contempt. Deliberately working to foster our awareness of beauty in its many guises would augment our enjoyment of others along with our acceptance of ourselves.

As a cure for the specific pathology of automatically deeming aging features ugly, I propose assembling a portrait gallery of women whom one admires.[5] Gather photographs of them taken in their later years, and display them where you'll see them often. The idea is to link respect for their accomplishments to enjoyment of their aging faces. Depending on your predilections, you might include Simone de Beauvoir, Janet Flanner, Coretta Scott King, Golda Meir, Louise Nevelson, Gertrude Stein, Virginia Woolf, Eleanor Roosevelt, Hannah Arendt, Jeanne Moreau, Rosa Parks, Mary McCarthy, Bella Abzug, Colette, Indira Gandhi, Kathryn Hepburn, Toni Morrison, Margaret Mead, Iris Murdoch, or Georgia O'Keeffe. Is it so horrible to look more like them? Just as one may have sought to emulate them in one's life, so one might hope eventually to resemble them in one's appearance. Thus, one might become reconciled to, even pleased with, one's own aging face.

If we got rid of an unduly stringent view of identity continuity, and if we opened up the concept of beauty, the facial legibility postulate would be more benign. Still, the reframings I have proposed may seem like palliatives, for I have said nothing about the relation between aging facial features and the aging body. One doesn't just see a less beautiful face in the mirror. One sees a face that is a harbinger of impending death—the ultimate Other that your appearance now personifies and that you are impelled to flee. I shall now turn to the problematics of gender, mortality, and aging faces.

Facing Up to Scary Heterogeneity—The Limits of Becoming and the Need for Feminist Critique

Feminism has had an important role in articulating complex, nonstatic conceptions of the agentic self. Typically, feminists view the subject as heterogeneous and thus as to some degree opaque to itself and to some extent in conflict with itself. But, by and large, we have seen heterogeneity as an impetus for change—for personal insight and development as well as for social critique and political activism. In other words, the self is construed as evolving—as capitalizing on heterogeneity to gradually gain understanding and enhance effective functioning. Since "evolution" carries connotations of improvement, Gullette would charge that we are building an autobiographical progress template into our account of the self, and she would be right. To some extent, this is an artifact of the questions that have been salient for feminist scholars. We have tried to discern women's agency in everyday life, often under severe economic and emotional constraints. Also, we have sought to understand how women can extricate themselves from repressive socialization and ideology and how they can take bold emancipatory action. Aiming to explain how women retain a measure of control over their lives despite male dominance and how women can resist and overcome their subordination, feminist accounts of the self accent the propitious side of heterogeneity.

A quick scan of the feminist literature suggests that this orientation has led to tunnel vision with respect to the body. The preponderance of feminist work on the body focuses on women's bodies insofar as they present problems that cultural critique and social policy could ameliorate. There are, for example, vast feminist literatures on reproductive freedom, on sexual violence and other forms of woman battery, and on eating disorders. Insofar as feminist thought has included the body as a dimension of the subject's heterogeneity, it has seen bodily heterogeneity as remediable. If only laws were changed, services provided, sexist attitudes and practices forsworn, women would stop experiencing their bodies as alien sites of danger. Women would be able to live in harmony with their bodies.

It seems to me that, despite a core of good sense, Gullette's proposal to replace progress and decline narratives with becoming narratives and my proposals to loosen the identity constancy postulate, to discredit the facial legibility postulate, and to defang the goodness-goes–with-beauty postulate do not escape this blithe mindset. Even if we acknowledge the formidability of the cultural and psychological obstacles to implementing these proposals, an undercurrent of Pollyannaish falsity lingers. I trace this suspect aura to the failure of these proposals to confront an intractable form of heterogeneity associated with the body—the eventuality of death.

Feminist discussions of heterogeneity pay scant attention to cruel, violent unconscious material—to the death drive, as Freud would say. They emphasize relatively tame unconscious material—material that can be accessed and used as a resource for critique, as opposed to material that is best left repressed or disguised through sublimation. Likewise, feminist discussions of the body sidestep its unassimilable aspects—unrelievable, insupportable suffering stemming from incurable disease or irremediable impairment, and death itself. Bodies don't evolve forever. The fatal potentiality—vulnerability to accident and disease—dwells within every body. If one isn't killed suddenly when one is still young, one's body will deteriorate. It will require more attention all the time, and it will become stiff, brittle, and weak regardless of how much attention one lavishes on it. Then death comes. But this fate awaits male bodies, too (by actuarial calculations, usually earlier). Why, apart from discrimination in the health care system, is eroding health and death a feminist issue?

I submit that it should be a feminist concern because of the symbolic nexus that links death to femininity. Insofar as mortality is embedded in theology, and death is conceptualized as a deity plucking a life, the agent of death is represented as gender-congruent with the life-conferring, life-taking andro-deity. Figured as the Grim Reaper, death is depicted as vestigially masculine—as an emaciated, skeletal male. However, a shift in psychodynamics and imagery accompanies the scientization of life and death. Life is reduced to a piece of biological luck, while death is conceived as an inborn eventuality and an unredeemable terminus. Medicalized, death is internalized—it is a consequence of genetic susceptibility, bad habits, or toxic infestation. Secularized, death is a personal tragedy—the annihilation of individual subjectivity. Unconscious fantasies, as Julia Kristeva and Luce Irigaray remind us, associating death with lack and dissolution, and associating lack and dissolution with the "castrated" female body and the engulfing maternal body, gain psychic momentum. Though repressed, this metaphoric background structures perception of women's aging faces and imbues them with symbolic significance. Gray hair, wrinkles, and the like are not symptoms of any malady, much less imminent death. Still, women's aging features have been shanghaied as figurative vehicles for decline and demise. Because death is symbolically linked to the female body, an aging female face issues a particularly sharp rebuke to cherished illusions of invulnerability and immortality.

Here we have another instance of the treachery of the facial legibility postulate. Although I'm not sure that we can altogether sever the potent (and hardly inapt) symbolic link between time-altered features and the realities of decline and death, I am confident that feminists should be working on severing the symbolic link between *women's* aging faces and these disturbing bodily heterogeneities. There's no reason why women's aging faces should bear the whole burden of anxiety about death.

Now, it's worth pointing out that Ann Ferguson's suggestion that we substitute an aesthetic of health for an aesthetic of loveliness is on a collision course with these underlying symbolic associations (Ferguson 1996, 116). Not only is it mystifying what health looks like—do my friends who look fine but who are undergoing chemotherapy for cancer look healthy?—but also this proposal solidifies, when it should be resisting, the facial legibility postulate—health and healthy looks pass as surely as youth and youthful looks. Moreover, by itself, this proposal is futile, for it denies the symbolic connection between the aging female face and deteriorating health and death without subverting this well-entrenched figuration and the misogynist discourse in which it is embedded. No alternative aesthetic of the aging feminine face has any chance of succeeding until women's bodies together with the concept of femininity have been freed from their phantasmic coupling with death and its medically mediated portents. It is imperative, then, that feminists undertake a counterfigurative politics aimed at defeating this figurative regime.

The cultural background I have sketched explains why aging women are compelled to refuse their faces—why so many of us know the face in the mirror is ours but still identify with a facial image frozen in our twenties. It's tough enough being the feminine Other. No one wants to become the ultimate Other. It explains, as well, why aging women do not consider their painstaking grooming and grueling fitness routines frivolous or vain—why they depict their efforts at self-beautification as virtuous (Furman 1997, 54–55, 70). If aging women do not hide the signs of age, conventional beauty ideals and the facial legibility postulate authorize us to read their faces as a mark of inner corruption—the Grim Reaper lurking within. Laboring to stay young-looking is a way of shunning devolution and defilement. Jo Anna Isaak is right:

> Contrary to Sartre's claim that after forty we get the face we deserve, women after forty get *the face they have the courage to present.* (Isaak 1996, 150, emphasis added)

No meaning is inherent in any face, and likening the aging female face to a death mask is a vicious slander. Yet, it is far from clear how a courageous woman is to respond. If discretion is the better part of valor, keeping one's aging face and its symbolic reminder of death under wraps is the courageous response to aging. On this interpretation of courage, women should redouble their efforts to conceal their age and dedicate themselves to self-beautification. But if surrendering to misogyny's symbolic tyranny is cowardice, women should follow Susan Sontag's stirring advice—they "should tell the truth" (1979, 478). On this interpretation, courage demands repossessing our purloined faces and wearing them unrepentantly.

Notes

I am grateful to the editor of this volume, Margaret Urban Walker, to the participants at the conference on Ethical Issues on Women's Aging (Ethics Center, University of South Florida, St. Petersburg), and to Phillip Koplin for helpful comments on an earlier draft of this paper.

1. Epigraphs are from the autobiographical essays in *Minding the Body* by Patricia Foster (1994).
2. I thank Martha Holstein for alerting me to this interview.
3. I'd like to say that I find Gullette's snide remarks about fit bodies insulting. My senior cyborg body enables me to climb mountains with ease and also to feel safe enough to relax on city streets. While I realize my strength and agility won't last forever, they have afforded me incalculable pleasure, which I refuse to disavow or to give up prematurely. So, I'm with Donna Haraway—I, too, "would rather be a cyborg than a goddess" (Haraway 1997, 525).
4. Cash and Pruzinsky document some noteworthy qualifications of the presumption that beauty entails goodness. They observe that, when attractive people do not reciprocate social overtures, their behavior may be read as aloof and therefore as evidence of self-centeredness, although shyness or deficient social skills could explain their behavior equally well (Cash 1990, 53–54). Also, there is, not surprisingly, a gender factor: Attractive women who apply for jobs that are conventionally coded masculine or who are employed in such positions may lose their advantage and may even be discriminated against (Cash 1990, 56–57). Along similar lines, we are all familiar with the stereotype of the dumb blond—pretty and sexy, but foolish and manipulable. In this regard, I would stress that beauty is not invariably linked to every imaginable good quality. Although the dumb blond lacks intelligence, she is often portrayed as having a heart of gold. She is an excellent candidate for marriage and motherhood, if not for the corporate boardroom.
5. This exercise is based on a suggestion made by Sara Ruddick.

References

al-Shaykh, Hanan. "Inside a Moroccan Bath," in *Minding the Body: Women Writers on Body and Soul*, ed. Patricia Foster. New York: Anchor Books/Doubleday, 1994.

Bersheid, Ellen, and Elaine Walster. "Physical Attractiveness," in *Advances in Experimental Psychology*, vol. 7, ed. Leonard Berkowitz. New York: Academic Press, 1974, 157–215.

Cash, T. F. "The Psychology of Physical Appearance," in *Body Images: Development, Deviance, and Change*, ed. T. F. Cash and T. Pruzinsky. New York: Guilford Press, 1990, 51–79.

Castle, Ted. "Interview with Ted Castle," *Art Forum* 2, no. 2 (1983): 36–41.

Davis, Kathy. *Reshaping the Female Body*. New York: Routledge, 1995.

Ferguson, Ann. "Can I Choose Who I Am? And How Would That Empower Me? Gender, Race, Identities, and the Self," in *Women, Knowledge, and Reality*, ed. Ann Garry and Marilyn Pearsall. New York: Routledge, 1996.

Foster, Patricia, ed. *Minding the Body: Women Writers on Body and Soul*. New York: Anchor Books/Doubleday, 1994.

Furman, Frida Kerner. *Facing the Mirror: Older Women and Beauty Shop Culture*. New York: Routledge, 1997.

Gullette, Margaret Morganroth. *Declining to Decline: Cultural Combat and the Politics of the Midlife*. Charlottesville: University Press of Virginia, 1997.

Haraway, Donna. "A Manifesto for Cyborgs: Science, Technology, and Socialist Feminism in the 1980s," in *Feminist Social Thought: A Reader*, ed. Diana Tietjens Meyers. New York: Routledge, 1997.

Isaak, Jo Anna. *Feminism and Contemporary Art: The Revolutionary Power of Women's Laughter*. New York: Routledge, 1996.

Meyers, Diana Tietjens. *Self, Society, and Personal Choice*. New York: Columbia University Press, 1989.

———. "Intersectional Identity and Authenticity? Opposites Attract," in *Relational Autonomy*, ed. Catriona Mackenzie and Natalie Stoljar. New York: Oxford University Press, forthcoming.

Morgan, Kathryn. "Women and the Knife. Cosmetic Surgery and the Colonization of Women's Bodies," *Hypatia* 6, no. 3 (1991): 25–53.

Sontag, Susan. "The Double Standard of Aging," in *Psychology of Women: Selected Readings*, ed. Juanita H. Williams. New York: Norton, 1979.

· *Part Two* ·

Lives

· 3 ·

Virtues and Age

Sara Ruddick

$\mathscr{A}$re there distinctive virtues appropriate to "old age"? Virtues that we might expect of the elderly and of ourselves as we grow older? I will suggest that there are such virtues. By this I mean that there are virtues salient in the lives of people temporally situated between a lengthening, unalterable past and short future, where loss is predictable but its timing and form is not. But I recognize that the connection of virtue with age is itself controversial. It can seem inappropriate, morally, to expect elderly people to be virtuous. Or it can seem misguided to invoke a category of "age" to which the virtues of the elderly are relegated. I begin by considering these objections.

"Virtue" in the Lives of the Elderly

Given the real losses as well as the contempt and discrimination that aging people suffer, isn't it unkind and even politically regressive to speak to them of virtue? Don't the elderly deserve rest, comfort, indulgence? Shouldn't they reserve whatever energy they can muster for resisting the social insults inflicted upon them?

Previous attempts to ascribe virtues to the elderly have not inspired confidence. As Thomas Cole has suggested, the alleged virtues of age often mirror the values responsible for ageism. "Old people are (or should be) healthy, sexually active, engaged, productive, and self-reliant," not, as ageists imagine, sick, sexless, poor, and disengaged. Both the praise and the blame value robust, cheery, activist independence; neither looks easily on vulnerability, dependence, or failure.[1]

In this vein, Martha Holstein has shown how the idea of "productive" aging, despite its authors' intentions, remains associated with paid work,

45

and with values of the market system. As a dominant virtue, "productivity" slights the unpaid caregiving that remains predominantly women's work. The idea that the elderly should be productive also undermines their claims for state support. If they are good, that is, productive, the elderly will largely be able to care for themselves.[2]

Productive aging is given a more "feminine" tone in the ideal of graceful aging: the good elderly woman, as Susan Wendell describes her, is "healthy, slim, energetic, discreetly sexy [and, in a more masculine register], independent, reliable, prosperous and productive." Such an ideal keeps elderly women who succumb to it "hating and fearing who we are."[3]

To these doubts I add my own. I fear that ideals characteristically become burdensome to the people who are meant to be governed by them. Notoriously, prescriptions for being a "good mother" intimidate and demoralize ordinary mothers who fail in quite ordinary ways on most of the ordinary days of their parental lives. Are portraits of productive and plucky "good elderly" as likely to intimidate people who are in ordinary ways often exhausted, sad, and fearful? The "good mother" is shadowed by the "bad," the scapegoat who is held accountable for personal and social failure; the woman who may reassure us by being so much worse than we are but who, on our bad days, becomes a damning self-portrait. Does the virtuous old woman also bring in her wake a "bad" sister who both reassures and frightens?

Finally, efforts of virtue presume capacities to form intentions and to undertake responsibilities, then to remember and to act on them in the future. Given the likelihood of mental deterioration, an elderly person cannot expect that she will retain the capacities that make virtue possible. To be sure, as Iris Murdoch once put it, virtue always transpires "in the midst of a scene where every 'natural' thing, including one's own mind, is subject to chance,"[4] where, therefore, the possibility of being virtuous is beyond one's control. Age is not so much an exception to as a reminder of the human conditions of virtue. Yet it is also true that mental deterioration acquires a different valence in age, becoming a lively and particular possibility rather than a general effect of nature and chance.

Each of these doubts serves as a useful warning. But I believe that there is another, equally realistic story to tell about virtue in the life of the elderly. Most elderly, like most people at any age, struggle to maintain conceptions of themselves as good people. Many also try both to preserve relationships and to do well by the people to whom they are importantly related. These efforts of virtue are intrinsically rewarding for the elderly themselves, confirming their sense of agency, accountability, and moral standing. Efforts of the elderly to be virtuous also benefit the elderly indirectly by benefiting the people they care for and who care for them. By contrast, excusing the elderly from moral discipline or judgment only repeats the condescension to which they are subject.

To be sure, some elderly lose, to varying degrees, accustomed physical abilities—to hear, see, or walk, for example. They must reshape old and invent new ways of exercising virtue. For some, losses of memory and other mental capacities even more seriously undermine basic capacities to be virtuous. But deterioration of mind and memory, when it occurs, usually occurs only slowly. It is possible to adapt to changing mental habits and acquire new ones—to compensate for memory lapses and warn others of them. Only slowly, if at all, does mental incapacity make efforts of virtue impossible. Moreover, in appreciation of chance as it "affects one's own mind," the elderly often try (and if social conditions permitted would try more effectively) to ensure that they will behave virtuously even after they have lost the capacity to do so.

In sum, I will assume that elderly people can and do try to act virtuously and that these efforts benefit them and those they care for. But I will bear in mind that current American cultural ideals of productivity, independence, and "feminine" attractiveness may exert an ineluctable pressure on elderly people and are especially damaging to women. Accordingly I will suggest a way of looking at virtue, in general, that is less apt to yield intimidating ideals. And I will close by offering a different reading of independence, one of the principal virtues encouraged in and by the elderly.

Virtues of "Age"

Elderly people are neither more nor less virtuous than people of other age groups. Like anyone at any age, the elderly often fail even to try to be virtuous, mistake their own or others' good, and despair of achieving the moral goals they set for themselves. The question I want to ask is not, How virtuous are the elderly? Rather, I am interested in whether, among the many virtues one might recommend to anyone, some are distinctly appropriate to, though by no means limited to, age.

Skeptics[5] might dismiss this question in advance because they are suspicious of the category "age" and of "the elderly" as a social class. We are aged, so their argument might run, not primarily by bodily processes but by culture. One way that a culture ages us is by creating the category of "old age" and then homogenizing the people who inhabit it. In fact, people in their early eighties, say, are at least as various as people in their early thirties and probably more various than eight-year-olds. At age 30 or 80, people's idea of virtue is rooted in the circumstances of their particular history, culture, and class. At 30 or 80, people develop virtues as individuals, within or in opposition to the mores of their class and culture. To identify some of those virtues as distinctly appropriate to age is to participate in creating a homogenizing fiction.

This fiction, so the argument continues, is rooted in a misconception of age as a biological state marked by physical and mental deterioration. Various symptoms are then attributed to processes of "aging." Age, for example, brings neurological and circulatory changes that in turn often bring memory loss. The failure to remember is then anticipated and diagnosed in terms of age. In fact, however, the ability to remember varies enormously among the aging. Moreover, loss of memory is culturally diagnosed. What would have passed as momentary forgetting for someone in midlife is taken as a portentous "senior moment" for someone over 65. Even if people over 65 (say) did start forgetting, it might well be possible to develop new techniques of remembering and to value differently different kinds of remembering.

Of course older people become ill and die. But aging is not *about* being sick or dying; nor are illness and death about age. Many of the very old are healthy; illness and death afflict all ages. Rates of illness and death may be revealing of many social factors other than age. (Consider, for example, infant mortality rates or rates of deaths among males from 12 to 25 that differ for people of different economic, ethnic, and racial groups.) Death is the terminus not of aging but of life. Processes of dying are various: sudden, prolonged, painful, painless, messy, and clean. Since death can come at any age, managing the fear of death is a lifelong task beginning, at the latest, in adolescence.

In trying to sort through this argument against categories of "age," I want to employ, provisionally, a common distinction between midlife aging and older aging. The argument for the cultural construction of age seems most appropriate to the alleged aging of people in midlife. Although people become ill and die in their fifties (to chose an age that seems incontestably midlife), their aging—insofar as we want to speak of age at all—is not *predictably* about illness and dying. Nor does aging through one's fifties predictably involve either social or psychological decline. People may change in their fifties or remain pretty much the same as they were in their forties; changes may be social, psychological, or physical, and they may be for better or for worse. Women's menopause, the one physiological change the cultural script insists upon noting, has quite various positive or negative social, psychological, and biological meanings for different women, including almost no meaning at all for some.

The situation seems different for older aging—that of people in their seventies, for example. To be sure, illness and death affect people of all ages, and many in their seventies are healthy. But people in their seventies *typically* and *predictably* have a different relation than people in midlife to illness, decline, and death. Put bluntly, they themselves are apt to decline, to lose capacities they once enjoyed without noticing them. Their own death is closer rather than farther off. Equally important, the decline and dying of other elderly—friends, lovers, spouses, comrades—becomes a predictable part of their lives. Moreover, their own and others' decline and dying begin to change the lives of younger people they care about, not only, but especially, their children.

In short, facts and fears of decline and loss are central in the lives of the elderly. This does not gainsay the old and new pleasures and in addition the enlightenment that are also part of those lives. Nor does it deny the heterogeneity of elderly lives, nor the possibility that some individuals may live through their seventies and eighties without experiencing their own decline or loss, or that of others dear to them. But the predictability of decline as well as the unpredictability of the form it will take make both chance and loss salient to the exercise of virtue in elderly lives.

I have suggested that midlife aging is a cultural construction that should be socially resisted while elderly aging is a physical and psychological process. I am not happy with this distinction. People in their fifties have a developing relationship to age. Their past becomes longer, their future shorter, their predictable but unpredictable losses nearer. People may feel old in their twenties; conversely the sense of lost futures, of time spent, is probably, at any age, connected with a sense of getting old. But the younger a person, provided she is "normally" healthy, the greater the chances of recuperation and compensation, hence the more likely her sense of a closed future will pass. For fifty-year-olds, dwindling futures are sometimes conjoined with signs that really do seem to signify age—whether "facing the mirror"[6] or a medical diagnosis of degenerative disease. Moreover, fifty-year-olds become sixty-year-olds who become (if they are lucky) seventy-year-olds. There is no comforting barrier between the merely aging and the old.

Conversely, social policies shape the conditions and the experience of loss and decline. Political, not individual, will determines the availability to some or all people of respectful medical care, varieties of home service, and elderly-friendly public transportation and home furnishing—to take only obvious examples. The experience of older aging is, as constructivists argue, profoundly shaped by cultural attitudes, for example, the beliefs that beauty is a sign of goodness and that the elderly are ugly, that even the healthy are just about to become ill, that aging people are helpless burdens, or, to take the case at issue, that the elderly are no longer interested in or capable of virtue. Indeed, the desire to alter attitudes and policies, and therefore age itself, inspires most of the counterstories about aging in this book.[7]

The Virtues of Age

I assume then, that it is possible to speak without insult or conceptual confusion of elderly people and that these people are not morally other but as interested in and capable of virtue as people of any other age. I will now attempt to say something about the virtues of age. In doing so, I am drawing on a general understanding of virtue I have formed while considering the work of mothering, the development of children, and now the lives of elderly people. Thus my account of virtue is centrally focused on relations between vulnerable needy people and those who help them. In this context of care, virtues more easily appear to be relational, change and uncertainty are clearly inevitable, and the danger of burdensome ideals is especially clear.

Most of the virtues of the elderly—honesty, kindness, compassion, and so on—are not related to age. But some virtues, though not limited to the elderly, seem especially appropriate to people whose future is dwindling, and who will very likely experience multiple losses and decline. I begin with a list of such virtues: curiosity; a capacity for pleasure and delight; concern for near and distant others; capacities to forgive and let go, to accept, adjust, and appreciate;[8] and "wise independence," which includes not only the ability to plan and control one's life but also the ability to acknowledge one's limitations and accept help in ways that are gratifying to the helper. More somberly, the elderly should be able to manage pain, to mourn and integrate the loss of people dear to them, to handle, without bitterness, their increasing disabilities, and to prepare for death and its effect on those they care about.

I have witnessed and admired each of these virtues as elderly people have expressed them; I have seen the good they bring to the lives of elderly themselves and to people they care about and who care for them. Indeed I believe that attending to the importance of these particular virtues in lives of the elderly should lead to a richer appreciation of their value throughout the life cycle. At the close of the chapter I will return to two of them: the capacity to forgive and let be, and "wise independence."

Nonetheless, I believe that the idea of virtue, as it is implied by this list, makes virtues unnecessarily burdensome. The fault lies, I believe, not in the particular virtues mentioned—any list will be partial and revisable. Rather, the trouble comes from representing virtues primarily as characteristics of individuals, whether these are described as states, dispositions, capacities, or traits of character. In addition to being unnecessarily burdensome, this individualist account of virtue also seems conceptually inadequate to represent the moral efforts of elderly people and their caregivers. I now want to reflect briefly on three defects of this representation and suggest an alternative way of looking at virtue as an ongoing and relational process.

The first defect, and at least abstractly the most easily remedied, is the failure of the list to make explicit room for "negative" and socially troubling capacities and attitudes. So, for example, elderly people should be capable of "energetic anger,"[9] which, among other uses, is necessary to protest the social insults that they suffer by dint of age. As Bernard Boxill has argued, even when it does not bring remedies (which it often does to some degree), protest against the injustices one suffers is (typically) necessary to maintain a sense of self-respect.[10] One might of course add righteous anger to the list of virtues, alongside hopefulness, the capacity to manage pain, and so on. In fact, however, I have read little praise of anger as a virtue aside from those who, like critical race theorists and feminists, are committed to protesting injustice.[11] Admirable, but more pleasant virtues, seem to crowd anger out. This seems especially likely if we are considering virtues of elderly women. Anger seems to be more fearsome, more quickly diagnosed, yet more easily trivialized when expressed by women. I suspect this may also be true of anger expressed by the elderly, partly because "we" fear their demands on "us," partly because we attribute irritability to the fact of age, and partly because the elderly are disproportionately women.

Suppose we did add capacity for energetic anger to the list of virtues. Then a second kind of difficulty arises. The capacity to be angry is not easily separable, psychologically or conceptually, from diffuse "rage at the dying of the light." Between rage at inevitable loss and angry protest fall the many complaints occasioned by small humiliations that are not easily classified as social or psychophysical, remediable or inevitable. Because appropriate and useful anger so easily mixes with "irrational" rage and "whining" complaints, praising the one risks encouraging the other. But if we legislate against the unpleasant emotions—or their expression—we lose anger and the capacity to protest, both necessary for self-respect.

Should we then suggest that elderly people keep alive the capacity for rage and complaint for the sake of anger and the protest it allows? More generally, should we determine to include many "outlaw emotions"[12]— bitterness, hysteria, and paranoia, for example—either because they are useful in themselves, like anger, or because, like rage and complaint, they are psychologically inseparable from those that are? It is probably better to include than censure, though if capacities for complaint, rage, and other outlaw emotions were taken as virtues, the idea of virtue might begin to lose its sense.

To pursue this line of thought, and to introduce the second, less remediable defect of lists of virtues, let me return to the "bad mother" and the "bad elderly person" who shadow their "good" counterparts. Like the standard virtues of productivity and self-reliance, the virtues on my list are also stalked by stereotypical vices. The bad elderly are *not* hopeful and curious but rather dejected and apathetic. No longer capable of pleasure or delight, they are sunk in their beds, neither accepting, adjusting, nor independent; they are wrapped up in their complaints, ruminating on their losses and fears but self-protectively indifferent to the concerns of others. These vices paint a demoralizing portrait (and self-portrait) of the "good" elderly—indeed of "good" people—on certain days or in certain phases of their lives.

Again, the fault of this shadowing does not, I believe, lie in the particularities of a list of virtues. Since we identify virtues partly in terms of the vices—or in Aristotelian terms the extremes—that they counter, it is unsurprising that wherever there is virtue there is also vice. The bad elderly person, like the bad mother, will haunt any account that makes virtue and therefore vice an individual achievement or failure. For this reason alone, I would rather speak of *ongoing efforts of virtue* than of characteristics—a disposition or trait—that an individual strives to acquire and maintain. An effort of, or struggle toward, virtue would be identified as much by the temptations it resists as by the goals it achieves. The idea of virtue as involving characteristic ongoing struggles and efforts also seems to me to more accurately represent the moral activities of caregivers and elderly as I have witnessed them.

So, for example, the virtue of curiosity is expressed in efforts to point out or attend, to share stories and to gossip, to question and express surprise, and so forth. But curiosity is also expressed in efforts to resist the impediments that destroy it. Curiosity can be destroyed in many ways throughout life—by parental abuse, indifferent schooling, demeaning jobs or none at all, painful illness, and repeated humiliation, just to name a few. Age, even in the absence of social isolation and injustice, offers particular impediments or temptations arising from the bitter sadness of loss, the sense of "knowing it all already," the "laceration of laughter at what ceases to amuse,"[13] and sometimes from chronic pain or fatigue. Of course one might resist some of these impediments, fatigue and chronic pain, for example, out of a variety of motives that have nothing to do with curiosity. It is the conjunction of certain positive expressions that nearly define curiosity—attending, gossiping, learning, investigating—with resistance to the impediments to these same expressions, that marks the efforts of this particular virtue.

On this view curiosity is not simply achieved—or lost—in either its positive expression or its characteristic resistances. People do not so much *reveal* their curiosity by engaging in the efforts of attending, listening, and so forth. Rather, through these efforts they create curiosity, more or less, on some days rather than others. And similarly people do not overcome fatigue, jadedness, or sadness. Rather, they resist them more or less, on some days more than others. Being virtuous is something one *sometimes* does, not something one is.

But this way of speaking—being virtuous is what "one" sometimes does—brings me to my third objection to depicting virtues as individual achievements. Even after turning from achievement to process, I have continued to represent virtue as individual. I believe, however, that virtue is in the first instance created between and among people; that it is, therefore, inseparable from relationships. This relational quality pertains to virtue at any age but it may be especially evident in the moral lives of the elderly, and of young children and their parents.

The point is really simple. An individual is able to enjoy, remain curious, manage pain, or reflect on death only if she can create the occasions, with others, for doing so. Curiosity itself, or pleasure, or the ability to manage pain comes into being within occasions of relationship. These can be as simple as sharing the excitement of a thunderstorm, going to a movie, or finding and purchasing a new sweater. Or they can be as complex as attentive conversation about wishes for dying and hopes for survivors, and as fraught as weighing the consequences of analgesics and demanding them. I do not mean to suggest that "others" do things for "the elderly." Rather, people together, of the same or different generations, create the encounters in which all parties, each according to their ability, enjoy, sympathize, converse, and demand in ways that express efforts of virtue. These cooperative activities of virtue are relational in a second sense: they rely upon a network of social relations and policies that give people the time, means, and facilities to watch thunderstorms, purchase sweaters, control some of the conditions of their death, and demand analgesics.

The idea that virtue is an achieved aspect of individual character is not simply wrong. People are more or less able to bring some but not other requisite capacities to a relationship or group. Curiosity, say, has a way of becoming lively in the company of some people, going cold in the company of others. Conversely, people can maintain or create a measure of curiosity in themselves, especially if they are attentive to the details of natural or urban life, enjoy the "view from the window," or can read or watch television alone. But efforts of virtue seem in the first instance cooperative, efforts that people make together.

So being virtuous is something people *sometimes* do together. I want again to highlight "sometimes" lest my discussion of the efforts of virtue create a new and burdensome super-virtue: the continuous effort to be virtuous. The idea of continuous effort—whether by one or several people—is as much a part of a work ethic as productivity. Whether or not one is elderly, there are days when one isn't up to creating virtue alone or with others. Hours, days, even weeks of sadness, sloth, and apathy are an integral part rather than an interruption of ongoing efforts to be virtuous. They do not mark a person as bad; processes of doing virtue are marked by vicissitude, not failure. Over a period of time, a virtuous person may do virtue more rather than less; if so her efforts will, I believe, benefit her, people she cares for, and people who care for her. But no one needs to be counting or judging.

Bitterness, Holding On, and Letting Go

I want to close by considering two efforts of virtue that are prominent in the literature of gerontology, appear often in the lives of aging people, and were represented on my list. The first can be described positively as the capacity to forgive and let be, negatively as the capacity to resist regret. It often makes use of "life review," which has itself assumed the status of a virtue among gerontologists. The second is independence, the capacity to plan and control one's life, *combined with* the willingness to acknowledge one's limitations and accept help in ways that are gratifying to the helper, a combination I dub "wise independence." These virtues include capacities to forgive, let be, give up, let go. They therefore counter, on a practical as well as an abstract conceptual level, the impression of a super-virtue of continuous effort.

According to Erik Erikson, the last stage of the life cycle involves a "struggle to accept the inalterability of the past" when one's personal future is both unknowable and predictably short.[14] This temporal situation could give rise to many struggles. One of these involves bitter regret, an inability both to remember and to forgive, to let be. T. S. Eliot considers this bitterness—the "rending pain of re-enactment of all that you have done, and been"—one of the "gifts reserved for age."[15] Although Eliot, and to a lesser extent Erikson, speak as if the target of regret is oneself, regret often involves other individuals in addition to and, most important, inseparably from, oneself. In particular, "All *you* have done, and been [and become]" often addresses children or protégés. People also express bitter regret over damaged, disrupted, lost relationships, both political and intimate, where both self and other are inextricably twinned targets of bitterness.

There are sources of bitterness—acts of betrayal, cruelty, injustice— that may be impossible or perhaps even wrong to forgive. But bitter regret is painful in itself, distracts from current pleasures, and spoils relationships— say, with children, or former lovers and comrades—whose past is inseparable from the one who regrets. Overcoming regret is therefore a blessing. For Eliot the only cure for bitter regret is religion. Erikson recommends instead (or in addition) a "solitary reviewing of the past" or "review" of one's past from a "life-historical" perspective."[16] Following Erikson, the capacity to engage in life reviewing has itself been represented as one, perhaps primary, virtue of elderly people.[17]

A "life review" differs from reminiscence in having some sort of focus and aim; its remembering is directed and purposeful, even if for some people the aim may be just to recover, hold on to, and then dwell in a coherent good enough past. For Eliot such a review would likely be prompted by a search for continuity among generations or for the origins and occasions of "sin" requiring confession. In Erikson's writing, and perhaps in the literature following him, life reviewing is prompted by a desire to create coherence in one's life, to recognize in one's lengthening past a consistent identity. Others search times past for explanation and understanding. James Baldwin speaks of coming to terms with "the enormous gap" between "what one wishes to become and what one is," which compels "some of us . . . around the middle of our lives, to make a study of this baffling geography."[18] Baldwin's sentiments are akin to the case I am considering in which someone reviews her life in order to resist bitter regret over her own choices and those of people she loves.

Neither life reviewing nor bitter regret are reserved for age. Young people in their late teens express acute regret. Almost every school of psychotherapy prompts, and may even require, a "life review," whatever the age of the clients. Yet "life reviewing" and regret are associated with aging for good reason—opportunities for recouping losses and inventing new options objectively dwindle. As one ages, one comes to terms not only with the apparent inalterability of the past, but with the insight that no future change will compensate for losses. Moreover the imbalance of a long past and short future, along with the experience of regret, seems to prompt in some but not all people the kind of focused, reflective introspection that goes under the label of "life review."

The usefulness of life review, and I am thinking particularly of review motivated by regret, depends upon the transformative power of its principal activity of directed remembering. Notoriously, memories are deeply felt, but their meaning is neither static nor self-evident. There is a sense in which the past is not unalterable but can be remade through focused remembering. Without denying facts or pain, a person may actually remember more compassionately, with a sharper sense of context and complexity. In the case of regret, remembering may shift the balance from denial to acceptance, from vengeful obsession to letting go and letting be, from bitterness to the "holy innocence of those who forgive themselves."[19] One of the great boons of this transformation is that remembering itself can be turned from obsessive reenactment of all that "you have done and been," transforming itself into a pleasurable experience of undirected, forgiving reminiscence.

At least since Socrates said that the unexamined life is not worth living, people have been making excessive claims for the benefits of the kind of reflection involved in a life review. I do not claim that such a review is inevitable, indispensable, or obligatory. Many people are temperamentally disinclined to reflective remembering. Others do not suffer from bitter regret, a sense of identity confusion, a desire for a coherent life story, or any other unease that would prompt such a review. On the other hand, for many people it is useful, and ultimately pleasurable, to engage in life reviews. Moreover, in my experience, and in the literature, neither the need nor the ability to engage in such reflective remembering seems limited to either sex or any class, though it might be thought bizarre in some cultures.

Both resisting bitterness and life reviewing are efforts of virtue, and both may be represented as ongoing processes rather than something an individual achieves. To be sure, as regret recedes (or as explanation satisfies, or as identity appears to persist) the desire to review may give way to reminiscence and present preoccupations. But life reviewing, like "thinking" as Arendt described it, is intrinsically unending so long as one engages in it. Last night's insights become the next morning's questions.[20] Nor is regret simply conquered, the innocence of forgiving simply achieved. There will always be reminders of roads not taken, "things ill done and done to others' harm."[21] Just as people create curiosity between them, more or less, on some days rather than others, so they review the past, and more or less let it be, or better still take pleasure in it, depending on particular challenges, moods, and energy.

Although Erikson speaks of life reviewing as "solitary," transformative remembering often requires another who serves as witness and prompter. Bitter regret involves disturbing emotions, such as bitterness itself, anger, blame, and self-blame. Moreover, regret is typically obsessive—a person goes over and over her unwise choices, avoidable or entirely accidental disasters, and moral failures. A listener who hears, legitimates, but also questions, can help a person both to bear and to give up the bitterness to which she is subject.

In many U.S. communities and cultures it is common for therapists to serve as listeners to those speaking bitterness. I strongly endorse current projects to make individual and group therapy available for elderly people, whatever their financial ability to pay for it. Friends, and often near strangers, in fact anyone with a sympathetic but critical ear, can join in life reviewing. Early on it may be nearly impossible for those who are targets of bitterness to participate in remembering. But when bitterness is nearly let go, even the comrade who betrayed, or the lover who abandoned, or the child who disappointed, can share in revising memories.

The last virtue I consider is occasioned by the challenge, and the facts, of physical and mental decline. I described it as "independence joined with willingness to acknowledge one's limitations and accept help in ways that are gratifying to the helper." Now I would redescribe this "wise independence" as an ongoing struggle against two temptations. As an elderly person, exhausted by loss, may be tempted to let herself go—forget her appearance, give up making or carrying out plans, and turn herself over entirely to the care of others. This is the opposite of productive, busy aging. Partly to resist this temptation, and also out of the desire to control her own life as much as possible, an elderly person may be tempted to refuse help, deny her limitations, assert her desires even over small matters, stay "in charge" and "independent."

In the midst of decline and loss, it is a difficult and ongoing task simultaneously to hold on to one's desiring, active self, and to let it go. Elderly people I have known succumb sometimes to temptations of passivity, sometimes to assertive willfulness. Yet partly because we hear less from elderly people than from their caregivers, it is willful self-assertion that seems more common and problematic. Passivity may pass as compliance; in any case, a person who gives up on herself may be easy to care for. By contrast, a helper faced with a frail, needy, but willfully assertive person may feel helpless, unable to provide the care that she is obligated, and also desires, to provide. In the worse, but not uncommon, case a helper resorts to near force—deception, drugs, coercive placement in a home—in order to keep an elderly person safe.

I have been involved in this conflict as a participant and witness, and therefore cannot offer simple resolutions. What I offer instead are rather abstract recommendations for those of us who care for elderly people we love or are on the verge of being elderly ourselves, and are therefore able and motivated to prepare ourselves to exercise the virtues of age.

First, I believe it is helpful if caregivers and elderly people understand that struggles between them are moral as well as psychological; that they deal not only with conflicts of will but with efforts to live and care well. It is here, of course, that ideals of wise independence could become burdensome and should therefore be replaced by conceptions of ongoing effort and negotiation. Both living and caring well involve a changing process of adjusting, accepting, and appreciating the living and caring that remains possible.[22] Even the best efforts to negotiate a stable relation are liable to be undone by the unpredictable vicissitudes of aging.

It should go without saying that "wise independence" is created between and among people. An elderly person should know "in her bones" that if she "falls," in the many kinds of falling she is prey to, others will put together the pieces of her care and that she cannot forestall their guilt or frustration, or the pain of seeing her in pain. A caring person should know that if she hovers and insists she may encourage in the person she cares for a despairing acquiescence that is as life-ending as the "fall" she would prevent. It should also not need saying that such a difficult relationship will require tolerance of outlaw emotions: impatience, resentment, anger, and disappointment, to name a few. These are not just way stations in a progress toward cheerier feeling. They provide necessary information to an elderly person and her helpers as they create between them and for each other a workable balance between letting go and holding on, assertion and acceptance, intervention and letting be.

In describing the relations of "wise independence" as I have witnessed it among people who are failing and dying and those who care for them, I may appear to have fallen into the error of identifying aging itself with decline and death. So let me repeat: seventy- and eighty- and ninety-year-old people differ from each other; some lead healthy lives full of projects. But this is no reason to turn away from a struggle that is common among elderly people and those who care for them. Still less should we make vigorous elderly individuals exemplars of virtue by which those who fail and decline measure themselves. The claim "I can do it myself" reverberates throughout the life cycle, perhaps becoming a dominant note in individualist competitive cultures. But except among the most defensive, isolated, and sheltered individuals, displays of independence mingle with other, albeit often quieter, requests: "help me," "catch me if I fall." In trying to create mutually helpful and respectful relationships in which we can fall and be caught "with dignity," we have at least as much to learn from elderly people who fail well as from the vigorously healthy.

Notes

I am grateful to Martha Holstein, Hilde Lindemann Nelson, James Nelson, William Ruddick, Margaret Urban Walker, and Marilyn Young for comments on an earlier version of this chapter and to Margaret Walker for organizing the splendid conference that inspired these reflections on age.

1. Thomas R. Cole, *The Journey of Life: A Cultural History of Aging in America* (Cambridge: Cambridge University Press, 1992), 229.

2. Martha Holstein, "Women and Productive Aging: Troubling Implications," in *Critical Gerontology: Perspectives from Political and Moral Economy*, ed. Meredith Minkler and Carroll L. Estes (Amityville, N.Y.: Baywood, 1998); and Martha Holstein, "Ethics and Public Policy," in *The Future of Aged-Based Public-Policy*, ed. Robert B. Hudson (Baltimore: Johns Hopkins University Press, 1997).

3. Susan Wendell, "Old Women Out of Control," chapter 8 in this volume.

4. Iris Murdoch, "On 'God' and 'Good,' " *The Sovereignty of Good* (New York: Schocken Books, 1971), 71.

5. I am drawing specifically on Margaret Gullette, *Declining to Decline: Cultural Combat and the Politics of Midlife* (Charlottesville: University Press of Virginia, 1997).

6. The phrase is from Frida Kerner Furman, *Facing the Mirror: Older Women and Beauty Shop Culture* (New York: Routledge, 1997).

7. I take the term "counterstory" from Hilde Lindemann Nelson. See chapter 5 in this volume.

8. The phrases are from Susan Wendell, this volume.

9. The phrase is from Furman, *Facing the Mirror.*

10. Bernard Boxill, "Protest and Self-Respect," in *Philosophy Born of Struggle*, ed. Leonard Harris (Dubuque, Iowa: Kendall Hunt, 1982). See also Boxill, "Self-

Respect," ch. 9 in *Blacks & Social Justice* (Lanham, Md.: Rowman & Littlefield, 1992).

11. The exception is Aristotle. If considering anger as a moral emotion—as contrasted with a therapeutically useful emotion—I would recommend, in addition to Boxill: Sue Campbell, *Interpreting the Personal* (Ithaca: Cornell University Press, 1997); Audre Lorde, "The Uses of Anger," *Sister/Outsider* (Trumansburg, N.Y.: Crossing Press, 1984); Peter Lyman, "The Politics of Anger," *Socialist Review* 11 (1981); Naomi Scheman, "Anger and the Politics of Naming," *Engenderings* (New York: Routledge, 1993); Elizabeth Spelman, "Anger and Insubordination," in *Women, Knowledge and Reality*, ed. Ann Garry and Marilyn Pearsall (Boston: Unwin Hyman, 1989); Patricia Williams, "The Death of the Profane," *Alchemy of Race and Rights* (Cambridge: Harvard University Press, 1991).

12. I take the phrase "outlaw emotions" from Alison Jaggar, "Love and Knowledge: Emotion in Feminist Epistemology," in *Women, Knowledge and Reality*, ed. Ann Garry and Marilyn Pearsall (Boston: Unwin Hyman, 1989). See also Diana Tietjens Meyers, "Emotion and Heterodox Moral Perception," in *Feminists Rethink the Self*, ed. Diana Tietjens Meyers (Boulder: Westview, 1997), which I have found enormously helpful.

13. The phrase "known it all already" is adapted from T. S. Eliot, "Love Song of J. Alfred Prufrock." The "laceration of laughter that ceases to amuse" is from "Little Gidding." Both are in T. S. Eliot, *Collected Poems and Plays* (New York: Harcourt Brace, 1952).

14. Erik H. Erikson, Joan M. Erikson, and Helen Q. Kivnick, *Vital Involvement in Old Age* (New York: Norton, 1986), 56.

15. Eliot, "Little Gidding."

16. Erikson, *Vital Involvement*, 141.

17. For a summary of "life review" literature and a different, more critical view of it, see Margaret Urban Walker, this volume.

18. James Baldwin, in a review of *The Arrangements* by Elia Kazin, cited by Janet Landmann, *Regret* (New York: Oxford University Press, 1993), 68.

19. Albert Camus, *The Fall* (New York: Vintage, 1962), 145. "Yes we have lost track of the light, the mornings, the holy innocence of those who forgive themselves."

20. Adapted from Hannah Arendt, "Thinking and Moral Considerations," *Social Research* (Fall 1971): 417–46.

21. "Things ill done and done to others' harm" is from T. S. Eliot, "Little Gidding."

22. Drawing again on Susan Wendell, this volume.

· 4 ·

Unplanned Obsolescence:
Some Reflections on Aging

Sandra Lee Bartky

Grow old along with me!
  The best is yet to be,
  The last of life, for which the first was made.
          Robert Browning,
        "Rabbi Ben Ezra" (1864)

*W*hat is there precisely about the "last of life" the poet thinks is best? In what sense is the first of life made for the last? The poet has fallen in love and rescued Elizabeth Barrett, whose youth had been spent under the thumb of a tyrannical Victorian father and in the grip of psychosomatic illness, both of which had colluded in her virtual imprisonment in the family home. But surely, these lines are meant to have a more general appeal; indeed, they are among the most quoted in English verse. They were quoted to me often by my father, usually on birthdays. My father was relentlessly cheerful, his cheerfulness barely covering a chronic mild depression. Naturally, his perpetual optimism produced in me an equal and opposite reaction: pessimism.

Unlike the poet and my father, I see old age, for the most part, as a series of losses. There is the loss of one's social or professional networks; the loss, if one lives long enough and if there is one, of a life's companion; the loss, if one is unlucky, of motility, or sight or hearing or the control of one's sphincters; the loss of one's home, if illness requires moving in with an adult child or else removal to a nursing home; inevitably, there is the loss of life in death. For purposes of this chapter I shall define "old age" as beginning at age 70. Of course this varies: some people are washed up in their forties, while many of the "elderly" are energetic, vibrant, creative, and attractive.

61

I shall enumerate some of the losses that aging brings: the list is not intended to be comprehensive and it is strongly influenced by what I myself fear. I write as a white, middle-aged professional woman with a secure income, health insurance, and the prospect of a pension I can live on comfortably. My situation thus protects me against two great evils, racism and poverty, whose effects fall even more heavily on a vulnerable population such as the elderly. Nor do I have aging parents or adult children or grandchildren for whom I must care. I am childless and my parents are dead. Where I see gains accruing to the elderly, I will mention them. I shall deal chiefly with the social and cultural losses of the elderly, rather than physically based losses of motility (that are often accompanied by chronic pain) or the loss of mental capacity.[1] When this exercise has been completed, I shall try to determine which of these losses are the consequence of social, that is, cultural construction, hence in principle alterable, and which are irremediable features of the human condition.[2] Finally, I shall speculate as to what might be done to mitigate their force and effect.

Polar Bears on an Ice Floe

As we age, our friends and colleagues die: our networks shrink or disappear entirely. This contributes to the loneliness and isolation that beset many older people. The old friends and colleagues with whom we have bonded for decades are not so easily replaced. It is easier to make friends when one is young and relatively unformed. As we age, we make important value commitments; we take on form and definition. Moreover, what my generation has seen, the history of which we were a part, is part of who I am now. With the passage of time ever fewer people will understand things that have great existential import for us. While it is important for generations to speak together, I need as intimates people of my generation who remember *what it was like*—not just cataclysmic public events, but the flavor and texture of the vanished popular culture of our youth.

Loss of Social and Professional Networks

Many of us have been active in organizing and sustaining professional networks. This has been particularly important for feminists like myself. One of the most successful examples of professional networking was the organization of a task force that became Division 44, "The Society for the Psychological Study of Gay, Lesbian and Bi-Sexual Issues," of the American Psychological Association. This organization succeeded in having homosexuality removed from the standard reference list of psychological diseases; the consequences of this have been extensive.[3] Feminist psychologists continue to struggle against the inclusion of categories that harm women by classifying as a matter of individual pathology patterns that are the result of patriarchal social relations, for example, "masochistic personality disorder." Over time, however, founding members of our networks die or retire; our caucus or network disappears or changes its focus; younger people appear who wish to take the organization in directions we may not approve. The old militancy appears to vanish even if the problems against which it militated have not been resolved. New people appear, who do not always share the vision of our cohort.

I have seen the effects of professional obsolescence on older men in my own profession. Formerly influential philosophers see their comrades die or retire; they lose influence, and sometimes appear lost and stranded, polar bears on an ice floe. This happened to my own dissertation adviser. The philosophical orientation of his generation gave way to something quite different, indeed something hostile to the orientation of that generation. He died shortly after retirement. His work was influential in its day; no one reads him now.

Of course, not all networks are professional, as are the academic associations I have been discussing. My Aunt Lill, my mother's only sister and her best friend, belonged to a purely social network, the Wednesday Club. "The Wednesday Girls," as they always called themselves, met weekly for almost forty years. There were eight or nine of them, close friends all, who shared each other's joys and sorrows for most of their lives. Their names were household words to me because even though my mother (much younger than my aunt) was not a Wednesday Girl herself, she knew them all. Aunt Lill (who didn't drive) and my mother (housebound with small children) spent hours every day on the telephone; the struggles and sorrows, the small victories and defeats of the Wednesday Girls were discussed in detail. This talk was background to my play.

The Wednesday Girls were daughters of immigrants. None had been to college, nor had their husbands. Most of the husbands were salesmen or small businessmen who managed to make enough money to keep their wives out of wage work (a marker in those days of middle-class status), though some of the women "helped out" in the family business, indeed, probably helped run it. But Wednesday afternoons were sacrosanct. I went one time at my aunt's invitation to a Wednesday gathering. This must have been someone's birthday or anniversary and Aunt Lill wanted to make the afternoon special. So she hired me, the family piano prodigy, to play Chopin quietly in the background while she served petit fours, finger sandwiches, and tea. Of course the Wednesday Girls made a terrific fuss over me: how pretty I was, how talented! They dressed for each other, in fashionable frocks or chic suits with padded shoulders and handsome Bakelite buttons. (They all sewed, and well.) They wore funny little hats. They were, by the standards of the day, slim. Their long fingernails were blood red, their hairdos à la mode, their shoes two-toned leather with open toes. After lunch and a lot of talking, these elegant ladies settled happily into their games of mah-jongg. Over the years, everything was shared—the success of a child, the failure of a business. What astonishes me now about the Wednesday Girls is the readiness and effectiveness of their emotional and material support of one another, the surprising cohesiveness of the group and its longevity.

In time, they aged. Then husbands grew ill, mostly with heart conditions. It was thought better for the husbands if they retired and moved south, mostly to Florida or Arizona. Or was it thought better *by* the husbands to move south where one could play golf year round? I wonder how many of these women really wanted to uproot themselves. Then the husbands began to die. The Wednesday Girls gave immense comfort and support to one another on these occasions. But as no one in the club was very rich and because they had no pensions in their own name, many of the Wednesday Girls found that they could not live on what their husbands had left them. So, increasingly, they moved in with adult children, rarely a happy arrangement. And the children were scattered, many to California. So little by little, the fabric of the Wednesday Club was rent, and then, one day, it unraveled. They kept only in sporadic touch with one another, to be sure, but the news from points south was never very good. As these lifelong friends of my aunt had become lifelong friends of my mother too, I sometimes saw them when they made brief stopovers in Chicago to see friends or family still in the north. As older women, they had lost their verve and chic; they looked dowdy, thicker, gray of face, defeated. Networks are born, mature, sustain us and our projects, and then almost certainly decline. We have drawn sustenance from such networks, and some measure of identity. When they disappear, we are diminished.

Intellectual, Moral, and Cultural Obsolescence

During my first year in graduate school, I remember joining in with other students to make fun of some elderly professors who were frozen intellectually in what had been fashionable in the early days of their careers; we had no idea that such a fate might well befall us.

The same thing is happening to me. I have tried to retool in order to figure out (and then somewhat imperfectly) what postmodernism is all about, this because it falls within my subject area and I feel an obligation to teach it. I feel now how powerful is the tendency to stay with what we know and what we know how to teach, rather than to assimilate ideas in what often feels like an impenetrable jargon. I feel sometimes how close I come to intellectual obsolescence insofar as graduate students are concerned; they take to some of this material more easily than I do, just as they find it easier than I do to master computer skills.

Intellectual obsolescence can come to people who are not professional intellectuals. My late mother-in-law, for example, could never get it through her head that meat and other substantial, high-cholesterol, and wildly fattening foods weren't good for you. She stuffed us full of high-fat, delicious stuff at family dinners, but worse, she insisted that we take at least two shopping bags full of the same kinds of food home with us. This woman had been virtually kidnapped by the Nazis from her homeland and sent to Germany to cook in a factory. She was a displaced person at the end of the war, stranded in Germany, and unwilling to be repatriated to a country that had been overrun by Russia. Who knows what she ate during these terrible times? Who knows how often she got to eat at all? At the end of the war, she was sent to England where, as a poor single mother, she worked in a sweatshop and had to endure poverty in a country already in the grip of postwar austerity. Can she be blamed for equating food, especially rich food and meat, with life? Teresa read little but the Bible and religious tracts. She did not understand why we were trying to eat vegetarian, why we wanted to avoid butter, cheese, and cream; surely, these were just crazy American ideas; lots of things about life in America seemed quite crazy to her.

The elderly may have expected to become, but are not, repositories of wisdom; they are seen more often as out of step with the times, hopelessly old-fashioned. This is, unfortunately, often the case, as whatever wisdom the elderly have gathered belongs to a different historical moment. Ours is not a traditional culture in which values are preserved from one generation to another. For many elderly people, it may seem as though their political visions, and even their most elementary sense of propriety, have vanished. My mother and her friends, for example, were genuinely shocked that feminine hygiene products were advertised openly on television. Both my parents completely disapproved of "living in sin," even though, as atheists, they didn't believe in sin, and even though they had close friends who, because they were of different religions and didn't have the courage to stand down their families, lived "in sin" for years. Now the allowability of premarital sex is trumpeted loudly in nightly sit-coms.

Loss of the Significant Other

As women live longer than men, the coupled heterosexual woman can, statistically, look forward to widowhood. The loss and the loneliness are no less, of course, for husbands who survive or for lesbians and gays who lose their life partners. This loss is perhaps the principal cause of loneliness in the aged. But some women are set free by widowhood, women whose caretaking of sick, dependent, childish, or querulous old men was burdensome in the extreme. My neighbor, Noann, became a prisoner in her own home. Whenever she tried to go shopping or to the hairdresser, her husband (whose mind was gone) would begin to wail so loudly and so piteously at the sight of the hired "sitter" that Noann's heart would soften and she would stay home, sending the sitter to the store instead. Noann's embrace of her version of the "ethic of care" instilled in women was such that she wouldn't consider sending Jack to a nursing home; hence, despite considerable resources, Noann put herself under house arrest for nearly five years and she was only set free by Jack's death.

And then there were Sarah and Jake. Jake was a cigar-chomping enormous man whose bulk seemed to fill most available space. He was kindly and funny, with a loud, booming voice that filled any space that still remained. Jake was an accomplished raconteur who grabbed the center of attention wherever he found himself. Sara was small and somewhat lumpish, with rounded shoulders and a body language that spoke of defeat. She had plucked her eyebrows almost all out, thirties style, and had penciled in two deeply curving lines above her eyes that spoke eloquently of sadness. Sarah always walked behind Jake, because he was too large to go through a doorway *with* anyone else. He ignored her, which encouraged everyone else to ignore her too. Since she couldn't speak when Jake was there (nor could anyone else), it was assumed that she had nothing to say.

In time, Jake died. When Jake died, Sarah came alive. She was found to have opinions, wit, and funny stories of her own. Was Jake, this kindly and generous man, really a succubus who had been feeding on her substance for fifty years? She began standing straighter. She totally revised her eyebrows. She bought a new wardrobe of light print dresses, just right for Miami Beach, to which she removed herself at the earliest opportunity—a suggestion Jake had always vetoed. She went to tea dances for senior citizens and hinted, on her trips back to Chicago, of a life devoted, if not to dalliance, then to flirting.

But these are not representative tales. For most of the widowed, male and female, there is profound grief and loneliness. There is also *skin hunger*, the need for physical touching. It has been well documented that infants deprived of physical contact can fail to flourish. Something of this sort is true of adults too: though terrible, its deprivation does not have the dire consequences it has for infants. Work once separated me from my partner for an extended time. After several months I realized that I was suffering a deprivation I had not anticipated: frequent and sustaining loving touch. Fortunate are the elderly who have families who can provide this. But the chief provider—the beloved partner—is gone. Some isolated older people are advised to buy dogs and the advice seems to be quite sound, yet sad. How can a terrier stand in for your beloved? A dog or cat may satisfy some of our need to touch and be touched, but not the quality of love, affirmation, understanding, and emotional support we got (ideally) from the intimate other. The idea that my life's companion will die before I do fills me with the same dread I have at the prospect of my own death. Yet, I believe that he will suffer terribly if I die first and he is left alone. This sums up my sense of aging: a lose-lose situation.

Loss of the Admiring Gaze

The loss of an admiring gaze falls disproportionately on women. We need to see but also to be seen and to be seen as attractive. Indeed, the capacity to draw admiring glances from others is a chief marker of femininity in our culture; a woman's worth, not only in the eyes of others, but in her own eyes as well, depends, to a significant degree, on her appearance.[4] This topic is treated extensively in Diana Meyers's chapter 2 in this volume, so I will only touch upon it here. The experience of becoming invisible is, for a woman who has passed through middle age, already familiar; it is superbly described in Doris Lessing's *Summer Before the Dark*.[5]

I have written elsewhere and at some length about women's embodiment in advanced industrial society.[6] The anxieties we have as young women often grow worse in middle age, but what about old age? This is something about which we know very little. I suspect that old age is welcomed by some women because the issue, indeed, the burden of appearance has been settled; one is now an unattractive old crow and that's the end of it. But many older women may still have the needs and anxieties they had in middle age and earlier, as young commodities on the "Meet

Market." We know that many older women are still consumers of the accoutrements of the beauty industry. Some elderly women have hit upon a strategy to attract an admiring gaze in spite of advanced age and the indifference of the generalized social other (more about this in the final section).

Loss of Opportunity for Sexual Connection

Here is another loss that falls disproportionately on women. Masters and Johnson did everyone, not just the elderly, a great service in finding that neither sexual capacity (especially in women, but in men too) nor sexual enjoyment must necessarily cease with age.[7] But a number of obstacles stand in the way of heterosexual elderly women's full utilization of this finding. First, the ratio of women to men in every passing decade increases: men die younger than women; also, when older men are freed by death or divorce to couple again, many prefer younger women. Second, there is the folk belief that sexual interest disappears with age, indeed, that it *should* disappear and that the continuation in the aged of a keen sexual interest, not to mention an active sex life, is not just inappropriate, but faintly disreputable. I suspect that this idea had its origin in the belief that sex was for reproduction only, but hardly anyone in this country still believes this. Nevertheless, geriatric sex seems always good for a laugh in the entertainment media. Finally, I believe that some elderly persons, particularly women, remove themselves from the admittedly slim chance of dalliance because of the belief that sex and romance are the rewards of youth and beauty. The old, hence ugly, do not deserve or cannot hope to generate sexual desire in anyone. While there is always talk about the beauty of older women's deeply lined faces (mostly from artists and photographers), the appearance of the outward signs of aging are not welcome. Sexiness and youth are conjoined continually in films, advertising, music videos, and magazines. Many older women may believe that younger women are more adventurous in bed, more up-to-date in their sexual technique. There is no evidence that this is the case: here a socially depreciated self colludes in its own depreciation, a classic self-fulfilling prophecy—the patriarchal gaze turned inward.

What Is to Be Done?

The losses to which I directed most of my attention are social, not biological. These include the loss of one's social and professional networks, the loss of intellectual and moral relevance and hence moral authority, as well as the loss of conventional physical attractiveness, and finally, the loss of opportunities for romantic and sexual experience. The fact that these losses are in some ways "socially constructed" does not mean that they are easily overcome. By identifying some major losses involved in the process of aging, I hope to start a conversation about what we can anticipate as we age and what steps we can take, if not to eliminate these losses, at least to soften their effect.

The elderly might do well to cultivate resignation, but resignation is not a North American cultural value; indeed, it might be argued that our highly mobile, yuppified, hard-driving and excessively individualistic consumer culture is hostile to resignation. Virtue ethicists have neglected resignation; the issue requires extended treatment. But recommending resignation to the elderly is premature, for there are more practical sorts of things that the elderly themselves, as well as we, who are not quite elderly, can do to prepare ourselves for at least some of the social disabilities of old age.

How to deal with the loss of social and professional networks? First, professional networks. It is necessary for professional networks to be open to younger people; this means that criteria for inclusion must be flexible. In order to do "outreach" one must be prepared to see the network altered and enlarged; this means that our age cohort will have to give up some measure of control; it means too that we must be prepared to see the network or organization or caucus move in directions for which we lack a certain enthusiasm. This requires flexibility, but how much flexibility can we muster without a loss of principle? This is not a question that can be answered in a general way; here, decisions must be made on a case-by-case basis.

In order to expand, the network must show younger persons that it can and will help them professionally. The stabilization and expansion of sustaining and supportive networks will make it more likely that they will be there for us when we need them. Where networks do not exist, elderly people who feel alienated need to organize, for surely, there are other old people who are feeling the same way. And the critical mass necessary for the success of a network—or just a "support group"—can be quite small. I have never understood why people often say proudly, "I'm not a joiner."

On social networks: the Wednesday Girls were, I believe, victims of institutional heterosexuality. Even though their network was, for many, far more sustaining than their marriages, they were compelled to define marriage and family as primary. Hence, instead of moving even closer to one another as they aged and/or were widowed, they made the conventional moves with and for their husbands, or toward their adult children. Given how things were then, this was inevitable. But their fate is, at least for me, exemplary: they held friendship too cheaply.

Their story is tied to questions about how and with whom we want to retire and what sorts of arrangements we need to be making now. Do we want to face the necessity of fitting ourselves into some retirement community with people who do not share our interests or values? Do we want to leave behind networks of friends and family to go off with just a partner to points south? What kinds of stress would this put on the relationship? How well would we flourish, sundered from so many of the people who have sustained us? Or do we want to begin to think now about shaping our own retirement communities, or settlements, or communes? We need to do something extraordinary: we need to imagine alternative institutional arrangements, new ways of living together that might never have been tried before. This task is particularly urgent for people like me who have no children, as well as for those who have families but would prefer not to live with them in later life.

Intellectual obsolescence: a tough call. Assume that old dogs *can* be taught new tricks. The greatest obstacle to learning is the belief that one is unable to learn, a common belief among the elderly. Find a class or pay a tutor to come to your home and teach you effective computer literacy. I have heard that the Internet and the Web are great resources for the housebound. Skim the appropriate journal or magazine so that you can become conversant (more or less) with developments in areas that interest you. But what *ought* to interest you? Open minds are always praised, but we cannot keep our minds open to everything. Here again, there is no *general* answer to this question.

People who are still professionally active, or active in community groups, will know what they need to know. A teacher's aide in a ghetto school should know something about rap, also that there is a substantial sociological literature on gangs. Someone teaching eighteen-year-olds from a perspective critical of the dominant culture ought, probably, to find out who all those people are on the cover of *TV Guide* and *People*; she ought to watch MTV and the more popular sit-coms. I admit to being quite unable to do this myself. On the other hand, I held rock music in some contempt until a friend forced me to really listen to the Beatles. How much I would have missed had this not happened—not just the Beatles, but Elvis, the Stones, Eric Clapton, Janis Joplin, Jimi Hendrix, and so on. I'm still twenty-five years behind the times, but so what? Do we need always to be *au courant*? We have devoted decades to our own intellectual, cultural, and political development. We need not be tossed hither and yon by every new intellectual or cultural fashion. A balance needs to be found between the ground we have laboriously secured and the new territory that beckons. Once again, no general formula can be forthcoming. We must not regard it as loss of face to admit that we need a teacher or guide, even though I have noticed that younger people are often quite condescending toward older students. Aging is not only not for sissies, neither is it for the thin-skinned.

On aging and wisdom: I do not know if younger people find me wise or not. Some younger students, I'm sure, find my ideas quaint and quite superannuated. I share with my graduate students the ordeals I faced in graduate school and as a junior faculty member, hoping that they can learn something from my experience. Mostly they listen politely but noncommittally. I notice that when they are in crisis or need advice they tend to go to younger faculty.

Now others may not believe that we are wise, but some of us know that we are wiser than we were when we were younger. Some older people are just as foolish as they were when they were young. I too am capable of major stupidities, but I believe that, in general, I am more mature, more serene, more accepting of my own limitations, less obsessed with issues of success and failure and with what other people will think of me than I used to be; in a word, less self-absorbed. This is, I think, one of the few things we gain in aging. Indecision and lack of confidence are twin tormentors of youth, but not as often of age.

I come finally to questions about the appearance and sexuality of the elderly, especially of elderly women. The usual fund of experience out of which people write about such things is not available to me, as I am close to but not yet elderly. I have found very little material in women's autobiographies on sexuality and embodiment, especially as they affect old women. There are no fashion magazines aimed at women in their seventies, telling them what to do with their bodies or even how to feel about their bodies, much less stories on "how to hold onto your man" if you are 75. I do not know of boutiques in or out of larger stores that display clothes for the elderly. My own mother died at 72. She and her friends were very concerned with appearance, but not more so than they were in their forties or fifties. There are no reports of widespread anorexia or bulimia in elderly women. A friend's mother described to me her sense of alienation when she would glimpse herself in a mirror. She felt young inside, she said, but her face was crisscrossed with deep lines of age. I myself have the same experience, but with fewer lines; I am shocked by the aging of my body, not just my face. Older women are not expected to "make the most of what they have" unless they live in very wealthy communities (e.g., Beverly Hills or Orange County, California) in which case they will be expected to have periodic face-lifts, liposuction, tummy-tucks, and personal trainers. Many older women have given up even the possibility that they can satisfy the requirements of ideal embodied femininity and believe they are now supposed to become invisible, to dwindle away into retirement villages or nursing homes, or to respond selflessly to the day care crisis by caretaking their grandchildren or even great-grandchildren.

I have written elsewhere about the need for a new and more democratic aesthetics of the body;[8] insofar as such has not surfaced, we must live in the world as it is. I find it most remarkable that some women have invented transgressive strategies that undermine the invisibility, at best, and at worst, the repugnance of the dominant culture toward their aged bodies. Many of the elderly widows who are my neighbors are still quite active. While I believe that some are, deep down, quite lonely, this is not the whole story. It is also the case that they have made some sort of society for themselves, traveling together on a downtown express bus to concerts, shopping, and the theater. I take this bus often myself. What these women have done, quite subversively, and, I am sure, quite unconsciously, is to create an approving and appreciative collective gaze with which they affirm one another's appearance. They look attentively at one another, noticing what is new, or what has changed. "I love what you've done with your hair," they say to one another; "What a gorgeous suit, is it new?"; "You're looking wonderful, Sophie, have you lost weight?" They are delighted and excited to be in one another's company; they have created a new gaze, not the gaze of standard-issue patriarchy or of dead husbands, but a democratic and inclusive gaze that installs something attractive in everyone. This is a tribute to the unplanned ingenuity of aging women and their determination to restore to themselves what the culture denies them—their self-esteem, their dignity, and their beauty.

I shall close with a fantasy I have about these women, my neighbors in a huge and faceless 1950s high-rise that, like so many other such buildings with similar populations, stands like a sentinel on Chicago's northerly lakefront. My fantasy would offend them deeply but I think it unlikely that any will ever learn of it. While these women have made a sort of society for one another, each lives alone; I believe that many are lonely in the way one is lonely who has friends, but lacks a certain kind of intimacy. I believe too that many have what I called earlier "skin hunger." Here is my fantasy:

these elderly widows abandon their deeply entrenched homophobia (for they too, like the Wednesday Girls and many of us, are victims of institutionalized heterosexuality) and, just as they have learned to meet each other's needs for visibility and admiration, they go one step further and begin to meet each other's needs for physical intimacy. This intimacy need not be sexual, but if it is sexual, so much the better. Perhaps there are women whose needs extend no farther than hugging and embracing, frequent nuzzling kisses, the comfort of a warm body touching one's own body in bed on a winter night. For the women who need sex and have not had it for decades, I fantasize wild sexual excitement and fulfillment and the special kind of confidence that comes with the knowledge that one has the capacity to arouse sexual desire in another. Their condo would come alive with couplings and rumors of couplings, dalliance, flirting, gossip, matchmaking, lovers' quarrels, *liaisons innocentes ou dangereuses*. Now these suddenly energetic sisters will have more to talk about than the ingratitude of their children, the day's ration of soap operas, or the thoroughly exhausted topic of the cuteness of their grandchildren.

Notes

I would like to thank Margaret Walker for her detailed and indispensable assistance in the preparation of this manuscript; also Diana Meyers, Sara Ruddick, Anita Silvers, and other contributors to this volume. However, I bear full responsibility for the ideas contained herein.

1. Anita Silvers discusses the understanding of such losses in some detail in chapter 12 of this volume. See also Susan Wendell, *The Rejected Body: Feminist Philosophical Reflections on Disability* (New York: Routledge, 1996).

2. The idea that the stages of life are "socially constructed" comes from two sources, Philippe Aries, *Centuries of Childhood: A Social History of Family Life*, tr. Robert Baldrick (New York: Knopf, 1962); and Margaret Morganroth Gullette's recent pathbreaking "deconstruction" of middle age, *Declining to Decline: Cultural Combat and the Politics of the Midlife* (Charlottesville: University Press of Virginia, 1997).

3. The *1994 Diagnostic and Statistical Manual of Mental Disorders IV* no longer lists homosexuality as a form of mental illness.

4. See Sandra Lee Bartky, *Femininity and Domination: Studies in the Phenomenology of Oppression* (New York: Routledge, 1990), especially ch. 3; and Susan Bordo, *Unbearable Weight: Feminism, Western Culture, and the Body* (Berkeley: University of California Press, 1993).

5. Doris Lessing, *Summer Before the Dark* (New York: Knopf, 1973).

6. Bartky, *Femininity and Domination*, ch. 5.

7. William H. Masters and Virginia E. Johnson, *Human Sexual Response* (Boston: Little, Brown, 1966).

8. See Bartky, *Femininity and Domination*, ch. 3.

Stories of My Old Age

Hilde Lindemann Nelson

$\mathcal{I}$n the film *Marvin's Room*, a hairdresser who has a troubled son and a hard life returns with her children to the house of her father, Marvin, an elderly man lying bedridden and speechless because of the strokes that have damaged his brain. Marvin's primary caregiver is his other daughter, whom the hairdresser scorns for having wasted her best years tending to the needs of their decrepit parent—a waste that is all the more tragic in that the sister's life is almost over, as she will soon die of cancer. In an epiphanic moment, however, as the hairdresser watches her sister hold up a hand mirror for Marvin that scatters light over his bed and walls like a blessing, she sees beauty and dignity shining forth from the old man and understands that her sister's life has not been wasted. She has spent it on something of infinite value. With this insight the hairdresser begins to heal her own broken life, and at the end of the film we see her taking up the precious burden of responsibility for Marvin's care that her sister must now lay down.

Narrative Figurations and Counterstories

Stories such as this offer certain kinds of aesthetic pleasure—among others, the pleasure of familiarity. They do this by setting into play a variety of narrative figurations, as Diana Meyers calls them, drawn from a vast cultural store.[1] They adopt ready-made plot templates and character types—the troubled adolescent, the ministering angel, the whore with the heart of gold—that please us because we can make sense of them, and we can make sense of them because we've seen these figurations so often before. We encounter them not just in the movies but everywhere: in the fairy tales we remember from childhood, in commercial advertising, in newspaper stories, psychoanalytic theories, video games. And, as Meyers and others have argued, we rely heavily on these figurations to structure our own and other people's experiences.[2]

In addition to offering the pleasure of the familiar, though, *Marvin's Room* engages in a specialized kind of moral work: the work of countering the figuration of "burdensome and useless old man." It takes up the stock plot of decline in old age and refigures it as a story of affirmation and love. It thus functions as a *counterstory*—a story that allows its teller, or those on behalf of whom it is told, to resist an oppressive identity by rejecting the invidious figurations out of which it is constructed and replacing them with more respectful and humane understandings of who the person is.[3] The difficulty, though, as I shall argue, is that *Marvin's Room* isn't a very good counterstory, because although it reidentifies Marvin in a positive way, it does so by cementing more firmly into place the master narratives that unfairly and coercively assign the brunt of unpaid family caregiving to women.

In this chapter I defend the idea that identities are narratively constructed. I argue that this construction is profoundly social, not only because the overlapping, self-defining stories a person tells on her own behalf are largely composed of narrative figurations drawn from the cultural stock, but also because others impose identities upon her, whether she wills them or not, through their own narrative activity. I then develop the concept of the counterstory, in particular as it functions with respect to the identities of the elderly and their caregivers. Finally, I turn to the seemingly intractable problem of getting people who have unjustly identified an elderly person as useless and burdensome, or childish, or set in her ways, to listen to a counterstory that resists such identifications. The difficulty lies in penetrating what Margaret Walker has christened the "epistemic firewall"—the barrier that is erected between the privileged and the disenfranchised by various practices that naturalize, normalize, hide, or legitimate coercive behaviors and relations.[4] The firewall makes a state of affairs seem so obvious, so in keeping with the right and good order of things, that the counterstory gets dismissed as offensive, tiresome, threatening, or ridiculous. Often, it receives no sort of hearing at all. The task, then, is to figure out how to push a counterstory of old age through the firewall. I close by suggesting some strategies for doing this.

The Narrative Self-Constitution View

In order to cash out my claim that under certain conditions, people can successfully resist oppressive identities of old age and reidentify themselves as persons of full worth and dignity by telling counterstories, I shall have to demonstrate that personal identities are the sorts of entities on which narratives have an effect. To do this, I am going to draw on work by Marya Schechtman.[5]

In *The Constitution of Selves*, Schechtman observes that questions about whether a person at one point in time is still the same as the person at an earlier point in time—which is what philosophers generally mean when they talk about "personal identity"—is not what most of us are interested in when we think about who a person is. Instead, we want to understand how the person thinks, feels, and acts, what matters to her, how she sees herself. Schechtman calls this the characterization question—the question about the set of actions, experiences, and characteristics that make a person that person rather than someone else. On Schechtman's account, the characterization question is an attempt to get at the relationship between persons and intuitions we have concerning four basic features of personal existence: moral responsibility, self-interested concern, compensation, and survival.[6] Unlike the question of whether one is still the same person at two different points in time, which demands a yes-no answer, the characterization question admits of degrees. "All of the characteristics that are part of a person's history are presumed to contribute to making up her identity. Some, however, play a more central role than others and are more truly expressive of who she is" (77).

Assignments of *moral responsibility*, Schechtman claims, centrally involve judgments about the degree to which an action expresses one's identity. Whether a particular action is something that merely occurs in my history, something that is quite solidly mine, or something that flows naturally from features absolutely central to my character is on Schechtman's view directly relevant to the degree to which I am responsible for what I do. I am, for example, less culpable for snapping at you for no good reason if my irritability is the result of chronic pain brought on by severe arthritis than if I am simply an irritable, disagreeable person. Conversely, if I fail to take responsibility, say, for the care of my frail elderly mother merely because I would find it depressing and inconvenient to do so, that says something about who I am, and that is what the characterization question seeks to establish.

Self-interested concern, conceived as the concern a person has with her future well-being, includes the desire to avoid unnecessary pain, to make a difference in the world, to pursue one's goals. Some of these desires, however, are more fundamental to our sense of ourselves than others, and so are more truly our own. While we all care to some extent whether our lungs remain in good working order, for example, this is of particular concern to me if I am a dancer, since the state of my lungs has a direct bearing on my ability to pursue my profession. When I become elderly, however, I might care more about my physical safety than about the things that mattered to me when I danced. As the degree to which we care about fulfilling any particular desire is typically a function of how strongly we identify with that desire, facts about characterization enter into any account of self-interested concern.

As Schechtman sees it, *compensation* too is linked to the characterization question, since the degree to which a person is compensated in the future for some present pain depends on how much the person identifies with the future reward. The question here is not simply whether the person who gets the new car is the same person who took a second job to pay for it, as personal identity theorists have supposed, but whether I care enough about owning a new car so that it counts as compensation for the sacrifice I made for it. Looking back on my life from the vantage point of old age, I might discover that I no longer care about what happens to the small business I began fifty years ago—that its present flourishing is not compensation after all for the decades of work I put into it. Because compensation is bound up with the question of what is worth giving up for something else, it cannot be explained without appealing to a person's values and commitments, and these say something about who the person is.

Finally, Schechtman argues, the kind of *survival* that is most important to us—psychological continuation—also admits of degrees and is linked to facts about characterization. That it admits of degrees can be seen by thinking of the varying extents to which personality change is associated with disease, torture, drug addiction, cult membership, or spousal abuse. That survival is linked to facts about characterization can be seen by considering that the degree to which a person survives disease, abuse, or addiction bears some relationship to the degree to which her actions, experiences, and characteristics are her own. "I was no longer the same person I had been before the assault," says Susan J. Brison after having been beaten, raped, strangled, and left for dead.[7] "I died in Auschwitz," writes Charlotte Delbo.[8] And, laments a family member of an elderly person suffering from Alzheimer's disease: "She's not herself anymore."

For Schechtman, then, "Who am I?" is a question that can be answered in terms of overlapping complexes of actions, experiences, and characteristics that vary in terms of their centrality. But if that is what we mean when we talk of personal identity, what is it about such identities that renders them susceptible to narratives? Schechtman's answer is that a person creates her identity by forming an autobiographical narrative (93). She argues that it is the act of weaving stories of one's life that makes an individual a person, and a person's identity "is constituted by the content of her self-narrative" (94)—by what she holds herself responsible for, what concerns she has for her future well-being, what counts as compensation for her, and to what degree she remains who she once was.

According to Schechtman's "narrative self-constitution view," the construction of an identity-constituting autobiographical narrative does not have to be self-conscious. Rather, the sense of one's life as unfolding according to the logic of a narrative "is the lens through which we filter our experience and plan for actions, not a way we think about ourselves in reflective hours" (113). On this view, the autobiographical plotline is an organizing principle of our lives, often implicit rather than explicit.

This plotline, says Schechtman, must be that of a "conventional, linear narrative" if the story is to be identity-constituting for persons (96). Schechtman's reason for insisting on this is that she believes the traditional, linear narrative is the only one employed by individuals "like us": individuals for whom moral responsibility, self-interested concern, compensation, and survival are basic features of existence. Indeed, she claims that beings who arranged their experience in nonlinear ways would be unable to "make plans, engage in long-term commitments, or take responsibility for the past" (101). Such beings, she supposes, couldn't be recognized by us as *persons*, as their self-conception would be too different from ours to fit under that category. This part of Schechtman's account is open to serious criticism, especially as it pertains to the identities of elderly people, and I will return to it later on.

The narrative self-constitution view, says Schechtman, puts two important constraints on identity-constituting narratives. The first is the requirement that even if the narrative we use to organize our lives is implicit, it cannot be entirely hidden from us. As Schechtman puts it, "An identity-constituting narrative [must] be capable of local articulation. This means that the narrator should be able to explain why he does what he does, believes what he believes, and feels what he feels" (114). She asks us to think of a man who sincerely believes he loves his brother, but frequently behaves toward him in ways that suggest hostility. Because he is unaware of this hostility, she thinks, it is not fully integrated into his life and so is attributable to him to a lesser degree than the parts of his autobiography that he can articulate. She claims that only the acts, beliefs, and experiences that we can give an account of are fully identity-constituting. This cannot be quite right, however. If a person is hostile, we may attribute hostility to him independently of whether he admits it. What a person knows of himself determines a good deal of how he will make sense of the experiences in his life, but the experiences he needs to make sense of may be strongly determined precisely by the fact that there are things about himself he doesn't know. This constraint fails to acknowledge that one's identity is not simply a function of one's self-knowledge.

The second constraint on identity-constituting narratives, in Schechtman's view, is that they cohere with reality (119). In this way she allows for the possibility that people can be psychotic, mistaken about the facts, or guilty of interpretive inaccuracies. While minor errors of fact or interpretation do not seriously compromise one's self-conception, "seeing the facts as having implications wildly different from those others see makes taking one's place in the world of persons virtually impossible" (127). Although the narrative construction of an identity is on Schechtman's view largely a do-it-yourself project, an autobiography is identity-constituting only if one's feet pretty regularly manage to touch the floor.

The Other Construction Workers

I have treated Schechtman's views at some length because they offer a basis for understanding how personal identities could be the sorts of entities on which stories can have an effect. If a person's identity "is constituted by the content of her self-narrative," then our stories make us who we are. But surely it is not only our own story that makes us who we are. While there is much of merit in Schechtman's narrative self-constitution view, it is nevertheless open to serious criticisms. The first and most important is that she vastly underestimates the extent to which our identities are of others' making. As Alasdair MacIntyre puts it, we are never more than coauthors of our life narratives. "We enter upon a stage which we did not design and we find ourselves part of an action that was not of our making."[9] When we are children, we live inside the larger narrative that is our family's history, and the stories our parents and grandparents tell us about their own and our other relatives' lives add to our sense of ourselves. When we go to school we learn the history of our culture, and this too produces in us an awareness of ourselves as members of various communities. And if we belong to a community that is generally despised, the master narratives that are told to explain our inferiority and keep us in our place contribute to our identities—as do the narratives we tell together to resist them.

Personal identity is in some measure a social construction. As such, it requires *recognition*. It is not simply a matter of how we experience our own lives, but also of how others see us. My sense of myself as a skilled office manager who knows the firm from the inside out goes nowhere if the new CEO thinks of me as the faithful old retainer who ought to be pensioned off. In cases of this kind, the question is not whether I am in touch with reality, but who gets to say what is real about me. Because the new CEO has the power to assign me to a marginal role in the office or make things so unpleasant for me that I prefer to retire, my very real capabilities will find no expression once he constructs a reality that denies them an outlet. At that point, even if my job is absolutely central to my identity-constitut-ing self-narrative, I can no longer play it out in my ongoing story. His identifying me in terms of the stock character "faithful old retainer" thus has a direct impact on who I can now be.

What is at issue here is not so much identity-constituting "actions, experiences, or characteristics," as *roles* and *relationships*. My role as office manager is open to me only if the person who stands in relation to me as boss makes it possible for me to exercise it. Without his cooperation, that role is no longer a part of who I am. Roles and relationships can be so central to our sense of ourselves that Christine Korsgaard has recently called them our "practical identities":

> The conception of one's identity in question here is . . . a description under which you value yourself, a description under which you find your life to be worth living and your actions to be worth undertaking. So I will call this a conception of your practical identity. Practical identity is a complex matter and for the average person there will be a jumble of such conceptions. You are a human being, a woman or a man, an adher-ent of a certain religion, a member of an ethnic group, a member of a certain profession, someone's lover or friend, and so on. And all of these identities give rise to reasons and obligations. Your reasons express your identity, your nature; your obligations spring from what that identity forbids [or requires]. . . . Some parts of our identity are easily shed, and, where they come into conflict with more fundamental parts of our identity, they should be shed. The cases I have in mind are standard: a good soldier obeys orders, but a good human being doesn't massacre the innocent.[10]

As Korsgaard's examples indicate, she conceptualizes personal identity as a matter of overlapping and sometimes conflicting roles, rather than as the acts, experiences, and characteristics that Schechtman sees as the an-swers to the characterization question. Note too that for Korsgaard, a person has an indefinite number of practical identities, depending on what set of people or social roles she identifies with as she contemplates a given course of action.

While Korsgaard's view of personal identity offers an insightful complement to Schechtman's narrative self-constitution account, she goes no further than Schechtman in acknowledging the extent to which our identities are of others' making. But if Korsgaard is right to see personal identity in terms of the roles and relationships with which we identify, then clearly, who I am is often a matter of who others say I am. Many practical identities require more than one person for their construction and maintenance. My identity as a competent adult crucially depends on others' recognizing me as such. My identity as a white person hinges on the acknowledgment of others that I am indeed white. And my identity as a wife is thrown into devastating confusion if my husband decides he no longer wants to be married to me. In all these instances and many more, a key component of identity is others' recognition that the identity is properly mine.[11]

Schechtman's account, then, gives us a way of understanding personal identity as constructed out of the actions, experiences, and characteristics that figure importantly in the person's self-narrative. To this we may now add that personal identity is also constructed out of the roles and relationships that do the same thing. None of the five elements—actions, experiences, characteristics, roles, and relationships—are solely of our own making. All require recognition.[12]

Master Narratives and Counterstories

My first criticism of Schechtman, then, is that her account of narrative self-constitution is too individualistic; it pays insufficient attention to the social nature of personal identity. My second criticism is that her insistence on a linear plotline for any identity-constituting narrative that we could recognize as belonging to a person arbitrarily promotes one ideal of a good life for persons over other possible ideals, and in doing so, it oppresses the elderly.

The actions, experiences, roles, and so on that are the elements of our identity-constituting narratives are *narrative* elements in virtue of their form: we arrange them into stories. But they are also narrative in virtue of their association with the narrative figurations that abound in our culture. At some point in your life, for example, you probably made sense of your relationship with a lover by arranging the episodes of that relationship according to the stock courtship and marriage plot that structures everything from "Cinderella" to *Mansfield Park*. A rider on the subway looks at the unkempt elderly woman sitting across from him and pigeonholes her as a "hag," with an unconscious assist, perhaps, from a "Scooby-Doo" cartoon character. You help a stranger in need and she identifies you in biblical terms: you are a good Samaritan. My understanding of my teaching role is compounded, in part, of absentminded professor jokes and *Goodbye, Mr. Chips*. Both the content and the form of the stories that constitute us may thus be drawn from the cultural cupboard.

If identities are constructed through this sort of interpersonal narrative identification and recognition, and if Korsgaard is right to speak of practical identities in the plural, then we have reason to think that identity-constituting narratives not only require many tellers, but also that they are far from linear in form—not, at least, if what is meant by "linear" is the coherent, Aristotelian sequence of tightly interconnected events that rises to a climax and then drops off in a dénouement. Schechtman is not the only moral philosopher to present the linear plotline as constitutive of the lives of persons. The "career self," whose life trajectory is described in this way, also surfaces in John Rawls's assumption that persons have a "rational life plan," and Alasdair MacIntyre's and Charles Taylor's supposition that person's lives are structured by a "quest."[13] The more or less explicit view of all four philosophers is not merely that human beings cannot make sense of themselves outside a narrative in which each meaningful incident counts as progress in positioning oneself properly with respect to the good, but that the good itself consists largely in planning for, striving after, and attaining some end. The career self presupposed by this view is the protagonist of an *Entwicklungsroman*, whose chapters record the early training, the "wasted" time, the "recovered" sense of a calling, the self-doubts and failures, the achievements and public recognition, and finally, the "tapering off" into old age.

But this is a stock plot drawn from the cultural cupboard, not a transcendent fact about persons. While the career self is a dominant ideal among professionals and business executives in postindustrial Western societies, it is only one of many ways to conceptualize personhood. To insist that one must be a person like this if one is to be a person at all is to deny personhood to individuals—including the elderly—whose lives do not conform to the "career" plot, and it says to elderly people who *have* understood their lives as progressing toward a climactic point in their careers, "What mattered about your life is now behind you. You have nothing further to live for." Because it identifies elderly people either as nonpersons or as useless, the biography of the career self is a story that oppresses them.

It's doubtful that anyone could actually live out all of one's life according to the linear plot, and it surely seems as if many people do not. Life narratives often appear to be a hodgepodge of narrative fragments, some giving meaning to very localized experiences, others forming a kind of umbrella tale that pulls together a number of local stories but possibly leaves an equal number out of account. For bits of some people's stories, the plot intertwines with the stories of others but goes nowhere in particular, and there might or might not be connections among the narrative strands out of which the social roles with which we identify ourselves are built. Some of those roles are deeply at odds with one another—think of an immigrant who belongs to two very different cultures and simply moves between them without any thought that they must somehow be reconciled[14]—while other roles, such as "wife" and "woman," are contained one within the other and so are part of the same narrative fragment.

Rather than insist on a linear plotline, Schechtman would do better to say that in constructing a personal identity, as in spinning a thread, "we twist fibre on fibre. And the strength of the thread does not reside in the fact that some one fibre runs through the whole length, but in the overlapping of many fibres."[15] But what of Schechtman's worry that unless one fibre really does run through the length, we can't make sense of moral responsibility, self-interested concern, compensation, or personal survival? It's not easy to see why Schechtman is concerned about this. She seems to take it as self-evident that the identity-constituting narratives of individuals "like us" have a "standard" linear form, and then reasons that because "those whose self-conceptions take a form sufficiently different from our own cannot lead the kind of lives we live," the linear form of self-conception must be necessary to anything we would recognize as a person. However, if it turns out that the stories constituting the identities of individuals like us don't have to take the form that Schechtman supposes, then the link between personal identity and the four features is not the linear form and indeed might not be any particular form at all, but is merely the presence of the overlapping narrative fragments that make us who we are. If Schechtman were to object, "There is something common to all these fragments—namely the linear form that unites them in a self-constituting story," we might offer her Wittgenstein's reply: "Now you are only playing with words. One might as well say: 'Something runs through the whole thread—namely the continuous overlapping of those fibres' " (remark 67).

The impact of other people on our self-constituting narratives is not exhausted by these considerations of form, but is also crucial to understanding various kinds of oppression.[16] The narrative figurations by which other people identify me can do me serious harm, as we saw in the example of the office manager above. The stock character "faithful old retainer" there became an identity that is imposed upon an elderly woman in such a way as to disqualify her from exercising a social role that is for her a primary practical identity. A great deal of discrimination against the elderly tends to work in this way. The elderly person, identified as a stock figure, becomes a character in what Margaret Morganroth Gullette calls a narrative of decline, and the person is then required to behave according to the specifications of that particular plot.[17] The decline narrative generally harkens back to a golden age in which the person possessed desirable qualities—beauty, a capacity for many friendships, physical strength, a sense of the *Zeitgeist*—and then moves to the present, in which the person has sadly, or in the nature of things, lost these qualities.

Decline narratives sometimes do capture accurately a most significant change in a person's life. A disfiguring stroke, an inability to keep up with technological developments, congestive heart failure, the death of most of one's contemporaries make it impossible for some people to act out certain practical identities that were once central to their sense of themselves. But narratives of decline are tools of oppression when they exaggerate the importance of a loss, use a decline in one aspect of a person's life to paper over strengths and abilities the person might still be developing, or insist that a particular loss now identifies the person as a whole. In particular, narratives of decline are oppressive when they are used to block or restrict a person's access to a valuable role or relationship that might otherwise still be acquired or retained as she changes in the course of her life.

A person who is caught in a narrative of decline or some other oppressive narrative needs a counterstory that allows her to sustain or reclaim a practical identity that is threatened by something or someone she can't control. People also need communities of storytellers with whom to create the moral space[18] in which counterstories can be told. The community might be a political action organization, such as the Older Women's League, or it might be a more informal community, such as the neighborhood beauty parlor, or it might be a yet smaller and more informal community, consisting of one's partner and a close friend who still helps maintain one's various practical identities. The moral space in which this sort of narrative reconstruction goes on might not be big enough to get the office worker's old job back for her (it would have to contain the new CEO if it were to do that), but it can at least be a place where she gets others' help in sorting out who *she* thinks she is, and how her boss ought to have identified her. Because oppressive identities are constructed by other people's telling our stories in ways that diminish us, and because we all tend to believe what other people tell us, it's helpful to have a community of sympathetic others who can confirm the dissonance between the way we see ourselves and the way our oppressors identify us. Just as valuable is a community that challenges us to see the dissonance in the first place.

Sometimes we have to take the lead in creating the moral space in which our identity-constituting stories can be told. Steven Sabbat and Rom Harré tell of an elderly man with Alzheimer's disease who was introduced to a visitor at his day care center as, "This is Henry. Henry was a lawyer." To which Henry gently objected, "I *am* a lawyer."[19] In this case the day care workers recognized what Henry was doing to maintain a practical identity that mattered to him, and they redoubled their efforts to help him with this. Here, obviously, there was no longer any real possibility that Henry could retain his position as partner in his old law firm, so identifying him as an ex-lawyer didn't unjustly deprive him of the ability to exercise his profession. But the decline narrative that prompted the identification as "ex" is nevertheless oppressive in that it recognizes Henry primarily in terms of his losses. Alzheimer's disease does a thorough enough job on its own of fragmenting a person's identity without receiving a premature assist in that direction from thoughtless people.

The counterstory underlying Henry's protest, which resists the decline narrative and substitutes for it a story of professional continuity, arguably reidentifies Henry as a career self. If, as I have claimed, the linear plotline that traces the life course of a career self is oppressive, then doesn't Henry's counterstory merely capitulate to ageism rather than resist it? And isn't it then a bad counterstory? But notice what Henry is doing to the linear plotline. Even if he does think of his life as primarily the story of the preparation for and practice of his profession, he is resisting the narrative form that requires a dénouement to the life trajectory of a career self. He is challenging the assumption that once his career has climaxed, he is useless and unimportant.

Although Henry's counterstory has a linear form, many stories that counter ageism have more complicated plotlines, darting backward and then forward as they assemble a corrected picture of a present self. Furthermore, if others are involved in the telling, the story also radiates outward to connect to these other tellers' lives, and thickens as each adds her own fibre to the narrative thread. Counterstories often correct particular practical identities rather than reidentifying the person as a whole, so whether a given counterstory constitutes merely a local splice or requires a major reweaving of the life story depends on how central to the person the practical identity was.

From Ageism to Sexism

Not just any story that counters ageism is successful. Counterstories misfire in a number of different ways and for a number of different reasons. A counterstory to deflect ageism might go wrong by leaving in place the moral understandings that devalue the aged. If, for example, a seventy-year-old woman were to resist the identity of old-and-ugly by agreeing that old is ugly and enacting the counterstory of the face-lift, she might be endorsing rather than repudiating an oppressive identity. On the other hand, she might be expanding the repertoire of what a seventy-year-old looks like, in which case the counterstory may not have misfired after all. A second way in which a counterstory might go wrong is when the person who tells it seriously misrepresents to herself the sort of person she has been all along. So, for example, a woman might resist nursing home placement on the grounds that she must continue to live "independently," even though in her quest for independence she is both heavily depending on and heavily discounting her daughter's financial and emotional support. A third way a counterstory might go wrong is when, as in *Marvin's Room*, it secures an elderly man's dignity and worth by portraying his daughter as bad until she is willing to take on not only his care, but that of the other members of his household as well. This counterstory resists ageism, but at the daughter's expense.

In all these instances, the story that counters an invidious identity of age simultaneously reinforces sexism in one way or another. The seventy-year-old who undergoes surgery might want a face-lift for any number of reasons, but one possibility is that she shares the oppressive assumptions both that elderly women cannot be beautiful and that women must always do what they can to make themselves beautiful. In that case her narrative enactment is multiply unfortunate, because it fails to resist either ageist or sexist norms. The mother struggling to maintain her independence wishes, perhaps, to combat the idea that elderly women must be frail and receive care from others, but her way of doing it is to exploit her daughter's care-giving without acknowledging either its value or the cost to the daughter of providing it. That counterstory resists ageist norms, but leaves a patriarchal trope in place and so contributes to the daughter's gender oppression. As for *Marvin's Room*—well, perhaps I have said enough.

In weighing the worth of these counterstories I do not mean to imply that the people who tell them are necessarily doing something wrong. One would have to know a great deal more about their options and what they are trying to bring about before one could make such a judgment. Instead, I want to show how counterstories invite us to generalize the values and social arrangements they endorse. The story that helps the individual person to refuse an oppressive identity has social implications as well, since an oppressive identity is one that categorizes the individual as a member of a despised group. The counterstory is thus also always about groups—not only the despised group to which the individual has been identified as belonging, but often other groups that stand in some sort of relationship to this one. Suppose the generalization the counterstory invites were to bene-fit one oppressed group at the expense of another. Suppose further that the counterstory were widely adopted and many people were wronged as a result. In that case we have a reason for judging the counterstory to be a bad one. Such a story would fail of its purpose, which is to resist oppression. It *cannot* remedy an injustice by leaving it in place, and it *ought* not to remedy an injustice by putting another in its place. However, there may well be times when the best we can do is to tell a bad counterstory, as I shall explain in a moment.

The Epistemic Firewall

If counterstories can fail for reasons that are internal to the story, they can also fail for external reasons. It is all very well to tell a story of resistance in a community of sympathetic and like-minded people so that there, at least, the elderly woman can be seen for who she is, but a problem arises when the counterstory is told to those who have identified her unjustly. They, having the most to gain from a social system in which the elderly are dis-counted, dismissed, and disempowered, are also likely to discount and dis-miss the counterstory.

What stands between such a person and the counterstory she needs to hear is what Walker calls an "epistemic firewall"—a "lattice of law, custom, expectation, and the familiarity of what is pervasive and repeated"[20]—that makes our practices of discrimination against women, elderly people, and other marginalized groups seem so normal that any objection raised against them comes across as improper, peculiar, or ludicrous. The firewall allows coercive, demeaning, or otherwise unjust practices to proceed without eliciting the moral outrage they would otherwise trigger, as it blocks recognition that the practices are injurious and that those who are hurt by them have a legitimate cause for complaint.

One way the firewall works is by *privatizing*. Confining "these people" to private spaces in a way that makes it seem natural that they should be so confined hides them from view and makes unkind or violent treatment of them disappear behind closed doors. Elderly people are privatized when, for example, their reflexes or vision no longer make it safe for them to drive cars, because the suburbs in which most Americans live are arranged around car ownership rather than public transportation. Cars are so crucial to people's daily lives that we literally become disabled without them—and then we treat the disability as if it were a natural part of old age. Being without a car puts pressure on an elderly person to stay at home, as does lack of easy access to public transportation. These material conditions feed into and reinforce the beliefs and gaps in knowledge that keep the person indoors: not knowing what bus to take, fear, and the belief that one mustn't rely on others all become further reasons to stay at home. Staying at home, she is invisible to most other people. And her invisibility means that others have little occasion to think or care about her.

Naturalizing, which involves the production of appearances of inevitability of certain facts about certain people, is another function of the firewall. If, for example, it is taken as simply a fact of nature that women lose their looks and sexuality as they age, then we will not see the different kinds of attractiveness that elderly women often actually possess. While it's always a pity to deprive ourselves of a source of aesthetic enjoyment, the "fact" that elderly women can't be beautiful is also a source of moral harm in a culture where feminine beauty is a measure of social worth. A "fading" beauty is an object of pity, and her attempts to restore youthful good looks not infrequently invite ridicule. Moreover, since physical attractiveness in women is linked to sexual attractiveness to a greater degree than physical attractiveness in men, then, if elderly women can't be beautiful, they obviously can't have sex, either. That elderly women *do* have sex goes unremarked, is not discussed, and is almost never depicted—and this in a culture whose obsession with sex is thought to penetrate every aspect of life.

Patterns of behavior involving the elderly are *normalized* when there is a ubiquitous presumption that the behaviors under consideration are standard and normal. That these behaviors should exist is taken for granted, and attention is focused on how to engage in them responsibly and well, rather than in wondering why that particular set of behaviors is necessary. I am thinking here, for example, of the caregiving that elderly women must often provide to their husbands or same-sex partners, or, less commonly, their disabled children. Because Medicare does not reimburse long-term care and covers home health care only if there is no one at home to provide it, elderly women are frequently required to continue the familial caregiving they once provided for their young children and then for their elderly parents, well into their own old age. Medicare and other third-party payors view this sort of caregiving on the part of women as normal, and take it as a basis for setting policy. But the question as to why the caregiving should be almost exclusively women's work remains hidden when practices of care are normalized in this way.

Privatizing, naturalizing, and normalizing are functions of the firewall, but they are also at the same time its key components, along with the master narratives that are required for their upkeep and maintenance. These are the elements that rig in subtle ways what many people can know about elderly women's lives and identities, but as Walker points out, other elements are less subtle. "Large portions of this firewall consist of physical confinements and exclusions, explicit barring from certain positions or places of authoritative speech, or disabling economic and intellectual conditions."[21] The subtle and less subtle components of the wall typically work together, as for example when master narratives of decline make it seem natural that elderly people are safer and more comfortable at home.

Because the firewall also contains expectations that the elderly will be childish, willful, discontented, and unreasonable, nothing they themselves might have to say about their condition is likely to be taken very seriously. For someone's knowledge—about astrophysics, dressmaking, one's self, or any other thing—to be *recognized* as knowledge, the knower must be socially authorized. If one lacks epistemic authority, what one knows about oneself is the very thing one is presumptively disqualified from speaking about. After all, the elderly are prone to self-pity and other forms of whining, aren't they? You simply have to jolly them along a little.

Penetrating the Firewall

If the firewall is anything like what I've just described, it's no wonder that a counterstory has a hard time getting through it. There are, however, one or two strategies for penetrating the wall that are worth considering briefly. Let me begin with one that I think will not work, namely, the appeal to the idea that those of us who are younger hope to be elderly ourselves one day. In this strategy, we are invited to identify with the elderly teller of a counterstory by feeling self-interested concern for our own elderly selves.

There are a number of reasons to be skeptical about this. For one thing, the portion of my life narrative that links me to my distant future contains many elements that I can't at present foresee, and some of these elements will be self-defining. So while I will know important things about that future person, the things I don't know make it difficult for me to identify with her. This point is linked to the previous point about privatization. Perhaps the most important thing I need to know about my future self is what it is like to be old, but if a driving belief of the firewall is that old people don't—shouldn't—get around much anymore, I won't be likely to know anyone who is elderly except, perhaps, for people in my own family. That makes it harder for me to imagine myself as elderly.

The difficulty isn't just with what we don't know, however. Even what we know full well about our future selves tends not to have a great deal of motivational force for us now. A twenty-five-year-old will readily agree that if he takes up smoking today, he courts health problems in forty years. But he prefers that his sixty-five-year-old self should pay for his present pleasures rather than the other way around. He figures that what he can enjoy now is a sure thing, while there's always the possibility that he won't have to pay later on after all. Besides, he doesn't much care about that old man—his existence seems impossibly remote.

And finally, there is still another reason why we find it hard to identify with our future selves. When I think of the elderly woman I will become, I can't help but do so in terms of the narrative fragments my culture uses to make sense of old age. Unfortunately, many of these fragments consist of negative stereotypes, and, as if that weren't bad enough, they have already been combined in the master narratives that "explain" why old age is entirely a time of diminishment and loss. The fragments therefore have not only their own meaning, but also the fuller and more powerful meaning they derive from their participation in the master narratives. Yet their power is hidden. Because master narratives are a part of the firewall, the narrative fragments interact with the wall's other elements to produce an appearance of seamless and unproblematic inevitability that old age should be like this. Unless I am aware of the fragments' epistemic location, it will not occur to me that I can criticize them or replace them with more positive figurations.

The situation seems hopeless. If even the thought that I too will be elderly someday has no power to penetrate the firewall, how can a counterstory hope to do so? The answer is, not easily. But here, oddly enough, we may look to bad counterstories for help. A bad counterstory, recall, is one that leaves a particular form of injustice in place, or substitutes one form of injustice for another; I argued that the counterstory can't do its job in the first case and oughtn't to do it in the second. But not all forms of injustice are equally evil. Abandonment of an elderly person who is utterly helpless is surely worse than the expectation that one will give care because one is a woman. If a woman has been unwilling to care for her greatly needy father, whom she characterizes as a burdensome nuisance, she may find it easier to give up the ageist characterization if she doesn't at the same time have to challenge the sexism underlying the familial caregiving she ought now to take on. A lesser injustice sometimes serves as a kind of common ground between a biased person and the person who tells a flawed counterstory. That ground might be precisely what enables the biased person to hear the story and recognize the greater injustice it is designed to counter.[22] The hope is that after the greater injustice has been addressed, the lesser one too will receive attention. The danger, of course, is that since various kinds of oppression tend to reinforce one another, the incremental approach I am advocating here might end up leaving everything worse than it was. This is a realistic fear. Yet a bad counterstory might sometimes be the best we can do. Even if it fails to right all wrongs, if it changes the minds and hearts of a number of those who are biased against a particular group of people, it is probably good enough.

I can think of one other strategy that might allow an elderly person's counterstory to be heard by people who are biased against the elderly, and that is for the story to be told on her behalf by someone in authority. Part of what it is to be biased against the elderly is to dismiss or belittle their claims to authoritative knowledge about who they are—to shrug off the counterstory as just another old person's kvetching. But if the story is told by someone whose knowledge is socially authorized, it may take on sufficient weight to penetrate the prejudices of the biased auditor. It may be objected that if you speak for a marginalized person instead of allowing her to speak for herself, you join her oppressors in silencing her, but this objection assumes that when a marginalized person speaks for herself, she will in fact be heard. The objection also assumes that only the elderly person herself has the right to tell her story. If, however, our identity-constituting narratives are invariably coauthored—if, that is, personal identities are social constructions made up of overlapping stories that require many tellers—then there might be nothing wrong with telling someone else's story, as long as the story that is told is accurate and knowledgeable. What is required here is a collaborative effort. The person who is in a position to be heard needs to apprentice herself to the elderly people on whose behalf she tells the counterstory, so that she can learn how the story ought to go rather than merely taking it over.[23] Feminists have a particular responsibility to speak to, as well as about and on behalf of, older women in all contexts. On the assumption, however, that the socially more powerful person has earned the right to tell the story, sponsoring an elderly person's counterstory might be a constructive way of helping the person repair her identity. It need not necessarily be disrespectful of the person.

Finally, it is worth remembering that no epistemic firewall is as seamless or impenetrable as it appears. Like the master narratives that cement it together, it has many cracks, fissures, tensions, and contradictions that can serve as points of entry for a counterstory. While the task of repairing elderly women's identities through the kind of narrative work I have been describing is by no means easy, it is sometimes possible to do it. And it is always worth trying to do. After all, we all hope to be elderly ourselves some day.

Notes

I am grateful to Diana Tietjens Meyers, James Lindemann Nelson, Sara Ruddick, Margaret Urban Walker, and the other participants of the Conference on Ethical Issues in Women's Aging, held at the Ethics Center of the University of South Florida, February 20–22, 1998, for their many useful insights. Loving thanks also to Ellen C. D. Robinson.

1. Diana Tietjens Meyers, *Subjection and Subjectivity: Psychoanalytic Feminism and Moral Philosophy* (New York: Routledge, 1994).

2. See, for example, Richard Nisbett and Lee Ross, "Judgmental Heuristics and Knowledge Structures," in *Naturalizing Epistemology*, ed. Hilary Kornblith, 2d ed. (Cambridge: MIT Press, 1994), 261–90; Diana Tietjens Meyers, "The Family Romance: A *Fin de Siècle* Tragedy," in *Feminism and Families*, ed. Hilde Lindemann Nelson (New York: Routledge, 1997), 239–43; Helen Haste, *The Sexual Metaphor* (Cambridge: Harvard University Press, 1994), 36–47.

3. Hilde Lindemann Nelson, "Resistance and Insubordination," *Hypatia* 10, no. 2 (1995): 23–40.

4. Margaret Urban Walker, *Moral Understandings: A Feminist Study in Ethics* (New York: Routledge, 1998), 173.

5. Marya Schechtman, *The Constitution of Selves* (Ithaca: Cornell University Press, 1996); numbers in parentheses refer to this work.

6. The discussion of the four features is taken from Schechtman, *Constitution of Selves*, 80–89.

7. Susan J. Brison, "Outliving Oneself: Trauma, Memory, and Personal Iden-

tity," in *Feminists Rethink the Self*, ed. Diana Tietjens Meyers (Boulder: Westview, 1997), 16.

8. Charlotte Delbo, *Auschwitz and After*, tr. Rosette C. Lamont (New Haven: Yale University Press, 1995).

9. Alasdair MacIntyre, *After Virtue*, 2d ed. (Notre Dame: University of Notre Dame Press, 1984), 213.

10. Christine Korsgaard, *The Sources of Normativity* (New York: Cambridge University Press, 1996), 101–2.

11. See Hilde Lindemann Nelson, "The 'Bad Coherence' Problem for Reflective Endorsement," presented at the Pacific Division meeting of the American Philosophical Association, March 26, 1998. See also Ian Hacking, "Making up People," in *Reconstructing Individualism: Autonomy, Individuality, and the Self in Western Thought*, ed. Thomas C. Heller, Morton Sosna, and David E. Wellbery (Stanford University Press, 1986); Charles Taylor, *Multiculturalism and the "Politics of Recognition"* (Princeton: Princeton University Press, 1992); Walker, *Moral Understandings*.

12. As Annette Baier has recently pointed out, agency involves not only capacities, competencies, and intentions that reside within the individual, but uptake on the part of others. Almost no act is complete in itself, as it requires the expected responses of other agents for its completion. See *The Commons of the Mind*, Paul Carus Lecture (Chicago: Open Court, 1997).

13. See John Rawls, *A Theory of Justice* (Cambridge: Harvard University Press, 1971); MacIntyre, *After Virtue*; and Charles Taylor, *Sources of the Self* (Cambridge: Harvard University Press, 1989). For a discussion of career selves, see Margaret Urban Walker, ch. 6 in this volume, and *Moral Understandings*, ch. 6.

14. For an excellent discussion of the multiplicity of a self, see María C. Lugones, "Playfulness, 'World'-Travelling, and Loving Perception," *Hypatia* 2, no. 2 (1987): 3–19.

15. Ludwig Wittgenstein, *Philosophical Investigations*, tr. G.E.M. Anscombe (New York: Macmillan, 1958), remark 67.

16. For a very interesting suggestion as to how W.V.O. Quine's concept of a web of belief might help us make sense of deeply internalized psychological oppression, see Robert Noggle, "The Web of Self: Reflections on the Structure of Personhood," presented at the Pacific Division meeting of the American Philosophical Association, March 28, 1998.

17. Margaret Morganroth Gullette, *Declining to Decline: Cultural Combat and the Politics of the Midlife* (Charlottesville: University Press of Virginia, 1997).

18. For the notion of a moral space, see Margaret Urban Walker, "Keeping Moral Space Open: New Images of Ethics Consulting," *Hastings Center Report* 23, no. 4 (1993): 33–40.

19. Steven Sabbat and Rom Harré, "The Construction and Deconstruction of Self in Alzheimer's Disease," *Ageing and Society* 12 (1992): 443–61.

20. Walker, *Moral Understandings*, 173.

21. Walker, *Moral Understandings*, 173.

22. I thank Diana Tietjens Meyers for this suggestion, which she made to me in conversation, February 21, 1998.

23. See María Lugones and Elizabeth Spelman, "Have We Got a Theory for You: Feminist Theory, Cultural Imperialism, and the Demand for 'The Woman's Voice,' " *Women's Studies International Forum* 6, no. 6 (1983): 573–81; and Laurence Mordekhai Thomas, "Moral Deference," *Philosophical Forum* 34, nos. 1–3 (1992–93): 233–50.

· 6 ·

Getting Out of Line:
Alternatives to Life As a Career

Margaret Urban Walker

For Mommy, who knew how to be here now.

*A*utonomy has been a central value in influential moral theories and liberal political conceptions in the twentieth century. Autonomy may be taken as part of a characterization of the nature of moral selves, a feature defining the kind of being that moral beings are. Alternatively, autonomy may be set forth as an aspirational ideal for human beings as moral beings and political actors. It is typical in moral theorizing that the descriptive and prescriptive senses do not stay in separate boxes: moral ideals in theory often take something human beings supposedly are as a key to something it is best for human beings to become. It is also typical for moral theorists to offer characterizations and advance ideals of moral personality and moral relations in general that are in fact abstractions and idealizations of historically specific cultural understandings. These cultural understandings are as "thick" as their philosophical counterparts are "thin": they are embodied in concrete imagery and intertwined with social roles, identities, and functions that are familiar or conspicuous in certain times and places.

In this chapter I want to explore a culturally thicker version of autonomous individuality, in order to explore why older people in our society, and older women in particular, may not be able to choose to meet concrete social criteria of autonomy or to emulate culturally familiar exemplars of the autonomous individual. While exclusion from culturally valued identities is a common form of marginalization, I want to reconsider whether we all ought to aspire to be "autonomous men" in this culturally thicker sense. In conclusion, I suggest we think about alternative pictures of well-lived and admirable lives, and ones that may be at odds in the concrete with the kind of individuality and autonomy that a certain kind of society elevates as an ideal.

Problems with Autonomy

The adequacy and desirability of autonomy in both its descriptive and pre-scriptive senses are open to discussion. Autonomy defines individuals and a kind of individualism that have been repeatedly questioned in recent moral thinking. Feminist critics, for example, have noticed a convergence be-tween features associated with autonomy—independence from external guidance, acting under one's own direction, being able to control and to express oneself, self-assertiveness, choice guided by one's own values and interests rather than social expectations or pressures—and those associated with traditional social norms for masculine, but not feminine, personality. If autonomy represents the nature, perfection, or dignified expression of moral agency, but "autonomous man" really is a *man*, how are we to un-derstand women's moral agency? Communitarian and historicist critics, on the other hand, accuse the autonomous agent of liberal individualism with being no one in reality. That agent's autonomy is seen as a destructive myth or an inappropriate norm. It conceals, distorts, or devalues the human real-ity of individuals who achieve identity and meaning from the cultures, traditions, communities, and roles in which they are embedded.

While some feminists continue to prefer the framework of liberal indi-viduality, other feminists have championed ideals of selves as relationally defined, mutually concerned, reciprocally trusting, and complexly interde-pendent. Ethics of "care," "trust," or "responsibility" see these relational selves as fundamentally and necessarily responsive to each others' worth and need.[1] Communitarians and historicists see moral actors as imbued with historically and culturally formed identities that give substance and meaning to moral relations in their specific communities. They argue we do not simply choose the places from which we acquire meaningful self-under-standing; these are social communities, not social contracts.[2]

Feminists are understandably uneasy with appeals to "tradition" in communities that have traditions of sex oppression, and those who argue a central role for community and tradition may suspect contemporary femi-nism of embodying too much of the individualist quest for autonomy that they find impoverishing. Yet common to these recent lines of thought is their resistance to autonomy as the dominant ideal of self. They claim that autonomy is at best a restricted or partial expression of human moral agency, and at worst an impoverishing aim for it. Autonomy cannot encompass the realities of human interdependence and community, nor explain the concrete conditions of responsibility, the commitments, and the attachments to others that move us to action. If autonomy is a value, on these views, it must be conditioned by and integrated with other values that express our social natures.

The ill fit between norms of autonomous, self-reliant, and self-interested agency and social reality is evident in the situation of aging persons who are vulnerable and dependent and those who are responsible for their care. The moral position of dependently frail, cognitively impaired, and in some cases severely disabled people is not adequately considered in terms of kinds of independence, self-control, or reflective self-direction that are typically associated with autonomy. Ideals of consensual obligation and contractual responsibility for autonomous actors also fail to address the common situations of caregivers to older people who have come to require others' care. Often demands for care fall—by small increments, or suddenly, by dint of disabling illness or injury—upon those, disproportionately female, who see no reasonable and humane alternative to providing it, even at the cost of severe economic disadvantage and practical and emotional strain.[3] These are areas where ideals of autonomous individuality do not meet concrete realities of aging.

Nor does a disembodied, abstract equality among persons defined by their "freedom to choose" help us understand the social situations and self-perceptions of many people whose humanity is defined differently from that of others on the basis of their physical construction, appearance, or state. Social theorist Iris Young calls this a "scaling of bodies" that is at work historically in gender, race, ability, and age stereotyping.[4] Some people live out their sense of personal agency in bodies socially targeted for the fear, disgust, control, or use of more powerful others. The devalued bodies or low-valued social positions of groups of which many people are members keep those people marginal or vulnerable to neglect, violence, or exploitation even as they remain individually theoretically "free to choose." They are also subject to ridicule, humiliation, and misunderstandings driven by others' malicious, patronizing, or prejudiced view of who they can possibly be, and what their actions can mean. Paul Benson argues that "free agency" may be compromised not only by lack of relevant capacities for self-direction, but also by an incapacity to adequately reveal to others in our actions who we are to ourselves.[5] For people marginalized, devalued, or stigmatized, the assumptions that guide many others' reactions to what they do may make it practically impossible to be seen by those others as they see themselves, and to give their actions the meaning in the others' eyes that the actions have in their own. This does not only mean that people will be thought about, stereotypically and repetitively, in ways they cannot control; it means that they will be treated and responded to in accordance with what others think about them in many contexts of daily life.

I have spoken above of theoretical conceptions of autonomy that philosophers advance or debate. But here I want to focus instead on the thick fabric of images and exemplars in everyday life and common cultural understandings that attach to, and concretely represent, those philosophical abstractions. Moral ideals such as autonomy cannot be fully separated from social understandings that give them concrete reference, and some social understandings, I claim, always lie behind philosophers' abstract idealizations.[6] It is important to examine, then, not only the theoretical idea or ideal of autonomy, but the concrete, culturally familiar examples or embodiments of it that inform social understandings. But social understandings often picture as morally ideal a social position or function that is not available to all people. While it is in the nature of ideals to escape fulfillment, moral ideals can be linked to social positions and opportunities in ways that make some people destined to fail at them in fact or in the eyes of others.

Autonomy, for example, has long been defined concretely in ways at odds with social demands for appropriate feminine behavior in women.[7] It has also been elaborated in ways that reflect middle-class expectations of stability and control.[8] On the other hand, Joan Tronto's politically informed ethic of care exposes the way caregiving in our society is assigned to, and its values of interdependence and attentiveness to need are in fact associated with, people of lower status: women, the working or lower classes, and people of color. Independence and executive control are linked to higher social status.[9] Other morally valued ideals such as integrity and dignity may be denied application to people who are poor, dirty, unlearned, sick, enslaved, or dominated by those who are "better" or stronger. We need to ask whether prominent conceptions of valuable lives and admirable character might embody assumptions and invoke exemplars that are not hospitable to the lives of older women, among others.

Autonomy in Broader Context: Our Lives As Careers

In search of a thicker characterization, I situate the idea of autonomy within a broader cultural theme with a longer history, the idea of *each individual life as a career.* This theme of the shape and proper direction of a whole human life has special relevance for thinking about aging and about women. For it is the more deeply rooted and robust picture of a certain kind of individual and that individual's life that gives concrete meaning to autonomy in our social world.

Historian Thomas Cole has persuasively traced the theme of life as a career to "quintessentially modern ideas and images . . . born in Northern Europe between the late Middle Ages and the seventeenth century."[10] Prior to this time, Western European philosophical and religious traditions viewed human life in terms of general "ages" of human existence, such as childhood, youth, maturity, and old age. What emerged in the early modern period was the individualization of each life's journey as a personal drama. Early Protestantism saw the individual's drama as one of personal salvation, achieved over a lifetime through progressive control over body and will, aided by self-examination, work, and devotion. But this theme of a self-controlled and self-superintended existence became steadily more secular with the growth of modern life and capitalism: the later modern idea of a "life course" suggests a track to stay on and a path to follow to success, or at least stability, in worldly life.

The idea of a proper sequence of roles and responsibilities pegged to age-defined "stages" of life was distilled in the seventeenth century in the symbol of the rising and falling staircase. It was "the standard bourgeois image of a lifetime for the next 350 years."[11] This motif was popular in the eighteenth and nineteenth centuries, fading only early in the twentieth. It is still reflected in the idea of being "over the hill" or "past peak." The image displays what is expected of individuals at different stages to achieve a well-ordered life. But the image has another central function: to teach *internalized self-control*, the ability to govern oneself, a capacity required by the economic and political institutions of modern life. The image reminds individuals of their responsibility to order their own lives properly in society's view. Predictably, from the seventeenth century there were different versions of the stages of life for men and women.

Women (or, at any rate, ladies, women of advantaged class standing) in this scheme were not in fact intended to seek or achieve full self-governance, but rather to set themselves to master roles within the household under the governance of men. Women's life course is depicted in stages of domestic and child-rearing responsibilities, which diminish in later life. Men, on the other hand, were to conduct themselves appropriately in the workplace and public life, with men most economically and socially advantaged being not only governors of themselves but of other men and women. What is reflected in this ideal, then, even down to the present day, is an emphasis on health and control of the physical body for "productive" life, and an inner discipline of conforming to the demands of one's station throughout life. This ideal has always been meant primarily to guide men of middle-class standing in being economically productive and law-abiding citizens. It requires a supplementary plan to guide their female counterparts into the role of wives, that is, women who provide the necessary and helpful complement to men's desired economic and legal behavior.

While the "rigid code of moral self-government" originated several hundred years ago, the "autonomous individual as the ultimate unit of secular authority" is entrenched in the values of the middle class today.[12] The image of the fit, energetic, and productive individual who sets himself a course of progressive achievement within the boundaries of society's rules and institutions, and whose orderly life testifies to his self-discipline and individual effort, remains an icon of our culture. This picture of autonomy, rather than abstract ideas of acting out of one's own interests and preferences or acting on principles that one can rationally endorse, is really our central cultural ideal. It is a picture of autonomy as energetic self-superintendence with a consistent track record over a lifetime to show for it. It is instructive to notice how this more robust picture of physical vitality, reliable performance, and cumulative achievement—*an individual's life as a career*—recurs in the late twentieth century both in studies of aging and in contemporary ethics.

My own work uncovers the idea of a *career self* shaping the views of very influential moral philosophers in the late twentieth century.[13] In John Rawls's theory of justice as fairness, a signal achievement of the century, Rawls conceives of a person as a human life lived according to a plan. He sees a person's good as determined by the most rational long-term plan of life for that person.[14] Bernard Williams, a strong objector to Rawls's idea of the planned life, thinks of human lives in terms of "constitutive projects," important commitments and attachments that carry us into the future with a reason for living.[15] Alasdair MacIntyre, harshly critical of many facets of modern thought, describes a human self as the subject of a lifelong narrative that gets meaning from the climax toward which it moves.[16] Charles Taylor, both critic and interpreter of the modern sensibility, endorses MacIntyre's idea of an individual life as a "quest." He judges severely those whose lives as a whole do not sustain a meaningful narrative: he says they have failed as persons.[17]

What is revealing in these otherwise ethically diverse views is the repetition of the idea of an individual's life as a self-consciously controlled career. It binds a whole life or lifetime together in a unified way for which the individual is accountable. The individual's ability to account for this life—to bring forward its plan, project, or narrative plot—testifies to the individual's *self*-control. The imagery in each case recycles the cultural theme of autonomous agency, with its self-conscious individual enterprise. We might expect this from philosophers like Rawls who are within the liberal tradition, but we find it deeply embedded as well in the views of other philosophers who are critics of that tradition. I believe that this view has cultural depth, traced historically in part by Cole. This view runs beneath explicit differences in theoretical moral views, yet its cultural entrenchment exerts a pull on theorizing about personhood and character.

On the side of humanistic aging studies, a parallel theme emerges in discussions of the meaning and value of later life. While philosophers in the latter twentieth century speak of narratives and projects that give a whole life meaning, many gerontologists and humanists emphasize *life review* as an appropriate, perhaps indispensable, activity for the old. Theorized originally by Robert Butler in 1963, aging expert Harry Moody describes it as "an effort by the older person to sum up an entire life history, to sift its meaning, and ultimately to come to terms with that history at the horizon of death."[18] Butler apparently thought of life review as a naturally occurring and universal tendency in the old—as reminiscence surely is—and saw it as an experience of integration and resolution.

Contemporary writers notice that belief in the therapeutic power of life review may be optimistic,[19] and that the drive for coherence within a single linear story may be "distinctive of Western culture from the Renaissance to the present."[20] That is, it is possible that the idea of needing a unified and coherent life-spanning story may fit historically shaped and culturally specific ideas about persons and their lives, rather than spontaneous and universal ones. Harry Moody, for example, believes that a successful life review, one that finds one's life to have been intelligible, purposeful, or satisfying, does show the meaningfulness of a life. But he admits that summing up one's life, in fact, is not the only way to find meaning in it. He points to the French essayist Montaigne, whose enduring writings show facets of life "at a particular moment, from a glance, over one's shoulder, so to speak."[21]

In light of its apparent cultural specificity, we might ask some questions about life review. Why is the privileged view of life the one from its ending? Even if that's the last word, must it be the most accurate one? Why is the review of life a primary task for the old? It would seem that older people's enjoyment of reminiscence is bound to be, like all memory, highly selective; so why does life review have to take in life "whole"? Is life review a fact or a therapeutic recommendation? Is it a universal function of aging or the culmination of a particular style of living in a certain culture?

I propose that whole-life narrative is not a necessary expression of human personhood. Instead, it is a recipe for the sort of selves that fit a specific economic and institutional environment. While this model of relentless self-definition and self-control strongly emphasizes individual responsibility for oneself, it eclipses our dependence on and vulnerability to each other, and it overshadows our life-defining connections to and responsibilities for each other. This view of persons when filled in concretely has negative implications for aging selves, and ambiguous implications for women aging.[22]

The ordered life course of our time is the modernized one, no longer with the ten steps of the rising and falling staircase, but with "three boxes." Youth, adulthood, and old age fit us for the school, the workplace, and retirement, which Moody calls the "bureaucratically ordained means" of enforcing these life stages for purposes of the economy.[23] But "retirement," unlike school and workplace, is not a place. It is not an activity, like education or work, nor a role defined by the development of skills or exercise of competence, like that of student or worker. Retirement is defined instead as the cessation of the adult role of worker.

In a society that views the life course as a kind of "career," retirement, without designated role, activity, or development, signifies the end of the life course, even if there's a lot of life left. And if the ideal of self is the career self, the enterprising self busy at its career, the retired person surrenders not only a job, but eligibility for a centrally valued moral and social identity. The robust ideal of autonomy that pictures life as a career is inherently unkind to those growing older: they must compete in an arena where many are eventually destined to lose out to those younger, or they must retire into a state of "postadulthood."[24] It should not be surprising that in much gerontological writing the way to meaning in later life is either through "productive aging" in which we keep "busy" and "active" as before, or through a final project of life review. We must either continue our life careers or do the only thing left when they are over: reminisce about and document them, to prove to ourselves and to others that at least we *were* socially acceptable persons before our adulthood expired.

The autonomous individual as the striving career self was never a self-ideal intended for women. But it is one to which more women today aspire or are compelled, especially in the literal form of lifelong paid work. Women stand in a persistently ambiguous relation to this ideal of self. In one sense, it is an achievement for women to lay claim to the kind of autonomous individuality to which our society attaches great value. But this kind of individuality in its socially salient forms is defined in terms excluded by some women's traditional domestic roles, where those roles require women to play socially subordinate supporting parts (rather than self-determining or self-determined ones) that both free and require men to assume the role of a career self focused on its linear trajectory. This kind of individuality is also precluded or its ascription is deflected by many women's lives of relentless but repetitive labor, paid and unpaid, of precisely the sort that never "goes anywhere," in terms of social status, occupational importance, or increasing economic power. Housework, personal or domestic service, and caregiving are such "women's" works that do not, in the public arena, add up to a "career"; often, these kinds of work are not perceived as skilled or intelligent. Some women may wish to be freed precisely from the constraints of gender roles that render them ineligible for a socially valued expression of selfhood. Other women may wonder whether they want to be allowed, and inevitably in turn required, to emulate privileged men's social behavior in order to qualify as selves of an estimable kind. They might also wonder who will then supply the other-directed labors that permit career selves to direct so much attention to themselves and their careers. And they might well ask why these are the choices.

At the same time, the recruitment of women to this paradigm of individuality visits on them a cultural life pattern that renders later life, or life after employment, an unmapped space at the end of the life course—a space not literally but by social definition "empty." This space is getting wider all the time. The emptiness of this space may be designated "leisure," but little is recommended to fill it by our society except the consumption of goods and services.[25] In the case of men, this may contribute to the sense of "rolelessness" often mentioned in aging literature. Women's social situation in later life, however, cannot be inferred from or modeled upon men's. For many women, later life is a period filled with unceasing caregiving demands, especially for parents and spouses, and not occasionally for grown children, grandchildren, and other people's children, that society does little to acknowledge, much less relieve.[26] The apparent assimilation of women to the male-identified model of "career" followed by "retirement" may then function ideologically, concealing the reality of continuing work by older women that society compensates neither materially nor socially.

The career self was never an option for many people whose lives did not offer substantial promise of successful self-control of particular, conspicuous, and paradigmatic types. Many of those who are poor, chronically sick, or very seriously disabled, or those who are objects of others' domination or control, will encounter practical barriers, sometimes insuperable ones, to performing the role of a career self, or to having their performance recognized as one of the type that counts.[27] And the life of continuous progress and achievement must level off or diminish even for the minority who can approximate it. Yet regardless of its lack of fit with many people's early lives and most people's later ones, the self-directing career self is a social norm that encourages people to try to fit themselves to basic structures of a certain kind of economic and social life. This kind of life demands that one continuously "discipline" oneself over the long haul of life to specific forms of socially acknowledged and rewarded competitive striving as a condition of the "success" that is offered to relatively few and achieved by fewer. But, we can ask, should people try to fit themselves to this mold? Are there alternatives to "life as a career," and to the correlative idea that one's individual life has only the meaning one can give it in retrospect "as a whole"? Are there alternatives that would render later life—and all of life—richer?

Ideals of Spirituality and Connection

Anthropologist Barbara Myerhoff suggests that "vertical" as well as "horizontal" integration can result in a meaningful life. Horizontal integration is precisely that achievement of continuity in which the individual's unidirectional stream of life is seen as adding up to "a life career."[28] Vertical integration instead stresses "timeless transcendent recognition" that endures and does not pass away, what has been called at different times: epiphany, moments of being, revelation, satori, transcendence.[29] Many cultures, including parts of our own at earlier times, have seen later life as a period for the culmination of a spiritual career, rather than a temporal one, or as a time of life ripe for contemplative, reflective, counseling, guiding, or spiritual work. The theme of the "wise elder," and the roles and practices that give it concrete embodiment, including orator, mediator, teacher, and chaperone, seem to have vanished from our society.[30] Feared and venerated ritual positions open to the old in other societies, such as shaman, witch, medicine man, wise woman, or sorcerer, are regarded as scary cartoons in our own.[31] These roles are not only alien or antique. They suggest forces greater than those of intentional human control, or suggest the need for human beings to entrust themselves at times to a wisdom that is not expert scientific knowledge. These suggestions are not easily integrated with the autonomous individual's mission of rational self-control throughout a lifetime. Even the idea of "practical" or "folk" wisdom, something often attributed to the old as a social resource, can be shamed or disqualified in many contexts in our society by comparison with expert discourse by people with professional credentials of recent stamp. Philosophers themselves, including moral philosophers, often do not treat kindly, and sometimes just ignore, the role of spiritual practice or religious worship in providing meaning and wholeness in people's lives.

However, U.S. Census data show significantly increased membership in churches from the fifth decade of life onward, and although it is a complex and contested topic, there is some research to the effect that women are more inclined to religious participation and to prayer.[32] In my own experience women are more often open-minded or curious about, and more likely to engage in, religious, spiritual, meditative, occult, or holistic (and not conventionally Western medical) health practices. It would be worthwhile to overcome commonplace theoretical neglect of, and generic philosophical disdain for, these sources of meaning, coherence, and connection in life to which so many people, perhaps more often women than men, turn. This might lead to more realistic recognition and objective analysis of the diverse ways people *in fact* continue to find value, interest, and sense in and between their own and others' lives in their later years. Perhaps religious commitment or spiritual discipline is a resource for meaning in women's later lives that already plays a significant role that is underestimated in both theory and practice. Differences in this respect among and within groups defined multiply by age, gender, ethnicity, class, religion, education, political affiliation, and so forth, should be a subject of empirical research as well as an object of philosophical interest. I suspect inquiries like this would make the "wholeness" of well-tended career selves appear more and more a very special preoccupation of a particular (and privileged) segment of society. It is a preoccupation conditioned by specific assumptions about what is rational and valuable; it may also presume access to resources and opportunities of specific kinds.

On a more mundane level, however, I would like to offer another idea of "integration" that might be broad enough to encompass diverse commitments and attachments, worldly and otherwise. It is a conception that supports the idea of individual meaning and responsibility, but finds this in connections that enrich but transcend individuals. I would call it a *lateral integration of life*. This kind of integration supplies not only the pleasures of individual memory but the satisfactions of loyalties and meanings that transcend one's individuality. They can even transcend one's life.

We might see our life's stages (whether linked to our chronological ages or not) as characterized by central lessons, tasks, pleasures, experiences, or bonds. These might endure only for certain times of our lives, but we can revisit them in memory, savoring them for their distinctness or uniqueness in our lives, rather than for their continuity or comprehensiveness. Instead of a review of life in which many smaller bits must all add up to parts of ourselves, the memory of these stages will recall times when we were a smaller part of something else: a relationship, a family, a political movement, a partnership, an enterprise, an institution, a creative process, a ritual event. To remember the meaning of our being a part of these things is to remember being parts of the lives of many others, or being parts of things whose existence preceded or will succeed our own. Our lives on this view are more like journeys than careers: our physical trajectories are continuous, but where we stop to visit and what affects us may not follow a linear path. Some of what affects us may transform us into discontinuity with who or what we were before.

Some of what happens will be fulfilling or exhilarating, but other times will be ones of loss or pain: roads that close, people who are lost to us, dreams that are not realized, pain that we cannot avoid. These losses, for which there is no place on the resume of the career self, may sometimes also have their value. From some losses we might take positive meaning. Where we cannot, we might at least be reminded of our vulnerability and dependence, a point of connection with all living beings, and of the unavoidability of suffering, which we share with all things that feel. Some episodes of this life will be simply delightful or amusing. They will not need to be anything else either to be enjoyed as we live them, or to be remembered with pleasure, wonder, or mirth.

Unlike "life as a career," there is no reason for us to cease *living* this life, even in very late years, short of grave incapacitation. It embodies no eventually unfulfillable demand for achievement or progress; it requires only normal awareness, capacities for feeling, and opportunities to belong to or with something other than or larger than oneself. The meanings in such a life are many, and we do not wholly control much less create them.

I suspect the valued reminiscences of many people, old or not, are of these sorts that link times in those people's lives to something beyond themselves. Empirical studies of remembrance as a valued experience for older people need not be controlled by the idea of life review. They might explore open-mindedly possibilities other than the narrative of a whole life in review. Philosophical ideals of personal integration might stress the extension of selves beyond themselves and *the integration of selves into other lives and collective experiences*, rather than the self-protecting continuity of a career self.

We need to explore and contrast the life-motifs, guiding images of meaning, and ideals of self of women and men in diverse cultural, religious, and ethnic communities. These might be found in autobiographies and memoirs, stories and sermons, rituals and ceremonies, music, artwork, and craftwork with which people identify their experiences in everyday life. Documentary and community projects could be invaluable in uncovering, recovering, and sharing vital images of life's later times from all of our constituent cultures and communities. There must be more for us there than the impending obsolescence of aging career selves.

Notes

I am grateful for the lively and searching conversation among all this volume's contributors during our working conference in February 1998 at The Ethics Center of the University of South Florida in St. Petersburg. Our thinking together about lives, agency, and aging has deepened my understanding and increased my sense of the complexity of all of these.

1. For example, Carol Gilligan, *In A Different Voice* (Cambridge: Harvard University Press, 1982); Sara Ruddick, *Maternal Thinking* (New York: Ballantine Books, 1989); Annette Baier, *Moral Prejudices* (Cambridge: Harvard University Press, 1995); Virginia Held, *Feminist Morality* (Chicago: University of Chicago Press, 1993); and Margaret Urban Walker, *Moral Understandings: A Feminist Study in Ethics* (New York: Routledge, 1998).

2. For example, Alasdair MacIntyre, *After Virtue* (Notre Dame: University of Notre Dame Press, 1981); Michael Sandel, *Liberalism and the Limits of Justice* (New York: Cambridge University Press, 1982); Michael Walzer, *Thick and Thin* (Notre Dame: University of Notre Dame Press, 1994).

3. An indispensable study of this is Elaine Brody's *Women in the Middle: Their Parent-Care Years* (New York: Springer, 1990). See also Emily K. Abel, *Who Cares for the Elderly? Public Policy and the Experiences of Adult Daughters* (Philadelphia: Temple University Press, 1991).

4. Iris Young, *Justice and the Politics of Difference* (Princeton: Princeton University Press, 1990). See also Diana T. Meyers, *Subjection and Subjectivity* (New York: Routledge, 1994).

5. Paul Benson, "Feminist Second Thoughts on Free Agency," *Hypatia* 5 (1990): 47–64.

6. This is a central theme of Walker, *Moral Understandings*.

7. See Diana T. Meyers, *Self, Society, and Personal Choice* (New York: Columbia University Press, 1989).

8. See Kathryn Addelson, *Moral Passages* (New York: Routledge, 1994), ch. 5, and Walker, *Moral Understandings*, ch. 6.

9. Joan Tronto, *Moral Boundaries* (New York: Routledge, 1993).

10. Thomas R. Cole, *The Journey of Life* (New York: Cambridge University Press, 1992), xxix.

11. Cole, *The Journey*, 19.

12. Cole, *The Journey*, 93.

13. Walker, *Moral Understandings*, ch. 6.

14. John Rawls, *A Theory of Justice* (Cambridge: Harvard University Press, 1971), 92–93; see also 407 ff.

15. Bernard Williams, "Persons, Character, and Morality" and "Moral Luck," in *Moral Luck* (New York: Cambridge University Press, 1981).

16. Alasdair MacIntyre, *After Virtue* (Notre Dame: University of Notre Dame Press, 1981), especially 197–202.

17. Charles Taylor, *Sources of the Self* (Cambridge: Harvard University Press, 1989), 47–51.

18. Harry R. Moody, "The Meaning of Life and the Meaning of Old Age," in *What Does It Mean to Grow Old?* ed. Thomas R. Cole and Sally Gadow (Durham: Duke University Press, 1986), 24.

19. Kathleen Woodward, "Reminiscence and the Life Review: Prospects and Retrospects," in *What Does It Mean?* ed. Cole and Gadow, 145.

20. Bertram J. Cohler, "Aging, Morale, and Meaning: The Nexus of Narrative," in *Voices and Visions of Aging: Toward a Critical Gerontology*, ed. Thomas R. Cole, W. Andrew Achenbaum, Patricia Jacobi, and Robert Kastenbaum (New York: Springer, 1993), 110.

21. Moody, "The Meaning of Life," 26.

22. See Sara Ruddick's chapter 3 in this volume for a more positive account of the role of life review.

23. Moody, "The Meaning of Life," 36.

24. Sarah H. Matthews, *The Social World of Older Women: Management of Self-Identity* (Beverly Hills, Calif.: Sage, 1979), 42.

25. Harry R. Moody, "Overview: What Is Critical Gerontology and Why Is It Important?" in *Voices and Visions*, ed. Cole et al.

26. Along with Brody, *Women in the Middle*, Sara Arber and Jay Ginn, *Gender and Later Life: A Sociological Analysis of Resources and Constraints* (London: Sage, 1991), ch. 8, discuss contributions of elderly persons to the care of others. Bayne-Smith reports a study by W. Stafford (1994) for the Borough President of Manhattan based on the 1990 census that indicated "(a) 36% of black households in New York City with children were headed by persons 45 years or older who were caring for children not their own and (b) almost a quarter of all households with children (21%) were headed by black women 45 years and older without a spouse"—Marcia Bayne-Smith, "Health and Women of Color: A Contextual Overview," in *Race, Gender, and Health*, ed. Marcia Bayne-Smith (Thousand Oaks, Calif.: Sage, 1996), 31–32.

27. Anita Silvers disagrees that autonomy is an inappropriate or unachievable ideal for people with significant physical disabilities; see chapter 12 in this volume.

28. Barbara Myerhoff, "Rites and Signs of Ripening: The Intertwining of Ritual, Time, and Growing Older," in *Age in Anthropological Theory*, ed. David Kertzer and Jennie Keith (Ithaca: Cornell University Press, 1984), 322.

29. Myerhoff, "Rites and Signs," 322.

30. Carol A. B. Warren, "Aging and Identity in Premodern Times" in *Special Issue: Constructing, Maintaining, and Preserving Aging Identities,* ed. Tracy X. Karner, *Research on Aging* 20 (1998): 24.

31. Barbara Myerhoff, with Deena Metzger, Jay Ruby, and Virginia Tufte, *Remembered Lives: The Work of Ritual, Story-Telling, and Growing Older* (Ann Arbor: University of Michigan Press, 1992), 125.

32. For percentage figures on membership in churches, see U.S. Bureau of the Census *Statistical Abstract of the United States: 1997* (117th ed.), Washington, D.C.: U.S. Government Printing Office, 1997, 70; No. 86, Religious Preference, Church Membership, and Attendance: 1980 to 1995. Elizabeth Weiss Ozorak, "The Power, But Not the Glory: How Women Empower Themselves Through Religion," *Journal for the Scientific Study of Religion* 35 (1996): 17–29, contains references on women's religious participation and attitudes. For a more cautious view of "women's" religiosity, see Margaret M. Poloma, "From Sex Differences to Gender Role Beliefs: Exploring Effects on Six Dimensions of Religiosity," *Sex Roles* 25 (1991): 181–93. I thank Peggy DesAutels for sharing her recent research on women and religion with me; see chapter 10 in this volume.

· 7 ·

Death's Gender

James Lindemann Nelson

$\mathcal{D}$eath, Wallace Stevens tells us in "Sunday Morning," is the "mother of beauty."[1] For David Jones, death is a prostitute; his World War I epic poem, *In Parenthesis*, speaks of "sweet sister death" who strides about the battlefield with "strumpet confidence."[2] And Diana Tietjens Meyers tells us in chapter 2 in this volume that art portrays the face of death as the face of an old woman, the face of an old woman as the face of death.[3]

Sexing Death

These invocations of poetry and the graphic arts suggest one sense in which death has a gender: death, like nature, chaos, the body, emotion, and evil, has been connected in cultural imaginaries with the female.[4] Any strict identification of this kind might be contested, of course—there seems nothing so very feminine about the Grim Reaper, for example, and Milton made Death the son of Sin by her father Satan. My purpose here, though, is not to sort out the various gendered forms in which the idea of death has been cloaked. I will be interested in a different sense in which death might be gendered—in whether the gender of those who die might not alter the character of death.

This might seem an odd enterprise. Death could well strike us, as it apparently did Epicurus and Lucretius, as preeminently characterless. Or, if it has anything in the way of a character—if it is best understood, say, as a total and permanent privation of all that could possibly matter to a person—that character would seem uniform, and uniformly negative. Although timing and circumstances of dying alter radically from person to person, everyone dies alike, and, so far as can be determined in the order of nature, all the dead fare the same: a dead person has no further experiences of any

113

kind; a dead body decays. Neither gender nor any other distinguishing feature of people would seem to affect this one whit.

The investigation into gender's impact on death also might seem an inappropriate enterprise for this collection. The importance of affirming the diversity of being old, and particularly of women's diverse ways of aging and being old, makes it natural for feminists to resist stereotypical thinking about elderly people. Accordingly, it is important to insist that being old is not to be fully or even chiefly understood in terms of morbidity or mortality; being old is not to be identified with being as good as dead.

The odd enterprise I wish to take on squarely. Much of what I will attempt here involves showing that death too is diverse in ways that the leading philosophical accounts do not fully accommodate. At the same time I don't want to deny that discussing people who are old in terms of one feature of their lives—their proximity to death—is problematic. However, it is because theory tells, and practice enacts, stories about the connection between death and being elderly that are importantly flawed, that I think this journey worth the taking. It would be unfortunate if concern about representing the lives of old people too simply should distract attention from the ways in which their deaths have been too simply understood as well.

I begin by showing how inviting it is for philosophers who are interested in the moral relationships among different age groups or differently aged people to make both too much and not enough of mortality. These analyses have special, and sometimes worrisome implications for women, but my particular interest here will be in showing how these thinkers more or less explicitly rely on inadequate understandings of how death constitutes a harm to persons.

I then explore how gender may in fact be relevant to what kind of harms death constitutes to us mortals. Here, I will be drawing on the idea that systematic differences in what people value are relevant to the magnitude of death's harm, and as well on the idea that gender differences may track those systematic value differences more or less closely.

Finally, I want at least to rough out the outlines of three implications of the account developed here. One concerns a characteristic move in well-known theoretical efforts to use age as a device for making distributive justice decisions. The other two concern practice: little-noted gender biases in some of the most prominent cultural strategies for finding consolation in the face of mortality, and equally obscure dangers in the shifts in values that may accompany ways women live today.

Death, Age, Class

The literary critic Morris Zapp, one of the characters in David Lodge's series of academic novels, finds that he has rather lost his enthusiasm for poststructuralism after being kidnapped by terrorists. Zapp explains this by saying that his abduction has taught him a lesson: "Death is the one concept you can't deconstruct."[5] A number of contemporary philosophers seem to agree with Zapp's idea that death is "on the other side of language." At least, their accounts of death and its significance seem to deny to death the multiplicity that has recently been recognized as a signal feature of other socially, politically, and morally important concepts. For example, unlike, "race" or "gender," "death" is not often portrayed as something differently shaped for different people by different collusions of social powers, values, and practices.

Age As Superfact

Daniel Callahan, for example, who has written with considerable sensitivity about the way in which social circumstances and shared meanings might render dying "wild," "tame," or "peaceful,"[6] develops his account of what the old and young owe each other in a way that makes the issue of the proximity to death the single most important feature that both defines what it is to be old and gives the old their characteristic moral tasks. Dying may be a complex and socially mediated phenomenon, but death itself is simpler; as a general matter, its significance for Callahan is crucially conditioned by age. The death of the young is typically "tragic"; the death of the old, "tolerable." The old have already enjoyed the opportunities to discharge their duties and to gain the goods life provides; if, sadly, their personal or social circumstances have made it impossible for them to do so, this situation is not likely to be remedied simply by living longer.[7]

Frances Kamm, in trying to determine how justly to adjudicate contests over scarce, life-prolonging resources, makes how long one has already lived a crucial criterion for determining the gravity of one's need to go on living: the longer the life, the less need for more. For when it comes to the allocation of life-prolonging resources, the younger, solely because they are younger, are generally the "worse off" when compared to anyone at all older.[8] And Norman Daniels, who sets himself the task of justifying systems of health care allocation that favor the young over the old as age groups, notes that all of us who do not die prematurely move through all life's stages. He argues that therefore we can sensibly imagine distributing a fixed set of resources throughout the different periods of our lives. From that perspective, he maintains, it would be irrational to prefer an allocation of social resources designed to extend our lives when already old to an allocation designed to improve the chances that we will get to be old in the first place.[9] Again, this assumes that death's significance is, in the general case, a function of age alone—it is worth more to forestall death at an early age than to stave off a later death.

It has hardly been lost on feminists that basing social duties and notions of justice on age (in Daniels and Callahan, specifically on being elderly) affects women in particular, as women have a greater chance than men of becoming old, of being old for a long time, and of requiring a good deal of health care during their lives as elderly people. That women's stake in these theories is persistently undertheorized by their authors has been argued repeatedly in the literature.[10] What I want to feature here, however, is that, despite their differences, all of these writers regard death as "aged"—that is, the kind of harm death is to a person, or the seriousness of one's claim to avoid it, is dominantly affected by one's age. For none of them is it otherwise marked—not by ethnicity, not by class, and not by gender.

The theoretical attraction of the idea that one's age is so strongly relevant to the allocation of social resources is clearly enormous. If one is in the business of trying to figure out how to divide limited resources justly, and there is a "superfact" to save the day, so very much the better. By "superfact" I mean a fact that characterizes a set of people in a manner so relevant to distribution of goods or assignment of duties that none of their other traits, nor any of the traits of potential claimants not in that group can, singly or in combination, defeat its dispositive relevance. Who in the distributive justice game wouldn't be intrigued at the prospect of such a device?

Renaissance Death

Suppose, however, that the general respects in which death is a harm are not uniform, but vary according to considerations other than age. If such were the case, it would be arbitrary to give to age superfact status. Michael Neill's book *Issues of Death* suggests that death's harms may indeed vary along other dimensions. In trying to make better sense of English Renaissance tragedy, Neill argues that one of the most unsettling features about death to Renaissance Europeans was its rough egalitarianism; aristocrat and pauper died and decomposed alike.[11] This was taken to be unnatural, an outrageous cancellation of fundamental structures of meaning. Neill quotes John Donne to good effect in making this point:

> we must all pass this posthume death, this death after death, nay this death after burial, this dissolution after dissolution, this death of corruption and putrefaction, of vermiculation and incineration, of dissolution and dispersion in and from the grave, when those bodies that have been the children of royal parents and the parents of royal children, must say with Job, *to corruption, thou art my father,* and *to the worm, thou art my mother and my sister.* Miserable riddle, when the same worm must be my mother, my sister and my self! Miserable incest, when I must be married to my mother and my sister, and be both father and mother to my own mother and sister, beget and bear that worm which is all that miserable penury; when my mouth shall be filled with dust, and the worm shall feed, and feed sweetly, upon me; when the ambitious man shall have no satisfaction, if the poorest alive tread upon him, nor the poorest receive any contentment in being made equal to princes, for they shall be equal but in dust. . . . This is the most inglorious and contemptible vilification, the most deadly and preemptory nullification of man that we can consider.[12]

This is, to say no more, a complex piece of prose, not least in its use of gendered images. But Neill sees Donne's main theme to be repugnance at death's role as the Great Leveler. His historical work suggests two points. One is that *widely spread social understandings can contribute to the ways in which death is taken to be a harm.* While our own contemporaries are not free of the temptation to see structures of social privilege as reflections of the natural order, I suspect that death's being a common fate is less annoying to people today than some of its other features. This is surely not because we are nowadays indifferent about our place in hierarchies. Perhaps it indicates that we have become more instrumental about them than were many among our cultural predecessors. Being above others is widely prized, but largely to the extent that it secures one greater access to other things that are coveted: income, power, prestige, and the rest of the litany. Death either eliminates these goods or is irrelevant to them, and it's the absence of the goods that is taken to be important nowadays. That death also eliminates hierarchial patterns of distribution of such goods is, for many of us, largely beside the point. Insofar as there is a shift in the reasons why hierarchial orders are valued, the response to their loss may shift as well.

The second point that seems implicit in Neill is that *one's place in a social structure can also affect the ways in which death is taken to be harmful*. Donne suggests that the poor have no consolation in becoming no worse dust than their betters in life, but I cannot help but think that death's egalitarianism was at least somewhat more nettlessome to those who would be going down in the (under)world than to those for whom death was a form, however limited, of upward mobility—death's "preemptory nullification" is more of a problem, that is, for princes than for paupers.

However it stood with people in Renaissance Europe, Neill's historical work allows us to imagine a way in which social understandings and specifically class position might well affect the respects in which people saw death as a harm. It thereby prepares the ground for a view of death's harms more complex than that envisaged by Callahan, Kamm, or Daniels, one that acknowledges the relevance of social markers. If death, or at least its harms, can be class-sensitive in Renaissance England, why not gender-sensitive now?

Death's Sting

Old aristocrats in Renaissance Europe no doubt had better access to whatever life-prolonging technologies were then on offer than did young paupers; could they have justified their advantage with the claim that, due to their class position, death constituted a greater harm to them than to the youthful poor?

This may strike us inheritors of the Enlightenment as counterintuitive, and there is a natural way of accounting for that response. It might be that different groups of people have *feared* death for different reasons, but it does not follow that these social beliefs about death reflect differences in what *actually* makes death a harm. Nor is it clear what the ethical implications of mere beliefs about death's harmfulness might be. The real problem, it might seem, is to show whether death itself is a harm of a different kind to some people than to others.

The Goods of Experience and Action

There is, of course, an old and surprisingly tough question about whether, and if so in what respects, it is a bad thing to die at all. This question is seldom discussed—at least nowadays—in ways that would suggest that death might be a different thing for people differently situated and constituted.[13] While I have drawn from Neill's work the suggestion that class location might change at least some of the respects in which death is harmful, I imagine this idea would not be well received by those philosophers who have done the most conspicuous and explicit recent work on how death might be a harm: I have in mind particularly Thomas Nagel, whose article "Death"[14] is surely something of a contemporary classic on this question, and Kamm, who has thought through this question very thoroughly indeed. Both would likely distinguish between, on the one hand, the varieties of disturbing beliefs that may be associated with death—that is, that death removes essential distinctions, or, to take a more familiar example, the fear of eternal damnation—and, on the other, those considerations in which the harmfulness of death really resides, quite apart from what anyone believes, that is, because it forever deprives us of all possibility of the goods of experience and action, to use Kamm's formulation.[15] What makes death bad in fact and not fancy, as Nagel and Kamm see it, is the same for all of us.

But *was* the Renaissance belief that death cancels out important distinctions simply false, and is the view of Nagel, as amended by Kamm, that death deprives us of the goods of experience and action (and makes things "all over" for us) in contrast straightforwardly true? So far as can be known, *both* the Renaissance and the Nagel-Kamm characterizations are correct—if there is a difference, it is that people care much less about death as a leveler than they do about death as, so to speak, an extinguisher. Different facts about death affect different people at different times in different ways, it seems, and the moral is that we need a less generic account of why death is so nasty than either Nagel or even Kamm provides.

Kamm's own formulation of what death takes from us provides a glimpse of what that alternative might be like. She highlights the point that death takes away a particular kind of goods—not "all possible goods," but the "goods of experience and action."[16] This distinction itself suggests the possibility that the severity of death's sting might vary as a function of the extent to which one valued the goods of experience and action vis-à-vis unexperienced goods. Kamm develops a variant on this theme; she notes that the "true goods" of wisdom and good character, while they make life better, are "to a large degree complete in themselves once one has them," and says that they are best regarded as ways of being rather than as ways of acting or experiencing.[17] Such goods, which are among the most important things in life, are the least threatened by death.

Goods Outside Awareness and Action

But these Socratic virtues are not the only things that may have value independently of experience and action. There are, for example, possible states of affairs that neither affect nor are affected by particular people, yet about which people are far from indifferent. I, for example, would much rather it be the case that the future fifty generations includes the existence and flourishing of many human beings living in harmony with each other, other animals, and their environment, than have the future be depleted of all that gives the present grace. I would rather it not be the case that I am at this moment being viciously slandered, even to people who don't believe a word of it, and even if I should never find out about the matter.

At first blush, some philosophers might not accept these examples of goods as pointing to goods of unawareness and inaction. Both examples are introduced with a phrase that seems to relate a state of affairs to my wants. But what I intend to convey with these examples is that I judge a future state of the world in which justice flourishes and the lion lies down with the lamb and suchlike to be better than less pacific and equitable alternatives—not, ex hypothesi, better for me, but better for those who inhabit that world, or, perhaps, better objectively. I think of a state of the world that includes my being selected as a target for foul yet-forever-undetected-by-me calumny to be worse—perhaps for those who have to hear such drivel, or for those who spout it, or perhaps just worse simpliciter—than a similar state of the world that contains instead someone holding me up to fair criticism.

While sentiments of this sort are fairly widespread, it is quite possible that people might place more or less store in values not involving action or experience. It's not hard to imagine someone—call him Jack—quite willing to say that he was not indifferent to the state of the world fifty generations hence, but all of whose true enthusiasms revolve around what he experienced and what he did. I think it also possible to imagine someone much more engaged by unexperienced goods—call her Jill. For Jill, her children's flourishing is enormously valuable. While she enjoys watching them at it, fundamentally, it doesn't much matter to her at what time their lives are going well—now, or twenty years after her death. Jill might well prefer an arrangement in which the children's lives go somewhat less well during her own life, if that were necessary for matters to turn out very much better for them after her death.

Noting that the inevitability of a catastrophe does not necessarily make it any the less bad, Nagel famously concludes "Death" with the phrase, "It may be that a bad end is in store for all of us." After all, death is an "abrupt cancellation of indefinitely extensive possible goods."[18] Nagel may have Jack's number—he may indeed be cruising toward a bad end. Jill's prospects, however, may not be quite so dire. Not all of what matters deeply to her is quite so vulnerable to death's privations. Even the permanent loss of what are in principle indefinitely extendable goods does not necessarily leave one in a bad state—much depends upon what is retained and how it is valued. Of course, Jill's special engagement with unexperienced goods leaves open the possibility that she is liable to harms related to her death of a kind against which Jack is better armored—suppose, for example, that her children's lives go on the whole badly after her death. But at least with respect to the currently leading philosophical accounts of the matter, Jill seems the better off.

I further want to suggest that the reasons why Jack runs into this problem and Jill does not are not completely idiosyncratic. There are social forces that incline Jack and Jill to value as they do—forces that are not accidentally related to their genders.

How We Die: Career Selves and Seriatim Selves

In Harold Pinter's *Moonlight*, the dying Andy lies in his bed among the shards of his life. Estranged from his sons, disconnected from his friends, he and his wife exchange bitter boasts about their infidelities. All he has to cling to is the most important feature of what he has been:

> I sweated over a hot desk all the working life and nobody ever found a flaw in my working procedures. Nobody uncovered the slightest hint of negligence or misdemeanor. Never. . . . I was a first class civil servant. I was admired and respected. I do not say I was loved. I didn't want to be loved. Love is an attribute no civil servant worth his salt would give house room to. It's redundant. An excrescence. No, no, I'll tell you what I was. I was an envied and feared force in the temples of the just.[19]

In Margaret Walker's *Moral Understandings*, Andy—or, rather, his ghost—makes another appearance, albeit anonymously. Walker discusses the prevalence within moral theory of a particular kind of self disturbingly like Andy, which she styles the "career self."[20] Roughly sketched, a career self sees his life (aspirationally, in any event) as a unified field, in which particular enterprises, values, and relationships are (in principle) coordinated in the form of a "rational life plan" (à la Rawls), or a "quest" (to use the term favored by MacIntyre and Taylor), or a "project" (as Williams is wont to say). It's tempting to describe such lives in terms of the chapter titles of a conventionally structured novel: "The Years of Preparation," followed by "The Years of Struggle" and "The Years of Achievement," and finally, as the telltale compression of the pages warn us, "The Years of Retirement." There is a shape to this life, both in principle and in practice: you go up through the ranks, get tenure, make Professor, and then get an endowed chair; you finish law school, get a good clerkship, become an associate at a top firm, and then make partner; an MBA, a key to the executive washroom, the million-dollar circle. Such conceptions of life typically put great stress on agency and individuality (*I* exercise *my* agency to envisage and attain my goals, slaying such dragons as have the temerity to present themselves along the way), on what I experience myself as getting, keeping, and doing, as well as on relatively distinct tasks for distinct phases of life.

The Goods of Agency versus the Goods of Relationship

Now, if this is at all on target, it would be natural to regard the loss of the goods of individual agency and experience as heavy indeed for career selves—something akin, perhaps, to the impact of the leveling effect of death on Renaissance aristocrats. It would also seem natural to see old age as having something of a unified and distinct character—typically, it will be the time after the dragons have been slain and the quest fulfilled, and the task remaining is to make a graceful exit. Thus, the career self trope fits nicely with Callahan's general analysis of age as a unified category robust enough to support a distinct set of duties. It also coheres with Nagel's and Kamm's discussion of the harm of death, further supporting Walker's point that the career self notion is theoretically ubiquitous, haunting the thought of otherwise very different philosophers. But a good part of Walker's point in introducing the career self notion, and drawing attention to its largely unmotivated presence at the heart of the thought of writers otherwise maintaining importantly different commitments, is to point out the possibility of living a life in ways importantly different from that described with notions such as "career," "quest," "project," or "plan"—indeed, of pointing out that such lives are in fact lived.

Hilde Lindemann Nelson has in discussion used the phrase "living life seriatim" to designate an alternative to the career trajectory. I take her to mean seeing life less as an overall unified project and more as a set of fits and starts. For "seriatim selves," what death portends by way of harms, and the idea of the appropriate tasks of later life as well, might be different from what they are for career selves. The career self's big job is over as he enters his twilight years, and the final task is to fill out the remains of the day with some dignity. But the seriatim self may see her life as made up of many jobs, lots of them quite big enough, thank you, but none necessarily life-defining, nor especially valued for the particular role they play in contributing to the achievement of a "rational plan" for the whole.

Rather, there's the time of going to school, and then the time of getting married and dealing with pregnancies and children. After that, there may be a time of going back to school, a time of having a job apart from family obligations. But that may not last, because there may be a time of changing locations because of the more exigent career demands of a spouse who is a career self. There may then be a time of starting out doing something else, and a time of caring for one's parents, and perhaps of tending the grandchildren.

The connections between being a career or a seriatim self and how one values the goods of experience and agency vis-à-vis the nonexperiential dimensions of the goods of relationship are, of course, not logically necessary. A career self could certainly pursue a seamless project of exemplary selflessness, in which expressing one's own agency and having gratifying experiences were largely incidental, not to the main point at all. A seriatim self could find goods of action and experience the most fulfilling feature of every stop along her variegated way. Yet, as Cheshire Calhoun has pointed out, nonlogical connections can be as philosophically important as logically necessary ones.[21] The patterns of social practice and understandings that make career selves so prevalent, in both theory and practice, are part of what she might call an "ideology of the moral life" that installs the view that there is nothing so natural (at least for those paradigmatic moral agents, otherwise privileged men) as striving to impose one's own vision on life, and that many of the relationships that come our way will be with people with similar desires, leading to something of a premium on cultivating what Aristotle called "friends for use." Agency and experience are big themes all the way through the pertinent philosophical accounts; there is surely nothing contemplative in the connotation of "quest" or even the less dramatic "project" or "rational life plan." They are big themes as well in the real lives that both give rise to and approximate these idealizations. But a seriatim self has escaped, more or less, the ideological pressures, as well as the ideological and material rewards that encourage people to identify themselves with their careers, and hence may live a life both more shaped by contingencies than by the expression of personal agency and more involved in relationships prized intrinsically, not because they are instrumental to achieving the agent's quest. Individual experience and agency are surely important to pursuing and nurturing relationships, but they may not be as important as the site where the value of such pursuits reside. Seriatim selves may, then, place a greater importance on the goods of relationship, rather than the goods of agency and experience. I don't mean to deny that creating, preserving, and getting the good out of relationships won't importantly involve what people do, think, and feel. Nor that the social forces that have inclined more women than men to lives oriented relationally and lived seriatim are benign in intent or effect; quite the contrary. But lives so lived may have a special access to the values of relationship, and among the goods of those relationships that are not altogether a matter of who is useful to whom, one must surely be an appreciation of the significance of the other quite on her own terms, not as a function of what makes me happy.[22] People who manage to make the good of others central to their lives in this way are importantly invested in something robust enough to withstand their deaths.

Death and Women's Aging with Dignity

Morris Zapp was wrong. Death doesn't wear its meaning on its face— univocal, stable, and uncontestable. Nor is age the only dimension along which its significance varies. There is reason to believe that its character is altered according to one's position in the system of class differences, and reason, too, to think that it alters with one's position in the system of gender differences, or at least that gender closely tracks patterns of human valuing with which the significance of death more directly varies.

I have already suggested that very influential age-based theories of distributive justice make the mistake of supposing that the harmfulness of death varies as a general matter with age alone, but I've yet to draw out the implications of the error, particularly as they affect women who are old. I have also implied that ignoring the sense in which death is gendered has unfortunate implications for social practices that involve women distinctively; something more needs to be said about that, as well.

Aging, Dignity, and Justice

Most feminist assessments of theories of intergenerational justice have been concerned that the interests of aging women were particularly at risk. In suggesting that at least many women may not be as vulnerable to losing the goods of action and experience as are many men, this feminist concern seems to have been given a curious twist.

In my view, however, the real lesson here is that handing out resources in ways that favor the young cannot be justified as straightforwardly as proponents would intend. If old people tend to differ by gender in the ways in which they are threatened by death, it does not follow that we should simply accept the framework of age rationing and deduct further "points" for being female as well as elderly. Such a framework rests on the misleading idea that the moral significance of selected human traits, such as age or gender, can be measured in a common scale, in a way largely detached from the full moral complexity of human life. This analytic structure needs to be questioned more rigorously. In figuring out how to direct health care budgets or hand out transplantable livers, comparing the stringency of the claims of the young qua young to those of the old qua old is a form of "false totalization," and thus is disrespectful, particularly (though not solely) to people who happen to be old. Avoiding such disrespect does not require abandoning the notion that age is relevant to issues of how to allocate scarce goods fairly, but to make age determinative is not only disrespectful, it is distracting. Making age a superfact oversimplifies the task of achieving justice in the distribution of scarce goods, but that's not the whole of the problem. So understood, the focus on age obscures other issues that are at least equally important. Why are we finding ourselves playing off Medicaid (medical support for children and the indigent) against Medicare (medical support for the elderly) in the first place? Why does health care cost as much as it does? Why do we so obsess about medicine, when well-being may often be more reliably secured by enhancing social environments? And, perhaps most radically, how would medicine and its social setting look if the central role of the goods of experience and agency in many people's lives were challenged, and hence the harm of death—or, at least the harm most theoretically apparent to philosophers now—diminished generally?

Gender and the Forms of Consolation

It seems reasonable to think that the forms of hope and consolation on offer in cultures would be specially tailored to the kinds of selves those cultures particularly prize. If, in the dominant culture, social power and authority are disproportionately in the hands of career selves, we might expect important strategies to include authoritative promises that what death crucially removes will yet be restored; that there is agency and experience beyond the grave.

This, of course, is just what we do find. Stories of personal survival, beatific visions, and resurrections of the body are not the only ways in which cultures offer hope and solace to their participants, but they clearly have had pride of place in Western societies for many centuries.[23] As important as these stories have been, however, they do little to highlight the resilience to death's harms that tend to come with ways of valuing that put less stress on action and experience. I don't mean to suggest that only hard-driving CEOs have found notions of heaven attractive; I'd be surprised if very many people, however marked by gender or class or ethnicity or age, were altogether indifferent to the goods of action and experience, and of course, certain actions and experiences constitute an important part of the value of relationships, even if they do not exhaust that value. But a more equitable society, and in particular a society with more on offer for the variety of people who are facing death soon, would do well to fill its collective imaginary with a greater variety of ways of thinking about the end of life. People who place more store on goods whose value is not altogether a matter of whether or not they themselves have certain experiences would be better served if more public discourse about death pointed to the enduring significance of such goods, about how their goodness can be relatively independent of awareness or even of temporal location. It would be a start if the very notion that death's harm can be, at least in part, a function of what and how a person values, were itself a more readily recognizable idea. To some extent, this was a common theme to the ancient philosophers who took philosophy's task to be therapeutic; now, we leave therapy largely to medicine, trusting to it to deliver us from death. About this, Dan Callahan is absolutely right—it is not going to happen. Maybe it is time again to look to philosophy for deliverance.[24]

Gender and the Sort of Selves We Are

Above, I've entered a plea that the resources society makes available to those facing death—proximately, at least people who are old, ultimately everyone—should be deployed in a fashion more responsive to the different ways in which death is a harm to us. In fact, it would be all to the good if more of us accepted the very possibility that something potentially a matter of human control—how and what we value—is strongly relevant to the kind of harms death presents to us. This would hold open the chance for people to shift to less classically individualist "career self" oriented patterns; if it also meant that a more egalitarian world led to more people adopting what had previously been characterized as feminine ways of living, no harm done.

Alas, what may be happening is just the reverse. If the Western world today is not more egalitarian in general, it at least presents more opportunity for women, particularly those privileged in racial, class, and other respects, to be more visible and more powerful in areas of social life from which they had previously been more rigorously restricted. This is certainly to be applauded, but everything has the defects of its qualities. It may be the case that women who today are not yet old, and perhaps therefore in a position to take greater advantage of new opportunities than their foremothers, may find themselves lacking in some of the strengths women now elderly tend to possess. In short, they may find themselves in this respect to be more like men—not necessarily in that they will die sooner than their foremothers, but that, having had as central parts of their lives the kind of careers traditional for men, they may die valuing more as men have valued. There are surely features in the lives of many women with careers that would tend to resist this assimilation. But it would be unfortunate if a more egalitarian world means a world in which more people are more like what many men traditionally have been, and in which the question of death's gender has been decisively settled.

Notes

Perhaps more than is usually the case, it is important to acknowledge that no one else can be held responsible for these ideas. However, I have received an enormous amount of help from Hilde Lindemann Nelson, Margaret Walker, Ellen Robinson, and the participants in the wonderfully stimulating Conference on Ethical Issues in Women's Aging with Dignity, held at the Ethics Center, the University of South Florida, in February 1998. I must in particular mention Sara Ruddick and Diana Tietjens Meyers. William Ruddick was also kind enough to read a late draft and share his thoughtful impressions with me. I wish I could have profited more from all their good counsel. Finally, I am also much beholden to Eric Nelson's performance as Andy in a production of Pinter's *Moonlight* performed at the College of St. Benedict, St. Joseph, Minnesota, in March 1998.

1. Wallace Stevens, "Sunday Morning," in *The Collected Poems of Wallace Stevens* (New York, Knopf, 1954), 66–70.
2. David Jones, *In Parenthesis* (New York: Chilmark, 1962), 162.
3. Diana Tietjens Meyers, chapter 2 in this volume.
4. For discussion of this theme, see Genevieve Lloyd, *The Man of Reason:*

"Male" and *"Female"* in *Western Philosophy* (Minneapolis: University of Minnesota Press, 1984).

5. David Lodge, *Small World* (New York: Warner Books, 1984), 373.

6. Daniel Callahan, *The Troubled Dream of Life* (New York: Simon & Schuster, 1993).

7. Daniel Callahan, *Setting Limits* (New York: Simon & Schuster, 1987). His characterization of a tolerable death is given on p. 66.

8. Frances M. Kamm, *Morality, Mortality,* vol. I: *Death and Whom to Save from It* (New York: Oxford University Press, 1993).

9. Norman Daniels, *Am I My Parent's Keeper?* (New York: Oxford University Press, 1988). See also his "The Prudential Life-Span Account of Justice Across Generations," in his *Justice and Justification: Reflective Equilibrium in Theory and Practice* (Cambridge: Cambridge University Press, 1996), 257–83.

10. For feminist discussion of Callahan, see Nora Kizer Bell, "If Age Becomes a Standard for Rationing Health Care . . ." in *Feminist Perspectives in Medical Ethics,* ed. Helen Bequaert Holmes and Laura Purdy (Bloomington: Indiana University Press, 1992), 82–90; Kathleen M. Dixon, "Oppressive Limits: Callahan's Foundation Myth," *Journal of Medicine and Philosophy* 19, no. 6 (1994): 613–37; and my "Going Gently into That Good Night: A Review Essay on Callahan's *Setting Limits,*" *Bioethics Books* 1, no. 1 (1989): 1–4. My "Measured Fairness, Situated Justice: Feminist Reflections on Health Care Rationing," *Kennedy Institute of Ethics Journal* 6, no. 1 (March 1996): 53–68, examines Kamm's and Daniels's work. Nancy S. Jecker's "Toward a Theory of Age-Group Justice," *Journal of Medicine and Philosophy* 14, no. 6 (1989): 655–76, takes on Daniels. See also Jecker's "Age-Based Rationing and Women," *Journal of the American Medical Association* 266 (1991): 3012–15.

11. Michael Neill, *Issues of Death: Morality and Identity in English Renaissance Tragedy* (New York: Oxford University Press, 1997). See also Terence Hawkes's review in the *London Review of Books* 19 (1997): 10–11, "On the Way in Which Tragedy 'Openeth up the Greatest Wounds and Showeth Forth the Ulcers That Are Covered with Tissue.' "

12. John Donne, "Death's Duel," in *Devotions upon Emergent Occasions Together with Death's Duel* (Ann Arbor: University of Michigan Press, 1959), 176–77, as quoted in Neill, *Issues of Death,* 11–12.

13. The philosophers of classical antiquity, who gave this question about death a good going over, seem to have been very interested in whether different ways of thinking and living could reduce the harm of death; see the discussion in Martha C. Nussbaum, *The Therapy of Desire: Theory and Practice in Hellenistic Ethics* (Princeton: Princeton University Press, 1994). This is certainly a less developed tendency in contemporary discussions. See, however, Derek Parfit's "Should We Welcome or Regret My Conclusions?" in his *Reasons and Persons* (London: Oxford University Press, 1984). Kamm, as will be noted, is also interested in the possibility that developing certain virtues could make one less vulnerable to death's harms.

14. "Death" is probably most readily available in Thomas Nagel's *Mortal Questions* (Cambridge: Cambridge University Press, 1979).

15. Kamm probes many other possible ways in which death is bad. One on

which she particularly focuses is the idea that death involves nothingness, which we regard as an "unexperienced bad." (See her discussion of "The Limbo Man" in chapters 1 and 3 of *Morality, Mortality*.) That we do so is shown by certain thought experiments that converge on the distinctive negativity of things being all over for us. This "Extinction Factor" Kamm regards as the most distinctive feature of our concern with death. But, on her own showing, death involves things being all over for us only in some (albeit crucial) respects. What is clearly all over is our access to the goods of experience and action.

16. Kamm, *Morality, Mortality*, 17. She points out that one finds unexperienced harms in death as well—for instance, a person might find death harmful because it truncated her chances of living so as to attract the admiration of future generations.

17. Kamm, *Morality, Mortality*, 61.

18. Nagel, *Mortal Questions*, 10.

19. Harold Pinter, *Moonlight* (New York: Dramatists Play Services, 1995), 13.

20. Margaret Walker, *Moral Understandings: A Feminist Study in Ethics* (New York: Routledge, 1998), ch. 6.

21. Cheshire Calhoun, "Justice, Care, Gender Bias," *Journal of Philosophy* 85, no. 9 (September 1998): 451–63.

22. See Marilyn Frye's discussion of the "arrogant eye of masculine perception," in her "In and Out of Harm's Way," from *The Politics of Reality* (Trumansburg, N.Y.: Crossings Press, 1983), 66–72.

23. I don't mean to suggest that these notions are only interpretable in ways that stress the significance of experience and action. It is not only in the East that there are eschatological traditions that are contemplative or mystical, and not much interested in the survival of one's personality. However, here again is a point where Calhoun's insight is helpful—what is logically entailed by a theory can be overshadowed in philosophical importance by what is ideologically enacted.

24. About the therapeutic task of philosophy, I again cite Nussbaum's *Therapy of Desire*. Callahan powerfully inveighs against the notion that medicine will someday cure us of all our ills, including mortality, in every book he has written in the past eleven years; his most recent, *False Hopes* (New York: Simon & Schuster, 1998), continues the jeremiad.

· *Part Three* ·

Looking at Health Care

· 8 ·

Old Women Out of Control:
Some Thoughts on Aging, Ethics,
and Psychosomatic Medicine

Susan Wendell

In Declining to Decline: Cultural Combat and the Politics of the Midlife (1997), Margaret Morganroth Gullette examines a widespread contemporary picture of midlife as the time when women and men start to become unattractive, chronically ill (with menopause now commonly represented as the inescapable chronic illness of women), disabled, unemployable, out-of-date and therefore expendable, and an overprivileged burden on the young. Gullette argues that expectations of midlife decline, although they are attributed to natural physical changes, are socially and culturally constructed; when we internalize them, we suffer from premature fears of aging and midlife crises of identity. She points out that depreciating images of middle and old age benefit current economic interests, such as the effort to eliminate job seniority, and she urges people of all ages to resist expectations of decline.

I am grateful for Gullette's description and analysis of middle-ageism. It forced me to confront the sense of dread that has intruded on my consciousness in recent years—dread that I was being pushed out of the stream of life, not (this time) because of my disability, but because I am going through menopause. I had come to terms with my experience of chronic illness partly by realizing that disability is socially constructed through our collective failure to recognize, appreciate, and accommodate the great diversity of human bodies and brains (Wendell 1996). I had even understood that, since aging is disabling (back to this later), many people older than myself had been pushed out of the activities they love by their societies' failures to accommodate people with disabilities. But I had not begun to

133

recognize the pervasive cultural construction of midlife decline that Gullette describes in *Declining to Decline,* much less to resist it.

Gullette's call for individual and collective resistance to the "identity-stripping" of middle-ageism has my heartfelt support. But I worry about the rejection of illness and disability expressed and implied in her book. When she criticizes the false equation, "old age equals sickness equals death" (206), Gullette comes perilously close to portraying middle-aged and old people who have disabilities as embarrassments to the images of their age groups.

Speaking of the scripted decline ushered in by midlife in her culture, Gullette says: "Aging-into-the-middle-years is actually a socially constructed disease with an adolescent or childhood exposure and a midlife onset" (6). Later she remarks that her culture "treats the problems of illness in old age as if they modeled normal old age, relying on our ageist ignorance of normal old age" (108). And she assures us that "at midlife people work harder and more efficiently, have less absenteeism, and are loyal" (231). These and other remarks throughout the book suggest that Gullette believes in *real* decline, as opposed to socially constructed decline, and that she equates real decline with illness, disability, and the inability to work as much or as well as one did when young. Yet disability, chronic illness, and even life-threatening illness do not "naturally" imply a decline any more than healthy, nondisabled (what Gullette calls "normal") aging does. Nor do they imply an imperative to move out of the labor market or the arenas of productive and creative work.

In arguing against the socially constructed midlife decline, it is important, for several reasons, not to insist on its opposite, the "wonderful" (Gullette's word, on 222 and elsewhere), healthy, energetic midlife and old age. First, to do so alienates large numbers of people (and increasing numbers with increasing age) from the benefits of identifying with an alternative vision of aging. Diana Meyers points out in chapter 2 in this volume that substituting a different but no more expansive standard of beauty is no solution to the problem of being excluded by age from identifying oneself, and being identified by others, as beautiful. So too, leaning on a distinction between normal and sick/disabled middle and old age is no solution to the problem of being excluded by age from identifying oneself, and being identified by others, as having a valuable present and future life. It benefits some—those who are aging in good health with little or no disability—at the expense of others, *including their probable future selves,* on whom the demeaning narratives of decline can and will be projected.

Second, insistence on "wonderful" aging does not reflect the truth.

Aging is not always and never *just* being sick or dying, but it is also these. Aging is also disabling, and especially disabling in societies where inadequate provision is made for the participation of people with nonideal, limited, or suffering bodies. Arthritis, rheumatism, heart and respiratory diseases, stroke, Parkinsonism, and hypertension, all of which occur more frequently after midlife, are major causes of disability in Canada and the United States (Health and Welfare Canada and Statistics Canada 1981, Statistics Canada 1986 and 1991, Pope and Tarlov 1991, LaPlante 1991, Bury 1978). Statistics Canada reports a steady increase with age in the number of people whose daily activities are limited due to chronic health conditions, from 23 percent in the 45 to 64 age group to 47 percent in the over-75 group. Hospitalizations increase steadily and dramatically too.

These facts are particularly relevant to women. The average Canadian woman has 1.5 more years of life without disability than the average man, but an additional five years with disability (*Report on the Health of Canadians* 1996). A woman's preparation for aging must involve planning for sickness, medical treatment, and disability. Moreover, my research on disability accommodation (and the lack thereof) has warned me that neither Canada nor the United States is prepared to accommodate the large numbers of disabled old women who are on the way. Both countries need to do some collective planning if disabled old women are to be enabled to participate in their societies and do the things they enjoy to the full extent of their abilities. Planning to accommodate disabilities is in most people's best interest, but it will be neglected if those who are not now disabled prefer to imagine that they will age and die without experiencing disability.

Gullette seems to think that the physical problems of aging are created primarily by unjust or inadequate social systems. In one of her few acknowledgments that such problems exist, she refers to "physical alterations and diseases that derive from discriminatory socioeconomic practices, environmental depredations, lack of access to information and health care" as "socially induced illnesses . . . not natural concomitants of aging" (15). While I agree that it is important not to allow damage caused by social systems to be misrepresented as expected consequences of aging, I think it is wildly optimistic to imagine that social justice, a healthful environment, and medical advances can eliminate most of the illnesses and physical limitations of middle and old age. Some of the most privileged middle-aged and old people in the world get sick now; spreading their level of privilege to everyone in the world, could it be done, would not be sufficient. But even supposing that it is not overly optimistic to hope for universal health and the elimination of age-related physical impairments, achieving them is unlikely to benefit the present midlife generation, their children, or their children's children.

Finally, to reject illness and disability as abnormal forms of aging, dangerous to the personal and political goals of people who resist socially constructed decline, lends support to the ubiquitous marketing of control of the body, to medical abuse and neglect of middle-aged and old women, and to all the social controls and punishments visited upon those whose bodies are seen to be out of control.

Ideals of Aging and the Marketing of Fear and Hope

Just as most of us are aware of the conventional North American expectations of midlife decline, so too we are aware of the conventional ideals of graceful aging: healthy, slim, energetic, discreetly sexy, independent, reliable, prosperous, and productive. We are allowed to have a few wrinkles and a little sagging, take more vitamins and go to bed a little earlier; we should not emulate the fashions and activities of the young (that's embarrassing), but we should be able to appreciate them. It may seem odd that expectations of decline and ideals of graceful aging occur together, but it fits the general pattern of social marginalization. Marginalized people are understood to be inferior, no matter what they do, but encouraged to pursue an ideal version of themselves, different enough from the "normal" group to remain "the Other" (useful for so many purposes), but similar enough to demonstrate the absolute value of the "normal" group. For example, people with noticeable disabilities are encouraged to look and act "normal" enough to avoid causing social discomfort in the nondisabled; making this effort demonstrates their understanding that "normal" is best. But they are discouraged from concealing their disabilities or acting too "normal," which would constitute a kind of refusal of their lower social status and prevent the comparisons by which the nondisabled know themselves as "normal." In the case of people who are marginalized by aging, the "normal" group is the young (or, more accurately, some of the young).

The middle-aged and old have been set up to strive for an ideal that keeps us hating and fearing who we are. For we are, among other things, bodies subject to wear, accident, infection, poisoning, mutation, and, of course, gravity and sunlight. We are bodies at once miraculously self-regulating and frighteningly out of our own control. Consequently, we are offered, for a price, many products and services to reverse our hatred and assuage our fear, including dietary supplements, hormones, drugs, surgery, and an incredible array of therapies—physical, psychological, and spiritual. More insidiously, we are offered ideologies of self-control that allow us, also for a price, to hope to avoid the bad version of old age; the price of these ideologies is taking the blame should we find ourselves sick or disabled.

Recently I started watching a public television fund-raising series that interested me because a woman gynecologist promised to discuss women's health issues, including menopause. She seemed well informed and funny, and I was just settling down to learn what I could, when I heard her say that she now understood that fibroid tumors (benign uterine growths) are creative impulses that a woman is not expressing, or something she has outgrown, such as a relationship or a job, that she hasn't given up. The same doctor had just told us that 40 percent of women grow a fibroid at some time in their lives; a few of us in the audience may have been astonished to learn that only 40 percent of women have unexpressed creativity or tiresome relationships or jobs (but perhaps the others grow another kind of tumor). The doctor went on to explain her version of the relationship among body, mind, spirit, and society, how we can prevent disease by managing our lives, and how, if we become ill, we can increase the effectiveness of other treatments by examining the meanings of our diseases. I confess my attention wandered. I wish I could say this sort of fare is unusual, but, on the contrary, it seems that the message "Heal Thyself" has become a staple of public television. Since PBS is aimed at the most educated television audience, I take this to be a sign of the growing influence of popular psychosomatic medicine.

There are, however, indications that the people who sell or propound popular psychosomatic medicine have realized that implicitly blaming those who are not in perfect health is offensive to significant numbers of their audience, and that they have tried to create more ethically sophisticated, blame-free versions of their message of hope and responsibility. For instance, the doctor I watched on the PBS fund-raiser explained that, although all our health problems express something wrong in our lives, we shouldn't be ashamed of our diseases, because no one can be expected to "get everything right," and we do not usually realize what is wrong with our lives until we become diseased. This may be consoling when the problem is a fibroid or the flu, but I wonder how it must feel to a woman who has advanced ovarian cancer. How big a life-error must ovarian cancer represent? Was such an error really unavoidable? Can it be consoling to think that you failed to notice that something *that* serious was wrong with your life, and that the solution still eludes you?

The blame problem of popularized psychosomatic medicine is hard to eliminate, because it is tied logically to the source of hope: If managing our lives or psyches properly will enable us to improve, retain, or restore our health, then, if we are very ill, we have made some terrible mistakes. The promise that we can control our bodies is a package deal that comes with the blame for not controlling them. Of course, sometimes those who sell or propound control do not promise *absolute* control; they speak of minimizing risks and maximizing health, and then blame is not implied in their offer of hope. But blame still lurks wherever concern is focused on controlling the body, because there the role of chance is minimized and deviation from the goal looks like failure. People will ask, "What did I (or she or he) do wrong," not "How can I live well with (or even appreciate) this different body?"

It may be that most people at midlife or beyond would gladly pay the price of blame for the illusion of control and the hope it seems to offer. The price may seem too high to me because I am on the wrong side of the divide, already among those who know that we, with our incurable and unacceptable bodies, represent failure to control the body. But there are other consequences of the popularity of mind-over-body medicine that need to be considered, including how it affects our treatment of people with illnesses and disabilities, how it increases our fears of becoming sick or (more) disabled, and how it colludes with our desires to avoid thinking, individually and collectively, about death (see Wendell 1996). Moreover, public support for psychosomatic theories increases their influence in medicine. Those of us facing fears of aging should ask ourselves whether we want to add our wishful thinking to the already powerful, and sometimes dangerous, influence of psychosomatic medicine.

Investigations into Psychosomatic Diagnosis

When I tell people that I am researching the ethics and politics of psychosomatic diagnosis, almost everyone tells me a story of a friend or relative (usually someone past midlife) whose doctor(s) persistently diagnosed their complaints as psychosomatic and who turned out to have some other, serious illness. These true stories often have an unhappy ending: By the time the real problem was discovered, it was too late to treat it successfully. Sometimes they have a "happy" ending: After months or years of fear, frustration, self-doubt, and social and economic losses, a person's experience of her or his body was validated by medicine and society when she or he was diagnosed as having a treatable illness or injury. Apparently, existing side-by-side with widespread enthusiasm for psychosomatic theories of illness, there is widespread experience of their dangers. Nevertheless, the tendency is to interpret these experiences as individual failures of medicine—the physician was prejudiced, ignorant, careless, or simply rushed off her or his feet. I have been reading the literature of psychosomatic medicine in order to discover whether there are so many stories about false psychosomatic diagnosis because there are many individual failures or because there are deeper problems at work in medicine—problems of systemic bias and/or confused theorizing about illness and disability.

The first problem I encountered is that definitions of psychosomatic illness vary widely among researchers, psychiatrists, and other physicians. The major reference work of psychiatrists, *The Diagnostic and Statistical Manual of Mental Disorders IV*, describes seven "somatoform disorders." These include much of what used to be called "hysteria" and "conversion." It warns that they "are often encountered in general medical settings" and reports that five out of the seven somatoform disorders occur more frequently in females than in males (1994, 445–69). In the medical literature, there is a great deal of controversy about how to define psychosomatic illness; many researchers and clinicians prefer to use broader criteria than those specified for "somatoform disorders" in the *DSM IV*. Researchers frequently equate any unexplained physical symptoms with psychosomatic illness. For the purposes of this chapter, I will use "psychosomatic diagnosis" to mean any diagnosis that attributes a patient's symptoms exclusively or primarily to psychological causes such as inner conflicts, anxiety, depression, or reactions to stress.

My research is revealing that some social groups are more likely to receive psychosomatic diagnoses than others. Although this is not in itself evidence of systemic bias (perhaps some groups really are more likely to get psychosomatic illnesses), the identity of these groups and the things said about them in the literature of psychosomatic medicine set off warning bells in my feminist brain. For example, at the beginning of a 1992 cross-cultural study of the incidence of psychosomatic symptoms, Canino et al. summarize existing beliefs about their distribution:

> Functional somatic symptoms (medically unexplained physical symptoms) are common occurrences in clinical settings. . . . In a broad sense, the term *somatization* is the one most often used to denote the somatic presentation of a putative psychiatric disorder. Somatization is observed most frequently among women, individuals from non-Western or devel-

oping nations, those from lower socioeconomic backgrounds, and those with significant depressive symptoms. (1992, 605)

It seems a remarkable coincidence that men of higher socioeconomic backgrounds from the developed Western countries are, in all the world, the people least likely to "somatize," given that they also happen to be the people who are accorded the most believability and authority in Western scientific settings. It is possible, of course, that women of all socioeconomic backgrounds from the developed West, women and men from non-Western or developing countries, poor men from the developed West, and people who have been diagnosed with depression (many more women than men, incidentally) suffer more psychosomatic illnesses, perhaps because they live with the greater stress of social disadvantage. It is also possible that they have more unexplained physical symptoms because medicine is less interested in explaining their symptoms (both less interested in investigating individuals' symptoms in the clinical setting and less interested in studying their bodies and diseases in scientific research), because their complaints are assumed to be less believable as evidence of physical illness, and because their authority to describe anything, including their own bodies, is less than that of privileged men.

The widely held generalizations about which groups are likely to "somatize" are being tested in recent studies, with varying results. For example, in their own study in Puerto Rico and the mainland United States, Canino et al. found that "female respondents of any age or cultural group reported higher levels of medically unexplained symptoms than did male respondents of similar sociodemographic characteristics" (1992, 608). But a large-scale study of patients in England (Popay et al. 1993) concluded that the hypothesis that women "somatize" more than men was not supported by the evidence and suggested that more attention be paid to the possibility that women's higher rates of minor physical illness *cause* their higher rates of depression. Piccinelli and Simon (1997) studied primary care patients at fifteen centers in fourteen countries around the world and concluded that their data "do not support the common belief that females somatize more than males or the traditional view that somatization is a basic orientation prevailing in developing countries" (433). The prevalent belief that Asians "somatize" their emotional distress more than Europeans or Americans has been challenged on both methodological and factual grounds in articles by Yuko Kawanishi (1992) and Sing Lee (1997).[1]

Challenges to the prevalent generalizations in the literature of psychosomatic medicine are encouraging, but it is the prevalence of these beliefs about certain groups that worries me, since it suggests gender, racial, and class bias in this branch of medicine (and in the thinking of general practitioners), and it is likely to put some people at greater risk of receiving false psychosomatic diagnoses than others. Women are particularly vulnerable because women visit doctors more often than men (van Wijk et al. 1992), because women reportedly have more "functional" complaints (complaints about symptoms for which a doctor finds no organic explanation) (Popay et al. 1993), because more women have histories of being diagnosed with depression (Rosser 1994), and because medicine knows less about women's bodies. Much medical knowledge was obtained by studying only white men's bodies. There has been little medical research on the health of women of color (Rosser 1994), and there is little medical knowledge about some of women's ordinary bodily processes, especially menopause. Lack of medical knowledge about a group of people puts them at risk for having "medically unexplained symptoms," which are liable to be diagnosed as psychosomatic.

In a recent review of progress in reducing gender bias in clinical psychology, Phyllis Chesler lists five areas of continuing clinical bias affecting women, including "women (and to a lesser extent, men) with medical illnesses are often, and wrongfully, psychiatrically diagnosed and medicated" (Chesler 1997, 37).[2] In an article in *American Family Physician* (Miller et al. 1986), Miller, Benson, Goldberg, and Gould, all neurologists attached to the Harbor-UCLA Medical Center, describe twenty-five patients with serious neurological diseases, all of whom had been diagnosed originally by other physicians as having "hysteria" or "functional disorder" (i.e., something is wrong, but it is not organic). Twenty of the twenty-five patients were women. Miller et al. warn that, in their experience, four factors seem to contribute to the risk of receiving a false diagnosis of hysteria: female gender; prior psychiatric diagnosis (including anxiety or depression); plausible psychodynamic explanations (often offered by patients) for the medical problems; and exaggerated physical findings (which the authors attribute partly to patients' fears that their physicians will not believe them). They say, "a diagnosis of hysteria is usually wrong" (157). They also cite two follow-up studies of patients originally diagnosed as having hysterical illnesses, in which 60 to 65 percent of the patients proved to have "significant pathology" (160).

Elizabeth A. Klonoff and Hope Landrine hypothesize that "the misdiagnosis of physical disorders as psychiatric in part accounts for women's higher rate of depression, anxiety, and somatization disorders" (Klonoff and Landrine 1997, xxii). They review studies that estimate that 41 percent to

83 percent of people being treated for psychiatric disorders have misdiagnosed physical disorders. Their book, *Preventing Misdiagnosis of Women,* describes a number of physical disorders that have some psychiatric symptoms and are more common in women than men, including hyperthyroidism (somewhat more common in African American women than in white women) and hypothyroidism (more common in older women), multiple sclerosis (more common in white women than in Asian American or African American women), and lupus (more common in African American and Native American women than in white women). The authors draw attention to particular dangers in the misdiagnosis of some of these illnesses: Certain common drug therapies exacerbate their symptoms, sometimes lethally, and some of these illnesses progress irreversibly if they go untreated for a significant period of time. For example, hyperthyroidism and hypothyroidism often present with symptoms of depression or anxiety, but antidepressants, lithium, and antipsychotic drugs are dangerous to patients with these disorders. Lupus, a progressive disease, can be slowed by appropriate (nonpsychotropic) drug therapies, but these work best when it is detected and treated early; thorazine, an antipsychotic drug, has been implicated in causing lupus.

Women of lower socioeconomic backgrounds, women immigrants from non-Western or developing countries, and women with previous psychiatric diagnoses of depression are particularly vulnerable to psychosomatic diagnosis because they fit into more than one category of perceived risk for psychosomatic illness. Moreover, a previous history of depression can be used as a ready explanation for many unexplained symptoms, especially severe and prolonged fatigue (which is, despite its apparent vagueness, an early symptom of many serious medical conditions besides depression).

Are women at midlife and older at greater risk than younger women? My study of the literature of psychosomatic medicine has not revealed a reliable answer to this. Some research in this field suggests a higher level of "somatization" among older people, but the researchers express concern that older age was correlated with lower education levels in their samples, which might affect tendencies to "somatize." One study of 3,798 people in the Piedmont area of North Carolina, having controlled for educational differences, found that "somatization" was associated with being female, 45 to 64 years old, and separated, widowed, or divorced (Swartz et al. 1989). However, older age is not usually included in the list of risk factors for somatoform disorders.

Nevertheless, there are several factors that midlife and older women should consider when assessing their risk of receiving false psychosomatic diagnoses in clinical settings. There is the lack of medical knowledge concerning menopause and the health of postmenopausal women. When physicians do not know how a woman should feel, and when they (like everyone else) have stereotypical expectations of menopausal and postmenopausal women, they may dismiss or underrate symptoms more readily. For example, Ellen M. Goudsmit reports on studies showing that women with coronary heart disease were given fewer diagnostic procedures and offered fewer treatments than men (1994). There is the fact that older people have more medical problems and therefore consult physicians more; physicians expect a substantial proportion of patients' complaints to be psychosomatic (Swartz et al. 1989), and they are under increasing pressure to reduce medical costs by not ordering diagnostic procedures that prove to be unnecessary. Finally, there is the influence of ageism. In the Western world, most menopausal and postmenopausal women have low social status. Low social status leads to low believability and authority, which, in Western medical settings, put a person at risk for receiving a psychosomatic diagnosis.

The Ethics of Psychologizing Illness

I would like to see some recognition that psychosomatic diagnosis is an issue of medical ethics. Unfortunately, medical ethics still focuses on the life-and-death issues most relevant to those who are expecting babies, acutely ill, or extremely old. It tries to tell us which fetuses may be created or aborted, who should get expensive life-saving medical procedures, and who may be ethically killed or allowed to die near the end of life. Yet most of us who are past midlife are more affected by what Paul A. Komesaroff (1995, 67) has called the "microethics" of interaction with doctors and other health care providers, the "unbroken continuum of ethical decision making" (68), engaged in by both doctor and patient in a clinical interaction, which can affect profoundly the patient's future health and the quality of her or his daily life. How and when doctors and patients psychologize illness are important aspects of the microethics of clinical encounters.

Reaching the conclusion that a patient's problems are psychological without a thorough medical investigation is an ethical decision that may have serious consequences for the patient, including premature, preventable death. Even suggesting to a patient that her problem is psychological before an investigation is complete has ethical implications; it is likely to start a chain of events that a physician should consider before making the suggestion. Most people have stresses in their lives or traumas in their histories that can plausibly be seen as causes of illness, once the assumption is made that an illness has a psychological cause. It is not a trivial matter to induce a patient to examine her life for stresses and traumas and consider whether she is handling them appropriately, to question her working conditions and all her relationships, to scrutinize her habits of thinking and feeling and even her spiritual life in search of a cause of her symptoms.

For the physician who does not rush to psychosomatic diagnosis, the more difficult ethical question is what constitutes a sufficiently thorough investigation of possible physical causes. Doctors must weigh such factors as the severity of the patient's suffering and the probability of serious disease or injury against such factors as the risks involved in a diagnostic procedure, its invasiveness or painfulness, and its cost. It is part of their microethical practice to make such judgments every day, and they cannot be expected to make the best judgment every time, much less to be right every time. The question arises, what should they do when all the investigations they believe to be justified show no organic cause? At that point, I would like them to consider the dangers of giving a psychosomatic diagnosis. It may be more ethical to tell the patient that they do not know, and that perhaps scientific medicine does not know, the cause of the symptom(s).

The dangers of giving psychosomatic diagnoses when medical investigation has revealed no physical cause of symptoms include at least the following: Patients may accept the diagnosis and stop looking for answers when, in fact, there is serious organic disease present. Patients may be given treatments that are at best unnecessary and at worst dangerous, especially the most commonly prescribed psychoactive drugs, tranquilizers, and antidepressants.[3] Patients with significant loss of function may lose their jobs because they are unable to work and do not fall into a category of illness that entitles them to sick leave, or because they need accommodations in order to continue working and psychosomatic disorders do not entitle them to accommodation. Patients who are unable to work may become impoverished because insurers and governments do not classify the psychosomatic disorders as diagnoses that qualify them for benefits. And many patients are liable to lose family and social support, no matter how sick they are, if the people they know believe that their apparently physical illnesses are "in their head." (See Wendell 1996 on the economic and social consequences of psychosomatic diagnosis.)

Both doctors and patients know that illnesses do not fall neatly into categories of physical or mental. It fits our experience better to say that health and illness are complex phenomena with physical, psychological, and social components. But societies (and physicians) also need to categorize illnesses. Not only what kinds of treatment a patient will receive, but what kinds of medical investigations will be done, are determined by the answer to the question: Is this probably a physical or a mental illness? The demand to categorize illness is often economic; insurers, employers, government bureaucracies, and courts need clear answers where there may be none. The very language of laws and policies demands clear distinctions in the realms of illness. If a woman needs accommodation in her workplace in order to continue working during or after an illness, whether or not she receives it will depend partly on her diagnosis. It is virtually certain that she will not be accommodated if she is said to have a psychosomatic problem. Patients in this category fall between the cracks; such an illness is neither a genuine physical disease nor the sort of mental disorder that has a prognosis, a treatment, and some social recognition. Although there are specialists in psychosomatic medicine, some of whom recognize that it is not the same as faking or exaggerating illness, or shirking responsibility, a diagnosis of psychosomatic illness is most often, in practice, a dumping ground for medical puzzles. Helping patients in this category is not a medical priority, and there are few if any agreed upon treatments.[4] Yet for patients, our future health, our future incomes, and the attitudes of the people around us depend on whether our problems are labeled as psychosomatic.

Thus, there is a fundamental conflict between the growing public desire for a more holistic approach to health and illness and the legal structures and social policies that demand that illnesses be categorized and then provide support and accommodation for some but not others. Moreover, there is widespread confusion about what it means to say that an illness is primarily (or even partially) caused by psychological factors, but it is often taken to imply greater personal responsibility than for "purely" physical illnesses. We need much more public discussion of the relationship between alleged psychological causes of illness and questions of treatment, accommodation, responsibility, and blame. We—patients, health care providers, caregivers, friends, and relatives—need to develop ethical responses to the conflicts and confusions generated by professional and amateur psychosomatic medicine.

There are two ethical responses that we can all adopt immediately. We can refrain from speculating about psychological causes of illnesses and accidents, and we can treat popular offerings of psychosomatic theories with skepticism. Informal psychosomatic theorizing about ourselves and our friends and acquaintances contributes to everyone's willingness to accept psychosomatic diagnoses from physicians, even when we should not.

In addition, remember that Miller et al. (1986) reported that plausible psychodynamic explanations for a symptom, *often offered by patients themselves,* were one of the risk factors for receiving a false diagnosis of hysteria. Informal psychosomatic theorizing presents a risk to our health care and a risk to our social believability when we need to be believed. These risks make it a matter of ethical concern. Instead of reaching into psychodynamics for a comforting explanation of why we or our friends became ill or had an accident (comforting because it helps to assure us that we have control), we might allow the misfortune to remind us of the vulnerability we share.

I titled this chapter "Old Women Out of Control" because I was struck by the contrasting cultural images of young women out of control—rebellious, transgressive, resistant, exciting—and old women out of control—sick, disabled, dying, needy, and socially costly. Middle-aged and old women are vulnerable to psychosomatic theorizing because of our embarrassment and fear in response to symptoms; any new illness or impairment threatens to confirm the cultural expectation of decline. Everywhere we turn, we are urged to "take control" of our bodies and lives, lest we become passive victims of aging. But this is social mythology. Anyone past midlife knows from experience that we control very little compared to what can happen to us, and that passive victimization is not the only alternative to trying to "take control." There are, for instance, the demanding arts of acceptance, adjustment, and appreciation. To cultivate these in relation to our aging bodies is another way of declining to decline.

Notes

The author thanks Valerie Oglov for her invaluable assistance in researching psychosomatic medicine, the Dean of Arts office of Simon Fraser University for research funding, and Simon Fraser University for study leave, during which this article was written.

1. The prevalent theory about Asians is that they are more reluctant to verbalize emotional distress than Europeans and Americans, and therefore they "express" their distress in physical symptoms. This theory would seem to be at odds with the claim that European and American women "somatize" more than European and American men; indeed, it would seem to predict that many white men would be ill with psychosomatic diseases. I have encountered no awareness of this irony in the literature.

2. In an editorial in the *Journal of Psychosomatic Research,* Donna E. Stewart notes with approval that "the first three Chairs of Women's Health appointed in

1995 in Canada, the United States, and Australia, are all psychiatrists, two of whom are psychosomatic researchers" (Stewart 1996, 221). That's a comforting thought!

3. Rosser (1994, 41) points out that overprescription of tranquilizers and antidepressants to women is still a major medical problem.

4. For example, a recent review of treatments for tension-type headache, a disorder generally accepted as psychosomatic, concluded that none of the current treatments, including drugs, biofeedback, and psychotherapy, appears to be more effective than the others (Biondi and Portuesi 1994).

References

Biondi, Massimo, and Giovanni Portuesi. "Tension-Type Headache: Psychosomatic Clinical Assessment and Treatment," *Psychotherapy and Psychosomatics* 61: 41–64. Basel: S. Karger, 1994.

Bury, Michael R. "Disablement in Society: Towards an Integrated Perspective," *International Journal of Rehabilitation Research* 2 (1) (1978): 33–40.

Canino, Ian A., Maritza Rubio-Stipec, Glorisa Canino, and Javier I. Escobar. "Functional Somatic Symptoms: A Cross-Ethnic Comparison," *American Journal of Orthopsychiatry* 62 (4) (1992): 605–12.

Chesler, Phyllis. "Women and Madness: A Feminist Diagnosis," *Ms.* (November/December 1997): 36–41.

Diagnostic and Statistical Manual of Mental Disorders, 4th ed. Washington, D.C.: American Psychiatric Association, 1994.

Goudsmit, Ellen M. "All in Her Mind! Stereotypic Views and the Psychologisation of Women's Illness," in *Women and Health: Feminist Perspectives,* ed. Sue Wilkinson and Celia Kitzinger. London: Taylor and Francis, 1994, 7–12.

Gullette, Margaret Morganroth. *Declining to Decline: Cultural Combat and the Politics of the Midlife.* Charlottesville: University Press of Virginia, 1997.

Health and Welfare Canada and Statistics Canada. *The Health of Canadians: Report of the Canada Health Survey.* Ottawa: Supply and Services Canada, 1981.

Kawanishi, Yuko. "Somatization of Asians: An Artifact of Western Medicalization?" *Transcultural Psychiatric Research Review* XXIX (1) (1992): 5–36. Montreal: Division of Social and Transcultural Psychiatry, Dept. of Psychiatry, McGill University.

Klonoff, Elizabeth A., and Hope Landrine. *Preventing Misdiagnosis of*

Women: A Guide to Physical Disorders that Have Psychiatric Symptoms. Thousand Oaks, Calif.: Sage, 1997.

Komesaroff, Paul A. "From Bioethics to Microethics: Ethical Debate and Clinical Medicine," in *Troubled Bodies: Critical Perspectives on Postmodernism, Medical Ethics, and the Body,* ed. Paul A. Komesaroff. Durham: Duke University Press, 1995, 62–86.

LaPlante, Mitchell P. *Disability Statistics Report (2): Disability Risks of Chronic Illnesses and Impairments.* Washington, D.C.: National Institute on Disability and Rehabilitation Research, U.S. Department of Education, 1991.

Lee, Sing. "A Chinese Perspective of Somatoform Disorders," *Journal of Psychosomatic Research* 43 (2) (1997): 115–19.

Miller, Bruce L., D. Frank Benson, Mark A. Goldberg, and Robert Gould. "Misdiagnosis of Hysteria," *American Family Physician* 34 (4) (1986): 157–60.

Piccinelli, Marco, and Gregory Simon. "Gender and Cross-Cultural Differences in Somatic Symptoms Associated with Emotional Distress. An International Study in Primary Care," *Psychological Medicine* 27 (1997): 433–44.

Popay, Jennie, Mel Bartley, and Charlie Owen. "Gender Inequalities in Health: Social Position, Affective Disorders and Minor Physical Morbidity," *Social Science and Medicine* 36 (1) (1993): 21–32.

Pope, Andrew M., and Alvin R. Tarlov, eds. *Disability in America: Toward A National Agenda for Prevention.* Washington, D.C.: National Academy Press, 1991.

Report on the Health of Canadians. Ottawa: Minister of Supply and Services Canada, 1996.

Rosser, Sue V. *Women's Health: Missing from U.S. Medicine.* Bloomington: Indiana University Press, 1994.

Statistics Canada. *The Health and Activity Limitation Survey.* Ottawa: Minister of Supply and Services Canada, 1986 and 1991.

Stewart, Donna E. "Women's Health and Psychosomatic Medicine," *Journal of Psychosomatic Research* 40 (3) (1996): 221–26.

Swartz, Marvin, Richard Landerman, Dan Blazer, and Linda George. "Somatization Symptoms in the Community: A Rural/Urban Comparison," *Psychosomatics: The Journal of the American Academy of Psychosomatic Medicine* 30 (1) (1989): 44–53. Washington, D.C.: The Academy of Psychosomatic Medicine.

van Wijk, Cecile M. T. Gijsbers, Annemarie M. Kolk, Wil J. H. M. van den Bosch, and Henk J. M. van den Hoogen. "Male and Female Morbidity in General Practice: The Nature of Sex Differences," *Social Science and Medicine* 35 (5) (1992): 665–78.

Wendell, Susan. *The Rejected Body: Feminist Philosophical Reflections on Disability.* New York: Routledge, 1996.

· 9 ·

Menopause: Taking the Cures or Curing the Takes?

Joan C. Callahan

Menopause is curable. . . . . The body changes typical of middle age can be reversed, and sexual functions can be restored, along with a fully feminine appearance. . . . . *Menopause is completely preventable.* No woman need suffer menopause or any of its symptoms if she receives preventive treatment *before* the onset of menopause. . . . In effect, the new medical possibilities double a woman's emotional lifespan. Forty no longer looms large as a dividing line. No longer is her life in danger of being broken in half by "the change." Now at last, her life can be a harmonious continuity not threatened by the sudden disruption of her womanhood, but marked by the growth and enrichment of that womanhood.[1]

So wrote gynecologist Robert A. Wilson in 1966, as he championed estrogen "replacement therapy" for all women approaching, undergoing, or after menopause.

Wilson's manifesto expresses two "takes" or conceptual constructions—the first of womanhood itself as disrupted by menopause; the second of menopause as a disease in need of medical intervention. In Part I of this chapter, I look at this received view on women's aging and menopause as a malady. In Part II, I look at the normal endocrine and physiological changes that are associated with menopause and their relation to what women actually experience. In Part III, I look at the hormone "replacement therapy" debate and its place in the construction of menopause as disease, and I consider the benefits and risks of prescribed hormones for women in general and for certain women in particular. It will be obvious that I have serious reservations about the administration of hormones; but let me make clear from the beginning that my overall concern in this chapter is with appropriate administration of hormones and with women's genuinely informed consent to hormonal intervention.

151

I. Cultural Constructions

In order to get a good start on an exploration of the cultural and physiological dimensions of menopause, we need an overview of the conceptual landscape. Several terms are used to talk about menopause, including *perimenopause, climacteric, premenopause,* and *postmenopause,* as well as *menopause* itself. The use of these terms is not entirely fixed. But Ann Voda suggests a helpful glossary that I shall adopt here.[2]

Voda defines *menopause* in the standard way, as the permanent cessation of menstruation resulting from loss of ovarian follicular activity, and she defines *perimenopause* phenomenologically, as the transition that begins with a woman's first hot flash and ends when a woman's hot flashes disappear.[3] As most women with the full experience of menopause know, this period is indefinite in duration, often beginning several years prior to menopause itself and continuing for several years after menopause. It is true that some women do not experience hot flashes. What is helpful about Voda's understanding of perimenopause, however, is its recognition that what we generally call "menopause" is not a discreet event at all, but rather a period of time of indefinite duration (although commonly three to six years) over which a woman moves into a new physiological life phase, which includes the cessation of ovulation and the lowering of hormone levels. What is commonly known as "menopause," then, is really perimenopause. We shall return to these definitions in Part II. First, though, I want to look at how women's aging, perimenopause, and menopause are currently presented in Western culture.

As Jacquelyn Zita points out, aging in general and menopause in particular are culturally represented as heretical changes in the female body.[4] As intolerance of the appearance of the aging woman's body increases, women are under more and more pressure to halt, or even reverse, these changes. Thus, cosmetic surgery ads like the one in figure 9.1 can be found in thousands of publications.

As another example, consider a number of contemporary representations of older women in film. Aging actresses, such as Shirley MacLaine, Anne Bancroft, and Vanessa Redgrave, have recently appeared in films representing older women as cranks, witches, characters, or fools of one sort or another.[5] One of the few exceptions to this is Gloria Stewart's 1998 appearance in *Titanic.* But even here, the director can't completely give up representing the aged Rose as a "character"—she travels with a small dog and, literally, a gallery of photographs that link the real meaning of her life to the past and, in particular, to her romance with a male passenger who perished when the great ship sank.

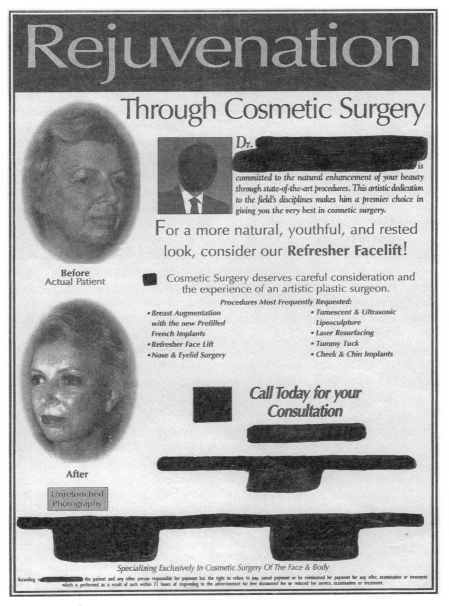

Figure 9.1

In line with such degrading cultural representations of older women, states and processes that are perfectly normal for women, such as menstruation, pregnancy, and menopause, are constantly medicalized. There is now an abundant literature on the history and cultural representation of menstruation and the very destructive construction of PMS as a malady that places women with regularity under the sway of "raging hormones." Pregnancy and childbirth have long been moved from the personal realm to the realm of professional medicine. And, as the baby boomers move into their fifties, menopause increasingly is billed as a malady requiring medical intervention. Since more than fifty million women in the United States alone will reach menopause by the year 2000, selling a drug to be taken daily by members of this group is a staggering fiscal prospect. Thus, it comes as no surprise that the pharmaceutical industry has become deeply invested in the medicalization of menopause and the marketing of drugs to "treat" it.

For example, current ads in widely read publications, such as *Newsweek,* press women to seek medical help for menopause. Wyeth-Ayerst, makers of Premarin, the oldest and most widely used estrogen replacement drug on the U.S. market, has been running an advertisement of "the Wyeth-Ayerst Women's Health Research Institute, devoted exclusively to the discovery and development of medicines that help women live healthier lives" (fig. 9.2).[6]

I'll turn directly to the question of hormone replacement therapy in Part III, but for now, I merely want to point to ads like this as part of the normalization of the cultural construction of menopause as a disease needing medical intervention. The pharmaceutical companies work this construction from at least three directions: by trying to enlist consumers through the direct marketing of drugs for so-called menopausal syndrome (sometimes by marketing the companies making these drugs, as in fig. 9.2), by enlisting the help of purportedly objective health associations, and by inundating physicians with their studies and remedies.

On marketing to consumers, Wyeth-Ayerst Laboratories serves as an example again. Consider the following report, reproduced as shown on the Internet by one of Wyeth-Ayerst's marketers, Yecies Associates.

LIVING SMART WITH PREMARIN
Organization: Wyeth-Ayerst Laboratories
Agency: Yecies Associates

- CAMPAIGN: Raise visibility and increase usage of Wyeth-Ayerst's Premarin, an estrogen replacement therapy (ERT) as a preventative and prescriptive treatment for osteoporosis.

When considering menopause and the consequences of its associated estrogen loss, consider the entire body of evidence.

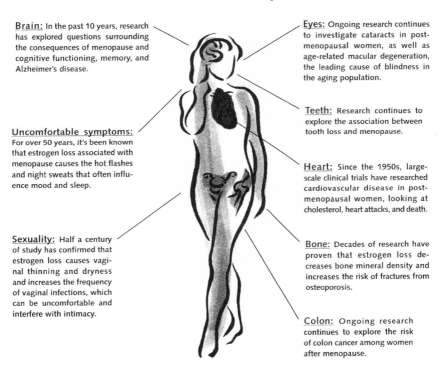

Brain: In the past 10 years, research has explored questions surrounding the consequences of menopause and cognitive functioning, memory, and Alzheimer's disease.

Uncomfortable symptoms: For over 50 years, it's been known that estrogen loss associated with menopause causes the hot flashes and night sweats that often influence mood and sleep.

Sexuality: Half a century of study has confirmed that estrogen loss causes vaginal thinning and dryness and increases the frequency of vaginal infections, which can be uncomfortable and interfere with intimacy.

Eyes: Ongoing research continues to investigate cataracts in post-menopausal women, as well as age-related macular degeneration, the leading cause of blindness in the aging population.

Teeth: Research continues to explore the association between tooth loss and menopause.

Heart: Since the 1950s, large-scale clinical trials have researched cardiovascular disease in post-menopausal women, looking at cholesterol, heart attacks, and death.

Bone: Decades of research have proven that estrogen loss decreases bone mineral density and increases the risk of fractures from osteoporosis.

Colon: Ongoing research continues to explore the risk of colon cancer among women after menopause.

Today, we know more than ever about the consequences of estrogen loss during and after menopause, and the effect it has on your entire body. So-called "selective" or "designer" estrogens may not impact a number of health issues associated with menopause. Talk to your doctor, because problems resulting from estrogen loss aren't always selective.

This message is sponsored by the Wyeth-Ayerst Women's Health Research Institute, devoted exclusively to the discovery and development of medicines that help women live healthier lives.

© 1998, Wyeth-Ayerst Laboratories   46960-01   Printed in U.S.A.   January 1998

Figure 9.2

- Yecies Associates conceived, developed, and implemented "Living Smart," a combination of specifically-targeted, hard-hitting corporate and community outreach programs and ancillary materials.
  - The programs attracted large audiences of women in peer group situations. By targeting peer groups, we overcame the denial and resistance usually associated with health problems. In peer group situations, people tend to make initial inquiries into new medical treatments, the first step toward one-on-one discussions with personal physicians.
- OBJECTIVES: The objectives of the campaign were to establish "Living Smart" corporate and community outreach programs, thereby raising the visibility of (ERT) among women over 40 and motivating this audience to discuss (ERT) with their physicians.
- RESULTS: Yecies Associates conducted extensive evaluations of program attendees attitudes and behaviors regarding health issues both before and after the programs. Over 80% of the women who attended the 100+ programs asked their doctors about (ERT) exceeding original expectations of 50%. There were over 300 million print and broadcast media impressions emphasizing the benefits of (ERT) for women.
- STRATEGY: In order to reach women over 35, we targeted large corporations with mixed gender emphasis, alumni associations, and women's organizations. We chose "Living Smart" as a theme encompassing many facets of women's health, including osteoporosis, menopause, breast cancer, cardiovascular issues, exercise, and nutrition. "Living Smart" gave a more positive positioning to the topic of women's health. It erased some of the negative issues of aging and addressed women's health in a more general way: what women can do to stay healthy after age 35.
  - To promote "Living Smart" after the programs, free exercise videos were available at every conference as well as opportunities to win sessions with nutritionists [*sic*] or personal trainers. We developed mailing lists from the programs and sent every program attendee a booklet on oseoporosis [*sic*].[7]

Notice the strategy here—to hide the push for Premarin in a general emphasis on women's health. And notice the age of the women targeted— women over 35—five years younger than Robert Wilson's choice of 40 back in 1966. As the age goes down, the market grows larger.

Various health groups, thought to be both commercially neutral and highly informed, participate enthusiastically in the medical construction of menopause and the marketing of medications for menopause. Consider, for example, a 1998 public service announcement from the American Heart Association (AHA), which appeared in publications around the United States (fig. 9.3). This particular announcement invites readers to visit the

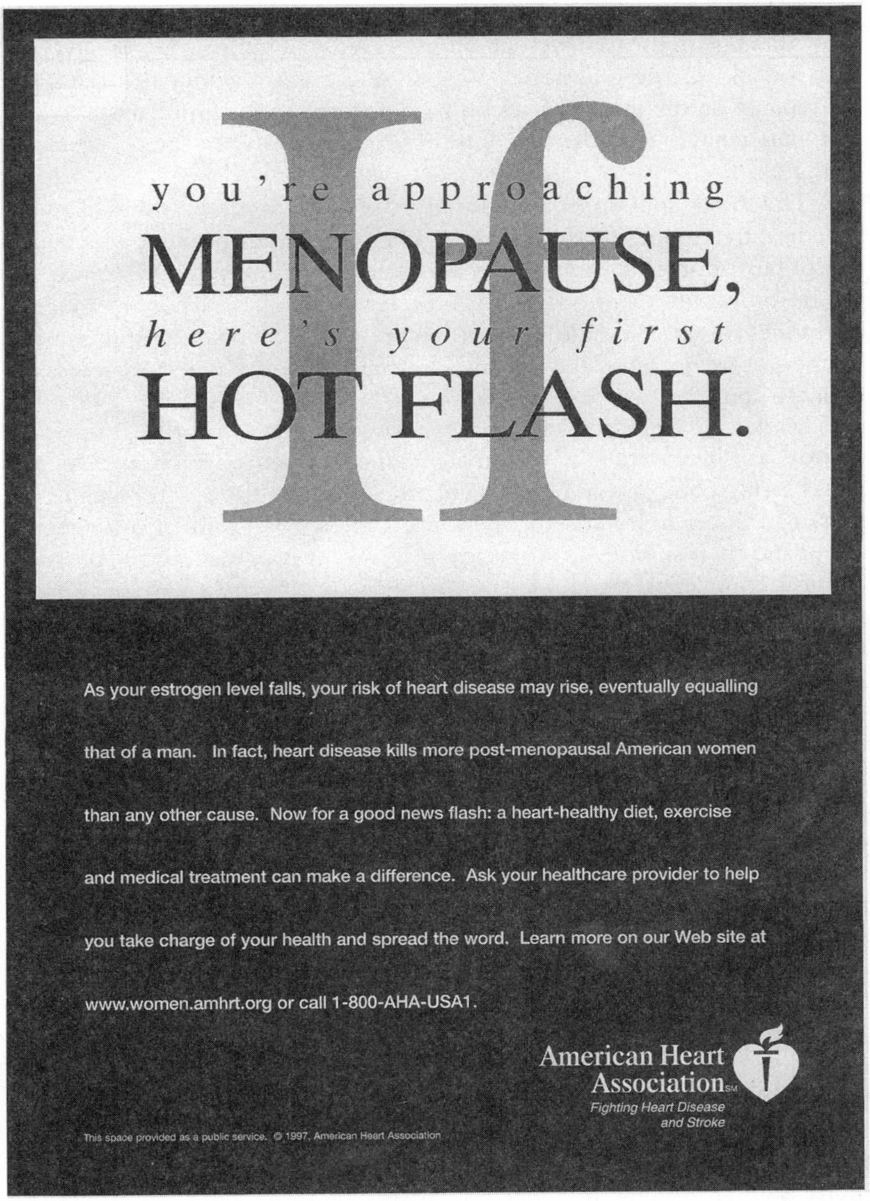

If you're approaching **MENOPAUSE,** *here's your first* **HOT FLASH.**

As your estrogen level falls, your risk of heart disease may rise, eventually equalling that of a man. In fact, heart disease kills more post-menopausal American women than any other cause. Now for a good news flash: a heart-healthy diet, exercise and medical treatment can make a difference. Ask your healthcare provider to help you take charge of your health and spread the word. Learn more on our Web site at www.women.amhrt.org or call 1-800-AHA-USA1.

American Heart Associationsm
Fighting Heart Disease and Stroke

This space provided as a public service. © 1997, American Heart Association

Figure 9.3

women's health portion of the AHA web site. Accepting the invitation will show that one of the two web site sponsors is the ubiquitous Wyeth-Ayerst. And a click on the question "What should I know about the effects of menopause on my health?" yields a page devoted to the problem of "estrogen deficiency" and the benefits of "hormone replacement therapy" (HRT).

This AHA announcement also urges women to see our physicians for "medical treatment" that can make a difference to our presumed increased risk of heart disease after menopause. Given the push on the AHA web site for hormone intervention, we can expect individual physicians to offer hormones to women as "treatment" to prevent heart disease. And, as most women of menopausal age are quick to report, their physicians almost invariably do this.

Marketing drugs to practitioners takes a number of forms. Individual doctors are given samples and small "reminder items," such as pens and pads bearing company and/or drug names. They are also given much larger gifts, handsome honoraria for speaking, and expense-paid trips for themselves and their spouses to attractive locations. It is estimated that pharmaceutical companies spend well over five billion dollars a year on various forms of marketing, much of it to physicians.[8] Further, pharmaceutical companies go to great lengths to find out what drugs physicians are prescribing or, more precisely, not prescribing, so that locating physicians as targets of marketing has itself become an important business in today's pharmaceutical industry. The visionary Physician Computer Network (PCN) was the first company to arrange to tap into physicians' computer systems to copy patient prescription records. In the late 1980s, PCN began offering physicians first-line computers and software at leases one-third below the going rate in exchange for direct access to patient files.[9] Such information gets fed back to pharmaceutical manufacturers, which then use the information to target individual physicians for drug marketing. And materials promoting various drugs are commonly published in medical journals in the form of "supplements" that barely distinguish them as advertisements.[10]

Physicians, of course, deny that pharmaceutical company marketing influences their prescribing practices. If they are right, the pharmaceutical industry is wasting billions of dollars in marketing their drugs to doctors. But, as I have suggested elsewhere, the pharmaceutical industry is not a bumpkin, and at least one series of studies has found that physicians seem pretty obviously to be influenced by pharmaceutical companies that sponsor continuing education sessions for doctors.[11]

As the baby boomers continue to age, contemporary advertising is changing. The "elderly" are increasingly represented as vibrant, and more and more products are targeted at the aging population. At the same time, pressure on women to address the marks of aging on our bodies increases—pressure to dye our hair, to have our faces "lifted," to do all that we can to preclude menopause. Is it so different from 1966, when Robert Wilson began urging us to be "feminine forever"? It seems not, except that the rhetoric of retaining femininity has evolved into a rhetoric of maintaining health. We need, then, to ask just what women's health at midlife genuinely requires, in particular, whether it generally requires taking hormones. In order to approach an answer to this, we need first to understand what menopause actually involves.

II. The Basic Endocrinology and Physiology of Menopause

Menopause involves hormonal changes. As "intercellular messengers," hormones are part of the body's regulatory system. When certain demands are made of the body, appropriate hormones are secreted into the system, where they "find and bind" with receptors on cells, which (ultimately) allows tissue to address the body's needs.[12] For women, transitions into and out of the reproductive years are marked by substantial fluctuations of the sex hormones. During puberty, a woman's reproductive hormonal system is gearing up; during perimenopause, her reproductive hormonal system is gearing down. Both are perfectly normal developmental stages, and both generally take from three to six years for completion.

The ovaries are the female hormone-secreting glands that produce the sex-steroid hormones necessary for reproduction.[13] The maturation and ovulation of eggs in the ovaries begins with puberty and ends with menopause.

Puberty is the transition into a woman's fertile years, signaled by menarche (the start of menstruation). At puberty, a series of events leads to the beginning of periodic increases in luteinizing hormone (LH) and follicle-stimulating hormone (FSH), which stimulate maturation of a group of egg-containing sacs (follicles) in a woman's ovaries. If a particular follicle produces enough estrogen, this causes another rise in LH.[14] Typically (but not invariably), a few hours after this surge of LH peaks, the follicle ovulates an egg, and the site of ovulation (the follicle—now called the corpus luteum) produces progesterone in addition to estrogen.[15] These changes in estrogen and progesterone cause a woman's uterus to build up a blood-rich lining. If conception occurs, the corpus luteum is sustained longer than if conception does not occur; but it eventually fades away, as the tissue that will be the placenta for the conceptus develops and takes up progesterone production. Thus, when conception occurs, a woman's uterine lining is maintained and enriched, making her uterus capable of supporting a conceptus. If her ovulated egg does not take in a sperm cell, there is no conception, and the corpus luteum stops producing hormones and fades away relatively quickly. When her progesterone levels drop to a certain point, the outermost, blood-rich lining of her uterus is shed. This is menstruation.

Reproductive maturity in a woman takes some time. Not all menstrual cycles actually include ovulation, and this is especially true in a woman's early and later reproductive years. As Susan Love describes it, puberty marks the initiation of a complicated hormonal "dance" that takes awhile "to get its choreography down."[16] At the other end of a woman's fertile years, the dance reverses, and that "choreography," too, takes awhile for a woman's body to master.

As a woman enters perimenopause, her ovaries are, basically, changing jobs. Remember, the ovaries do more than just contain eggs and ovulate some of them over a woman's fertile years. The ovaries are endocrine glands—glands that produce hormones. Through perimenopause, menopause, and postmenopause, the ovaries continue to produce hormones. The main difference is in the quantities of homones the ovaries produce.

During a woman's fertile years, a main job of the hormone estrogen in her system is to stimulate cell proliferation in the endometrium (uterine lining). Estrogen encourages cell proliferation in cells with estrogen receptors, which are commonly found in the endometrium and the breast. If breast tissue or endometrial tissue includes mutant cells that are malignant as a result of genetic inheritance or exposure to carcinogens (or some combination of these), the presence of estrogen encourages proliferation. This is why estrogens are associated with uterine and breast cancers.

Progesterone is antagonistic to estrogen; that is, it interferes with the proliferative effects of estrogen. Basically, progesterone "tells" the endometrium to stop rapid cell division and fill with secretions that will nourish any conceptus that implants in the uterine wall. During the menstrual cycle, the natural withdrawal of progesterone stimulates the shedding and reabsorption of the uterine lining. Whatever is present in the outer layer of the endometrium (including cancerous cells or a conceptus) is also shed or reabsorbed.[17] Estrogen, then, is clearly connected to the proliferation of cells that are estrogen receptive, and progesterones curb estrogen's proliferative effects. This will turn out to be an important consideration in the hormone replacement therapy debate, as we shall see in Part III.

As we have already seen, menopause is the cessation of menstruation resulting from the cessation of ovulation. As we have also seen, menstruation involves the shedding/reabsorption of the outermost layer of the uterine lining. That lining is built up and sustained by estrogen and progesterone. As a woman approaches menopause, her quantities of these hormones fluctuate. Thus, in perimenopause, a woman can experience effects of *both* high and low estrogen levels. That is, *low* estrogen levels (which are associated with hot flashes) can cause a woman's system to suddenly "wake up" and overproduce estrogen. This can then cause phenomena associated with *high* estrogen levels, such as headaches and breast tenderness, or, in combination with low progesterone levels, may cause phenomena commonly associated with so-called PMS.[18] Thus, these fluctuations in hormone levels explain why perimenopause can be a time of rapid and sometimes apparently inconsistent changes for a woman.

Negative features of these changes can be moderated by diet, exercise, and other "lifestyle" choices. But, as what we have seen in Part I suggests, women are constantly encouraged to seek medical intervention for menopause; and when women seek this intervention, we are commonly encouraged by physicians to take so-called hormone replacement therapy as we enter into perimenopause to ease our "symptoms" and/or prolong our health. Although the dominant rhetoric has changed from Wilson's emphasis on staying feminine forever to the rhetoric of "living smart," Wilson's recommendation that women take what is now known as "hormone replacement therapy" is more strongly and uniformly recommended by physicians than ever before. It is time to ask whether women should accept this recommendation.

III. The Hormone Replacement Therapy Debate

One clear articulation of the current dominant "take" on menopause is provided by Theresa Crenshaw, M.D.: "Menopause is not a natural condition; it is an endocrine disorder and should be treated medically with the same seriousness we treat other endocrine disorders, such as diabetes or thyroid disease."[19] Given that all women will experience menopause if they live long enough, it is certainly difficult to understand how menopause is not a natural condition for women. Further, as Susan Love points out,

until menopause became big business, American women were always told their symptoms were in their heads. With the new business of hormone therapy, there's been a complete flip-flop. Not only have the symptoms become "real," but all women are expected to experience all symptoms, and with the same degree of severity.[20]

We have already seen that there are significant endocrine changes associated with menopause, and that physicians now recognize women's felt experience of those changes as "real" is, without question, a good thing. What is so problematic, however, is that this recognition has taken place within a construction of menopause as a hormone deficiency disease. The movement is a breathtaking one, from "It's all in your heads" to "You are all ill and in need of medical intervention."

But surely there is an in-between. A woman's reproductive years are virtually saturated with estrogen. Breast and uterine cancers are associated with estrogen. Indeed, Susan Love says these cancers are "both caused, in part, by an oversupply of this hormone. So," says Love

> we could argue that, since nature intended us to have ten or twenty children, rather than the two or three most women have, this constant fertility, unchecked by regular pregnancy, keeps all that estrogen circulating and creates its own disease—let's call it "estrogen surplus disease."[21]

Now, no one has seriously suggested this. And if someone did, it would be a fine example of the double bind women always seem to face— our normal states would just be even more solidly represented as disease states. What is of interest here, though, is that a woman's overall exposure to endogenous (her own) estrogen seems to be relevant to her risk of cancer, particularly breast cancer. Early menstruation (prior to age 12) and late menopause (after age 55) contribute to lifelong exposure to endogenous estrogen. So does a woman's never having children, since pregnancy disrupts naturally occurring high concentrations of estrogen. Bone mass is now thought to be one marker of cumulative exposure to estrogen. Studies are beginning to find that postmenopausal women in the highest quartile of bone mass are at higher risk for breast cancer than those in the lowest quartile.[22] One of the major questions in the debate about exogenous (from outside the body) hormones is precisely whether exogenous hormones play a role in the occurrence of cancer in women taking them. I shall return to this question shortly. First, though, we need to consider the reported benefits of exogenous hormones for peri- and postmenopausal women.

The Reported Benefits of Exogenous Hormone Intervention

Before going further, I need to make explicit that it is important to resist the current language of hormone replacement therapy, since this language gives too much to the construction of menopause as a deficiency and a disease. Because there is no reason to simply assume that a woman *should* have the same hormone levels during and after her reproductive years, instead of talking about hormone replacement therapy, I'll adopt the language of exogenous hormone intervention (EHI) and administration of exogenous estrogen (EE).

The earliest forms of EHI actually appeared in the 1940s, and included estrogen only. This was known as estrogen replacement therapy (ERT), and in the early 1970s, administration of EHI in the form of EE only was widely prescribed. By 1975, Premarin, the most popular EE, had become one of the most frequently prescribed medications in the United States. At the same time, however, epidemiological studies had begun to link EE to endometrial cancer,[23] and prescriptions for EE dropped by 40 percent.[24]

By the early 1980s, progestins (progesterone-like compounds) were prescribed with estrogen and the language changed from estrogen replacement therapy to hormone replacement therapy. Since progesterone is, as we have seen, antagonistic to estrogen's proliferative effects, the addition of progestins to estrogen was celebrated as preventing the potential cancerous effects on the uterus of taking estrogen alone. Prescriptions for Premarin combined with the progestin Provera soared. As EHI is marketed increasingly aggressively as preventive of cardiovascular disease and osteoporosis, prescriptions have continued to rise, and in the late 1990s, Premarin is dispensed more than any other brand name drug in the United States.[25]

As we have seen, perimenopause is a time when a woman's system is undergoing substantial change. These changes are not limited to our reproductive organs—*many* cells in our bodies are affected by the hormonal fluctuations taking place in perimenopause, and women commonly have a varity of experiences that are consequent to these changes. It is important to realize, however, that these experiences vary *significantly* across women. Some women experience a few hot flashes, which barely bother them, and little else.[26] Other women have much more distressing experiences—hot flashes that continually wake them from sound sleep, serious skin and vaginal dryness, urinary incontinence and urinary tract infections, headaches, and severe mood swings are among the most frequent of these. Further, women suddenly cast into menopause (by, say, chemotherapy or surgery) commonly have more severe and discomforting menopausal experiences than women who undergo a "natural" menopause. There is, then, no question that for some women, the perimenopause is a difficult transition.

There is also no question that EHI, particularly EHI containing estrogen, is effective in relieving these felt effects of hormonal changes at menopause. For most women, these experiential phenomena will stop in a relatively short period of time. However, a number of women accept EHI to help with their most distressing experiences; and for many of these women, short-term use of EHI is an appropriate and substantial help to their comfort during perimenopause.

Long-term use of EHI, however, is a more worrisome matter, and in recent years women have been urged more and more strongly to adopt EHI for the long term (use for ten years or more). Heart disease is the major killer of postmenopausal women. Osteoporosis can lead to fractures, substantially decreased quality of life, and even death for some postmenopausal women. It is now continually claimed in the media and in physicians' offices that women should take exogenous hormones to lower their risk of both heart disease and osteoporosis. What was argued on the basis of femininity in the 1960s is argued on the grounds of longevity in the 1990s. But what do we *really* know about these alleged benefits of long-term EHI?

Studies in 1991, 1996, and 1998 report that EHI with estrogen reduces cardiovascular risk by approximately 50 percent in postmenopausal women.[27] What exactly, though, does this mean? The received view is that women's estrogen provides a kind of natural immunity to heart disease, which vanishes with menopause. But there is no indication that women's lifetime exposure to endogenous (our own) estrogen (as determined by the factors discussed previously, such as pregnancy and age at menarche and menopause) has any effect on our rate of heart disease (as opposed to our rate of breast cancer, to which I shall turn momentarily). Despite this, the claim is made that EHI lowers cardiovascular risk. This is very puzzling, and suggests that something else might be providing cardiovascular help to women taking exogenous hormones.

As it turns out, researchers are beginning to suggest that the conclusion that estrogen alone lowers cardiovascular risk is much too simple. For example, we now know that women who take exogenous hormones tend to be of higher socioeconomic status than those who don't, they tend to be better educated, they are thinner, they are likely to have had a hysterectomy, and they are more likely in general to have their health closely monitored—in short, we now know that women on EHI tend to start out with a better cardiovascular risk profile than those who are not on EHI.[28] Since this is the case, and since no controlled studies have been done to determine in a precise way what EE contributes to reducing cardiovascular risk, we do not know what, if anything, EE actually does contribute here. This is further complicated by the fact that the cardiovascular survival benefits EE is thought to contribute diminish with longer duration of use. All of this is not to say, of course, that there are no cardiovascular benefits of EE. But it is to say that if there are any benefits attributable to EE alone, they remain unclear; and it is to say that a woman's risk of developing heart disease increases as she ages, whether she takes exogenous estrogen or not.

Where there do seem to be measurable, understood cardiovascular benefits of EHI, these seem to be in the reduction of so-called bad cholesterol (LDL) and the increase in so-called good cholesterol (HDL) in the blood. But cholesterol can often be controlled by diet and exercise, which have additional health benefits and don't include the known and unknown risks of exogenous hormones.

Further, the cholesterol benefits of taking estrogen are highest during the first six to twelve months of use, after which they begin to decrease; and when a woman stops taking estrogen, her risk of heart attack shortly returns to what it would have been had she never taken it. Thus, for estrogen to be helpful in preventing a heart attack, a woman must be currently taking it. Past use, even for many years, offers no protection shortly after a woman stops taking it. In other words, to gain the full cardiovascular benefits of EHI, a woman must stay on EHI for the whole of her postmenopausal life.

Finally, estrogen's effects on blood cholesterol levels can only account for 25 to 50 percent of the cardiovascular benefit thought to be gained from taking EE.[29] What other mechanisms are at work, and any additional effects of these other mechanisms, remain unknown, adding to the riskiness of taking exogenous hormones without a clear account of why they help when they help and how they might be harmful. Thus, even if taking EE does have the effect of lowering a woman's cardiovascular risk (at least while she is on it), this effect diminishes over time and it is not clear that EHI is any given woman's best route to lowering that risk.

The other major claim most frequently made for EHI is that it helps to prevent osteoporosis. Osteoporosis is currently defined as "a disease characterized by low bone mass and microarchitectural deterioration of bone tissue, which lead to increased bone fragility and a consequent increase in fracture risk."[30] But, as Susan Love points out, one of the problems with this definition is that presently there is no way to test the microarchitecture of bones; so diagnoses of osteoporosis are made simply on the basis of bone density tests, and this is pressing the common understanding of osteoporosis as equivalent to low bone density, which, as we shall see in a moment, is simply inaccurate.

A woman's bone density is at its peak when she is around 35.[31] What any individual woman's peak bone density will be is determined largely by her genetic inheritance and her life habits. So, for example, women who have higher bone density at 35 because of genetics, diet, exercise, and/or other behavioral and environmental factors will likely be less at risk of osteoporosis as they age. Starting out with more bone, they have more bone to spare.

After 35, a woman loses more bone than she grows. Because of this, current modes of diagnosing osteoporosis test for bone density in comparison to what is taken to be the normal peak bone density for a 35-year-old woman. Since bone loss is virtually universal after 35, it is obvious that women over 35 are going to turn up deficient, if not fully diseased. As Susan Love puts it, "If you define *tall* as 'over six feet,' you'll have fewer tall people than if you define it as 'over five feet.' "[32] In precisely the same way, if we set the standard for normal bone density high, most older women will fall into the "diseased" category, which, Love observes, "is very nice for the people in the business of treating disease."[33]

This is not to fail to take osteoporosis and the risk of osteoporosis seriously. The quality of life of women affected by severe osteoporosis is profoundly compromised. But it is to call for attention to how the language gets used here. And *most* importantly, it cannot be emphasized strongly enough that despite all the contemporary warnings and worries about osteoporosis, 75 percent of women will never develop it.[34]

That said, observational studies do suggest that EE helps substantially to slow down the rate of bone loss, and may even help restore some bone density, at least while a woman is taking it. This makes EHI an attractive option for women at particular risk for osteoporosis. But, again, it needs to be emphasized that most women are *not* at particular risk for osteoporosis, and it needs to be emphasized further that, as in the case of cardiovascular disease, it is not clear what mechanisms are at work insofar as EE does help to prevent bone loss. Two studies suggest that the key to fractures currently associated with bone loss in U.S. women, particularly white women, might be the result of women's decreased production of other hormones after menopause.[35] Still other studies indicate that at least some women of color are at lower risk of osteoporosis than white women, but the reasons for this are unclear.[36]

Further, and as in the case of cardiovascular disease, risks of osteoporosis can be lowered by a diet with adequate calcium and vitamin D, and exercise, such as walking or running[37] and weight lifting. One of the ironies here is that heavier women, who may be at greater risk for cardiovascular disease, tend to have greater bone density than do slight women—in general, the fatter a woman is, the greater her bone density. This may be because of more stress put on the bones, helping them to grow, and/or because hormone conversions in fat tissue contribute to higher bone density.[38]

Finally, studies now indicate that other, nonhormonal compounds, such as alendronate sodium, can be used for treatment and prevention of osteoporosis. Currently marketed under the brand name Fosamax, alendronate has been shown to be effective not only in preventing bone loss, but in increasing bone density in postmenopausal women, at least for women under 60 years of age, and at least over several years of use.[39]

EE, then, does seem to contribute substantially to slowing down bone loss. However, the mechanisms by which it does this remain unclear and, as in the case of cardiovascular risk, the benefits of taking estrogen often can be gleaned in other ways that do not include the known and unknown systemic risks of exogenous hormones. Given these risks, a woman should not be encouraged to accept EHI, particularly over the long term, unless it is very, very clear that she is an appropriate candidate for this intervention.

The Known Major Risks of Exogenous Hormone Intervention

The most serious risks of EHI are breast and endometrial cancers. Since it is now estimated that one in eight American women will develop breast cancer, even a small increase in risk is an enormous concern. What activists in the women's health movement have long worried about is increasingly well documented—EHI is strongly linked to increased risk of endometrial and breast cancers.

As we saw earlier, when it became clear in the mid-1970s that women taking EE alone were at increased risk for endometrial cancer, prescriptions dropped off precipitously. By the early 1980s, progestins were given with estrogen, which counteracted estrogen's proliferative effects. This, combined with lower doses of estrogen, has been effective in substantially reducing, if not completely eliminating, the risk of endometrial cancer from EHI. Further, as we have seen above, EHI use seems to reduce cardiovascular risk. But studies are showing that the apparent benefit to women of reduced risk of mortality from heart attack decreases because of increases in death from breast cancer among women on EHI.[40] And researchers are beginning to suggest that even shorter-term use of EHI might increase a woman's risk of breast cancer.[41] What is more, new studies suggest that high bone mineral density might be an important risk factor for postmenopausal breast cancer. At least one study suggests that the risk of breast cancer associated with EHI might be greatly underestimated because of this, and that EHI might put women with high bone density at substantially increased risk of breast cancer.[42]

Given that lowering one's risks of cardiovascular disease and osteoporosis so often can be accomplished by diet and exercise, and leaving out consideration of endometrial cancer, why should women increase our known risk of breast cancer by taking exogenous hormones unless this is the last feasible option?

It might be appropriate at this point to move to suggestions of various natural foods and "remedies" for addressing the effects of perimenopause and menopause. But, in all candor, I am reluctant to do that. Foods (such as soy and flaxseed), creams (such as those made from yams), supplements (such as vitamin E), and herbs (such as black cohosh) that help with hot flashes often accomplish that help by their estrogenic effects; thus, taking them or using them might be dangerous for women at high risk for breast cancer.[43] Even cow's milk, constantly presented as the most wholesome of foods, might put us at greater risk for hormone-receptive cancers. A prospective study reported in May 1998 in the British medical journal *Lancet* links insulin-like growth factor-1 (IGF-1) to breast cancer in premenopausal women.[44] It is not clear whether IGF-1 plays a causal role in these cancers or whether elevated levels of the growth hormone simply accompany some other factor that plays a causal role. What is clear is that IGF-1 in blood is associated with larger relative risks for "common" cancers than any other factor yet discovered.[45] What is also clear is that elevated levels of IGF-1 are produced in dairy cows injected with genetically engineered bovine growth hormone (rBGH), which is administered to dairy cows to extend their periods of lactation.[46] IGF-1 in cows is chemically identical to that in humans, and can be passed on to human milk consumers. As Peter Montague notes, "rBGH is just the tip of a very dangerous iceberg" in contemporary agriculture.[47] But that is another topic for another time. My point is just that the causal factors that enter into our cancers remain largely mysterious, and there simply is not enough information currently available for us to know with great certainty much about what causes our cancers and what doesn't. But whenever we are clear on a risk factor, as we are in the case of EHI, all women need to be fully informed about it.

Conclusion

I am several years past menopause—mine was very easy. But since I am at risk for cardiovascular disease (my father died of a heart attack at 53) and osteoporosis (my mother had it), in February 1997, I decided to take my internist's advice and start on EHI. I'd been worried about the breast cancer risk, but another physician of my acquaintance told me that the benefits of EHI are certainly worth the risk of breast cancer. I lasted a month on EHI because I had some allergic symptoms.[48]

In May 1997, I was diagnosed with breast cancer. I do not believe that my breast cancer was a result of my month on EHI—there are *no* studies to indicate that such minimal exposure is in any way linked to breast cancer. I tell the story simply to make a final point, namely, that having undergone six months of chemotherapy followed by a mastectomy, now living with the possibility of recurrence, and recently having lost a friend to breast cancer, I respectfully disagree with that physician of my acquaintance. This is not a risk anyone should increase without the very best of reasons. Physicians who attempt to persuade virtually all their patients of menopausal age that they should accept EHI—and they are *legion*—act irresponsibly. There is no question that EHI can be helpful to many menopausal women. But prescribing EHI is a risky business, and women need to be fully informed of *their knowable individual risks*. That so many women are prescribed EHI without genuinely diligent consideration of their individual risks is one of the most egregious moral failures of contemporary medical practice.

Notes

I am grateful to Mary Anglin, Susan Bordo, Patricia Cooper, Jennifer Crossen, Susan Fernandez, Keith Schillo, Monica Udvardy, and Margaret Walker for helpful conversations, questions, and suggestions.

1. Robert A. Wilson, *Feminine Forever* (New York: Evans, 1966; reprinted New York: Pocket Books, 1971). Quote from the Pocket Books edition, 17 and 20. Wilson does allow that fertility cannot be restored by medical intervention (17).

2. See Ann M. Voda, *Menopause, Me and You: The Sound of Women Pausing* (Binghamton, N.Y.: Haworth Press, 1997). For some slightly different definitions, see the World Health Organization, *Scientific Group on Research on Menopause in the 1990s* (Geneva: World Health Organization, 1996).

3. Menopause itself is never actually directly experienced or demonstrated—it is inferred one year after a woman's last menstrual bleed.

4. Jacquelyn N. Zita, "Heresy in the Female Body: The Rhetorics of Menopause," in *Menopause: A Midlife Passage,* ed. Joan C. Callahan (Bloomington: Indiana University Press, 1993): 59–78.

5. See, for example, Shirley MacLaine in *Madame Sousatzka, Steel Magnolias, Guarding Tess;* Anne Bancroft in *Critical Care, Great Expectations, G. I. Jane;* Vanessa

Redgrave in *Howard's End* and *Two Mothers for Zachary*. Redgrave's Mrs. Dalloway (though true to Virginia Woolf's character) is also a profoundly foolish woman. For an expanded discussion of older women in film, see Jean Kozlowski, "Women, Film and the Midlife Woman's Choice: Sink or Sousatzka?" in *Menopause*, ed. Callahan, 3–22.

6. The cost of taking Premarin is roughly $20 a month. In 1998, this single drug commands a billion-dollar market.

7. This web site (http://www.prcentral.com/c96premarin.htm) is version 1.0 of a service provided by EMMI, publisher of *Inside PR and Reputation Management*. Copyright 1996 EMMI, Inc.

8. See, for example, Joan C. Callahan, "Professions, Institutions, and Moral Risk," in *Professional Ethics and Social Responsibility*, ed. Daniel E. Wueste (Lanham, Md.: Rowman & Littlefield, 1994): 243–70; and "Pushing Drugs to Doctors," *Consumer Reports* (February 1992): 87–94.

9. Michael W. Miller, "How Drug Companies Get Medical Records of Individual Patients," *Wall Street Journal*, (February 27, 1992): A1.

10. *Consumer Reports*, "Pushing Drugs to Doctors," 90–93.

11. See Callahan, "Professions, Institutions, and Moral Risk"; and *Consumer Reports*, "Pushing Drugs to Doctors," 91–92.

12. See, for example, Ann Voda, "A Journey to the Center of the Cell," in *Menopause*, ed. Callahan, 160–93.

13. For an expanded description of women's reproductive anatomy, physiology, and endocrinology, see James W. Knight and Joan C. Callahan, *Preventing Birth: Contemporary Methods and Related Moral Controversies* (Salt Lake City: University of Utah Press, 1989), ch. 3 and 4.

14. Most oral contraceptives work by interfering with this surge in LH production, thereby interfering with ovulation. If there is no such interference, the ovulated egg is swept off the surface of the woman's ovary and moved along toward her uterus through one of her fallopian tubes (or oviducts). At the same time, any sperm received in the vagina are transported up through the woman's system, into the oviduct. Once in her oviduct, opposite motions move the sperm toward the egg, which is being moved toward the uterus. Thus, despite popular misconceptions to the contrary, sperm do not engage in a swimming race toward a woman's egg—her system basically draws sperm onward. This is why Ann Voda calls conception "the egging of the sperm." See Voda, *Menopause, Me and You*, ch. 2.

15. Scientists do not yet understand why a cohort of four or five follicles (typically) begin to mature in a woman's cycle while others remain dormant. Nor do they understand why (normally) only one of these will fully mature and ovulate.

16. Susan M. Love with Karen Lindsey, *Dr. Susan Love's Hormone Book* (New York: Random House, 1997), 6.

17. RU 486, the controversial "new" oral "contraceptive" does not work by interfering with conception. It works by inducing menstruation. Thus, if there is a conceptus/embryo implanted in a woman's uterine lining, it will be shed/reabsorbed with her endometrium if she takes RU 486. This is why opponents of RU 486 nicknamed it "the abortion pill." It should also be noted that most of the

endometrial buildup in the menstrual cycle is actually reabsorbed. If there are cancerous cells in the uterine lining that are reabsorbed, these can be rendered harmless by a woman's own immune system.

18. See, for example, Love with Lindsey, *Dr. Susan Love's Hormone Book,* 6.

19. Marie McCullough, "Hope or Hype?" *Philadelphia Inquirer* (May 13, 1996), cited in Love with Lindsey, *Dr. Susan Love's Hormone Book,* 18.

20. Love with Lindsey, *Dr. Susan Love's Hormone Book,* 20.

21. Love with Lindsey, *Dr. Susan Love's Hormone Book,* 18.

22. See, for example, Y. Zhang, D. P. Kiel, B. E. Kreger, L. A. Cupples, R. C. Ellison, J. F. Dorgan, A. Schatzkin, D. Levy, and D. T. Felson, "Bone Mass and the Risk of Breast Cancer among Postmenopausal Women," *New England Journal of Medicine* 336 (February 27, 1997): 611–17; and L. H. Kuller, J. A. Cauley, L. Lucas, S. Cummings, and W. S. Browner, "Sex Steroid Hormones, Bone Mineral Density, and Risk of Breast Cancer," *Environmental Health Perspectives* 105 supp. 3 (April 1997): 593–99.

23. See, for example, D. Smith, A. Pentice, J. Donovan, and W. Hermann, "Association of EE and Endometrial Cancer," *New England Journal of Medicine* 293 (1975): 1164–67; H. K. Ziel and W. D. Finkle, "Increased Risk of Endometrial Carcinoma among Users of Conjugated Estrogens," *New England Journal of Medicine* 293 (1975): 1167–70; N. Weiss, D. Szakely, and F. Austin, "Increasing Incidence of Endometrial Cancer in the U.S.," *New England Journal of Medicine* 294 (1976): 1259–62; and T. Mack, M. Pike, B. Henderson, R. Pfeffer, V. Gerkins, M. Arthur, and S. Braun, "Estrogens and Endometrial Cancer in a Retirement Community," *New England Journal of Medicine* 294 (1976): 1262–67.

24. See, for example, Kathleen I. MacPherson, "The False Promises of Hormone Replacement Therapy and Current Dilemmas," in *Menopause,* ed. Callahan, 145–59; and V. Ernster, T. Bush, G. Huggins, B. Hulka, J. Kelsey, and D. Schottenfeld, "Clinical Perspectives: Benefits and Risks of Menopausal Estrogen and/or Progestin Hormone Use," *Preventive Medicine* 17 (1988): 201–23.

25. Love with Lindsey, *Dr. Sharon Love's Hormone Book,* 36.

26. See, for example, Mary Lou Logothetis, "Disease or Development: Women's Perceptions of Menopause and the Need for Hormone Replacement Therapy," in *Menopause,* ed. Callahan, 123–35. Logothetis reports that fully 75 percent of the women she interviewed indicated either no distress or minimal menopausal distress, and only 7 percent of the women she interviewed indicated severe menopausal distress.

27. M. J. Stampfer and G. A. Colditz, "Estrogen Replacement Therapy and Coronary Heart Disease: A Quantitative Assessment of the Epidemiologic Evidence," *Preventive Medicine* 20 (1991): 47–63; F. Grodstein, M. J. Stampfer, J. E. Manson, G. A. Colditz, W. C. Willett, B. Rosner, F. E. Speizer, and C. H. Hennekens, "Postmenopausal Estrogen and Progestin Use: The Risk of Cardiovascular Disease," *New England Journal of Medicine* 335 (1996): 453–61; and A. Nasr and M. Breckwoldt, "Estrogen Replacement Therapy and Cardiovascular Protection: Lipid Mechanisms are the Tip of the Iceberg," *Gynecological Endocrinology* 12, no. 1 (February 1998): 43–59.

28. K. A. Matthews, L. H. Kuller, R. R. Wing, E. N. Meilahn, and P. Plantinga, "Prior to Use of Estrogen Replacement Therapy, Are Users Healthier Than Nonusers?" *American Journal of Epidemiology* 143/10 (May 15, 1996): 971–78; C. Schairer, H. O. Adami, R. Hoover, I. Persson, "Cause-Specific Mortality in Women Receiving Hormone Replacement Therapy," *Epidemiology* 8 (1997): 59–65.

29. Nasr and Breckwoldt, "Estrogen Replacement Therapy and Cardiovascular Protection."

30. Conference Report, Consensus Development Conference: "Prophylaxis and Treatment of Osteoporosis," *American Journal of Medicine* 90 (1991): 107–10, cited in Love with Lindsey, *Dr. Susan Love's Hormone Book,* 79.

31. Bone is a dynamic tissue that is constantly being torn down and rebuilt. Thus, bone loss is a normal phenomenon that occurs at all ages and in men and women. Osteoporosis is not peculiar to women; men experience it too. The main difference between men and women is that men generally have more bone mass than women and, therefore, have more bone to spare when they reach a point where they are not building as much bone as they lose.

32. Love with Lindsey, *Dr. Susan Love's Hormone Book,* 83.

33. Love with Lindsey, *Dr. Susan Love's Hormone Book,* 83.

34. See, for example, "Menopausal Hormone Replacement Therapy," *Cancer Facts,* National Cancer Institute, National Institutes of Health; http://rex.nci.nih.-gov/INFOR_CANCER/Cancer_facts/Section3/FS3_10.html (accessed May 10, 1998).

35. One of these studies found that although rural Mayan women live thirty years after menopause and experience the same loss of estrogen and the same amount of bone density loss after menopause as do U.S. white women, these women do not get osteoporosis. The only endocrine difference the researchers found between these Mayan women and U.S. white women was that the testosterone produced in the Mayan women's ovaries was unaffected by menopause. See M. C. Martin, J. E. Block, S. D. Sanchez, C. D. Arnaud, and Y. Beyene, "Menopause Without Symptoms: The Endocrinology of Menopause among Rural Mayan Indians," *American Journal of Obstetrics and Gynecology* 168/6 (1993): 1839–45. Yet another study suggests that testosterone might play a definitive role in sustaining bone density. Researchers found that adding a small amount of testosterone to the hormone regimen of women with chemically induced menopause reversed the bone loss they were experiencing without the testosterone. See M. C. Pike, A. Pike, R. Rude, D. Shoupe, and J. Richardson, "Pilot Trial of a Gonadtropin Hormone Agonist with Replacement Hormones as a Prototype Contraceptive to Prevent Breast Cancer," *Contraception* 47, no. 5 (1993): 427–44. However, even these effects might be attributable to the aromatizing of testosterone to estradiol (a form of estrogen), thereby increasing a woman's actual amount of estrogen.

36. See, for example, J. H. Tobias, D. G. Cook, T. J. Chambers, and N. Dalsell, "A Comparison of Bone Mineral Density between Caucasian, Asian and Afro-Caribbean Women," *Clinical Science* 87 (1994): 587–91.

37. Susan Love classifies these as forms of weight-bearing exercise. See Love with Lindsey, *Dr. Susan Love's Hormone Book,* 86.

38. See, for example, Love with Lindsey, *Dr. Susan Love's Hormone Book,* 86.

39. Alendronate sodium is a biphosphonate, which turns off the cells that break down bones. See, for example, D. Hosking, C. E. D. Chilvers, C. Christiansen, P. Ravn, R. Wasnich, P. Ross, M. McClung, A. Balske, D. Thompson, M. Daley, and A. J. Yates, for the Early Postmenopausal Intervention Cohort Study Group, "Prevention of Bone Loss with Alendronate in Postmenopausal Women Under 60 Years of Age," *New England Journal of Medicine* 338 (1998): 485–92. Fosamax was approved in the United States by the Federal Drug Administration in September 1995 for treatment of osteoporosis in postmenopausal women and in April 1997 for prevention of osteoporosis in postmenopausal women.

40. Editorial, "Hormone Replacement Therapy—Breast versus Heart, versus Bone," *New England Journal of Medicine* 332 (1995): 1638–39; P. G. Tonilo, M. Levitz, A. Zeleniuch-Jacquotte et al., "A Prospective Study of Endogenous Estrogens and Breast Cancer in Postmenopausal Women," *Journal of the National Cancer Institute* 87 (1995): 190–97; F. Berrino, P. Muti, A. Micheli et al., "Serum Sex Hormone Levels after Menopause and Subsequent Breast Cancer," *Journal of the National Cancer Institute* 88 (1996): 291–96; and F. Grodstein, M. J. Stampfer, G. A. Colditz, W. C. Willett, J. E. Manson, M. Joffe, B. Rosner, C. Fuchs, S. E. Hankinson, D. J. Hunter, C. H. Hennekens, and F. E. Speizer, "Postmenopausal Hormone Therapy and Mortality," *New England Journal of Medicine* 336 (1997): 1769–75.

41. F. Grodstein and W. C. Willett, Correspondence: "Postmenopausal Hormone Therapy and Mortality," *New England Journal of Medicine* 337 (1997): 1389–91.

42. L. H. Kuller, J. A. Cauley, L. Lucas, S. Cummings, and W. S. Browner, "Sex Steroid Hormones, Bone Mineral Density, and Risk of Breast Cancer," *Environmental Health Perspectives* 105, sup. 3 (April 1997): 593–99.

43. There are now a number of books available with advice on these matters. See, for example, Dee Ito, *Without Estrogen: Natural Remedies for Menopause and Beyond* (New York: Random House, 1994); Love with Lindsey, *Dr. Susan Love's Hormone Book;* Susan Perry and Kate O'Hanlan, *Natural Menopause: The Complete Guide,* rev. ed. (New York: Addison Wesley, 1997); Voda, *Menopause, Me and You;* Susan S. Weed, *Menopausal Years: The Wise Woman Way* (New York: Ash Tree, 1992).

44. S. E. Hankinson, W. C. Willett, G. A. Colditz, D. J. Hunter, S. Michaud, B. Deroo, B. Rosner, F. E. Speizer, and M. Pollak, "Circulating Concentrations of Insulin-Like Growth Factor I and Risk of Breast Cancer," *Lancet* 351/9113 (May 9, 1998): 1393–96. Earlier in 1998, another prospective study linked IGF-1 to prostate cancer. See J. M. Chan, M. J. Stampfer, E. Giovannucci et al., "Plasma Insulin-like Growth Factor-I and Prostate Cancer Risk: A Prospective Study," *Science* 279 (January 23, 1998): 563–66.

45. J. Holly, "Insulin-like Growth Factor-I and New Opportunities for Cancer Prevention," *Lancet* 351/9113 (May 9, 1998): 1371–75.

46. See, for example, Peter Montague, "Breast Cancer, rBGH and Milk," *Rachel's Environment and Health Weekly* 598 (May 8, 1998); http://www.monitor.-net.rachel/. See also Monsanto's rBGH information at http://www.monsanto.com,

which uses the trade name of rBGH, Posilac®. Monsanto is in the process of increasing production of Posilac®. The company will open a new plant to manufacture the drug in Augusta, Georgia, in 1999. See "Monsanto Announces Plans to Construct New North American Polisac® Manufacturing Plant," Monsanto news release, St. Louis (June 17, 1996), in which Art Fitzgerald, president of the Monsanto Dairy Company (a division of the Monsanto Company), says: "The new Monsanto facility will accommodate projected market growth for POSILAC globally with the potential to significantly reduce manufacturing costs. It also will bring production closer to our largest market and our rapidly expanding customer base." The release also says: "Since POSILAC was introduced in February 1994, approximately 17,000 dairy producers, about 15 percent of all U.S. producers, have purchased the product. In just two years, it has become the largest selling dairy animal health product in the U.S. Sales continue to increase significantly—for example, in the first half of 1996 sales volumes are up 40% from the comparable period in 1995." See http://www.monsanto.com/ag/_asp/Monsanto.asp?MKTID=9999&PDTID=0&UID=0.

47. Montague, "Breast Cancer, rBGH and Milk."

48. As many as two-thirds of women who start on EHI stop taking it within two years. See, for example, "Hormone Replacement Therapy: Customize, Don't Compromise," *Mayo Clinic Women's HealthSource* (June 1997); http://www.mayohealth.org/mayo/9705/htm/hrt.htm (accessed May 22, 1998).

· 10 ·

Religious Women, Medical Settings, and Moral Risk

Peggy DesAutels

As we think about the ethical issues surrounding women and aging, it is important to ask the following questions. What do women in our society actually experience at various stages of their life cycle? Which of these experiences put women at moral risk? In what situations are women's senses of moral value and selfhood likely to be ignored or discounted? I, along with a number of feminist philosophers, advocate approaching feminist ethics by starting with women's actual situations and experiences.[1] No doubt, a wide variety of aging women's experiences call for moral analysis. I focus here on the medical experiences of older women with religious commitments. I argue that when older religious women find themselves in medical settings, their most deeply held values are at special risk of being disrespected and disregarded.

It may be helpful to give a few examples of ethically troubling medical situations involving older religious women.

- A woman who strongly believes that the experience of suffering and/or death is accompanied by valuable spiritual growth, and who prefers to be fully aware rather than in a drugged state as she nears the end of life, nonetheless lets her strongly assertive physician sway her into following his recommended "complete pain management" regime.
- A nun who sits on a hospital ethics committee knows that the patient in a case being discussed holds religious views similar to her own and that these views would affect the course of treatment most preferred by that patient, but fails to speak up and feels silenced by the expectation that discussions on ethics committees should remain secular.

175

- A patient who has in the past relied exclusively on prayer for healing and experienced what she considers to be several "spiritual" healings of serious medical conditions, now wishes to try an exclusively spiritual approach for a new "medically serious" condition, but neither her reports of past healing experiences nor her current wishes are taken seriously by her family or her physician.

These scenarios are just a few of many potential situations that can involve older religious women, medical settings, and moral risk. Below I first discuss why such situations should not be but nonetheless have been ignored by feminist and biomedical ethicists. I then analyze the significant risk to moral value and selfhood for the women in such situations. Finally, I recommend ways to address and lower these risks.

Religious Women, Feminist Ethics, and Biomedical Ethics

To date, those writing in feminist ethics have mostly ignored the fact that many women have a strong religious orientation and close ties to religious communities.[2] But for feminists interested in women's actual experience, the fact of the matter is that in the United States, over 60 percent of all adult women and over 80 percent of women over the age of 65 are members of either a church or a synagogue (*Statistical Abstract of the United States* 1997). These statistics should be of special interest to feminist ethicists for a number of reasons. First, the guiding values of religious women are likely to derive, at least in part, from their respective religious traditions. Second, the ethical decision-making processes of such women will often incorporate prayer. And third, the moral community of most significance to many older women is none other than a church community (Ozorak 1996, 25).

Why is there such avoidance by feminist ethicists in general, and feminist biomedical ethicists in particular, of the morally relevant religious commitments of so many women in our society? There are several contributing factors. An obvious one is the fact that currently both feminist ethics and biomedical ethics are embedded within the philosophical ethical tradition—a tradition with secular assumptions, secular terminologies, and secular methodologies. For example, philosophical ethicists do not assume that God exists; nor do they assume an afterlife. They do not use such phrases as "saving souls," or "spiritual growth," or "God's grace." And they advocate neither prayer nor the consulting of a religious authority as a means to making sound moral judgments. By focusing almost exclusively on philosophical concepts and theories in ethical debate, philosophical ethicists attempt to avoid the difficulties associated with including dogmatic and often conflicting religious assumptions and values.

There is another contributing factor to why feminists in particular do not sympathize with religious women. A major goal of feminism is to challenge those institutional structures, group practices, and belief systems that harm women as a group. Because religious institutions are notorious for their rigid patriarchal structures and sexist views of women, feminist philosophers tend to view women who actively participate in and feel positively toward their churches/synagogues as contributing to the perpetuation of the patriarchy. As a result, many feminists neither support nor defend religious women. Rather, they encourage religious women to divest themselves entirely of their patriarchal religious institutions, socialization, and ways of thinking.

Biomedical ethicists are also influenced in a number of ways to take a secular perspective on ethical issues that arise in medical settings. Although biomedical ethics as a field was shaped originally by religious traditions, it is now influenced primarily by the philosophical and legal traditions.[3] Discussions center primarily on patient *rights* and universal *principles* of bioethics. Patients are encouraged to make autonomous health care decisions in light of their own values, including religious values, but public discussion of religious values and how they can or should affect medical decision making has all but disappeared.

Finally, there are reasons why religion in general is likely to be discounted in medical settings. These have to do with the fact that the practice of Western medicine is closely allied with the practices of medical *science*. Religion assumes a spiritual aspect of reality and promotes spiritual values. Science assumes a matter-based reality and promotes secular values. Because medicine is closely allied with medical science, the materialistic methodologies, assumptions, and values of science automatically take precedence over religious methodologies, assumptions, and values. Scientific practices tend to exclude the use of divine power, view human purposes as biological, and focus on mind as brain. True, many medical practitioners and scientists have private religious commitments. They may well believe in an afterlife; they may value spiritual growth or have faith that prayer can heal. But the *practice* of medicine itself focuses on and most values the use of material means and technologies to keep the body healthy (pain-free and functioning properly) in *this* life. The prestige and authority of medicine depend on its claims to scientific validity. But even if physicians' practice of medicine is viewed as science, from a patient's perspective, the fundamental life choices to be made are moral and spiritual ones, even when the choices concern a patient's health and medical care.

Older Women and Religion

The typical faithful member of a church or synagogue is often stereotypically conceived of as an older woman. Just how accurate is this conception? Studies tend to corroborate that, in fact, women are more religious than men, and older persons are more religious than younger. Women pray more frequently than men, are more likely to be regular church/synagogue goers, are more apt to report having experienced a "faith" healing, and are more likely than men to view themselves as having a personal relationship with a loving God (Feltey and Paloma 1991, Ozorak 1996). Similarly, older persons pray more frequently than younger persons, are more apt to report having religious experiences, are more likely to attend church/synagogue, and are more likely than younger persons to perceive themselves as having a close relationship with God (*Statistical Abstract of the United States* 1997, Feltey and Poloma 1991).

Recent studies suggest a number of possible explanations for why women are more likely than men to be regular attendees at a church or synagogue. When interviewed about their church experiences, most women stress the centrality of caring, community, and service to others to these experiences (Ozorak 1996, 27–28). But it can still be asked why so many women choose traditional church organizations instead of other possible venues for caring and community. One plausibility is that girls are socialized to be more affiliative and conforming (Argyle and Beit-Hallahmi 1975). Another factor may be more structural. Because most women, until recently, have not worked outside the home, involvement in church has been one of the few ways to make a difference in their communities and societies (De Vaus and McAllister 1987). In addition, child-rearing has traditionally been relegated to women. Some women attend church primarily to ensure that their children attend (Lindsey 1990, Sapiro 1990).

Older persons are more likely to be religious than younger persons for some of the same reasons. When those who are now older were growing up, there were stronger general social pressures to attend church. And because many retired older persons have neither the workplace nor an at-home family, for many, their church community becomes a significant means for countering loneliness and isolation—a way to feel meaningfully connected to others, useful, and of service. In fact, many women, both young and old, when interviewed, directly refer to their congregation, or a subset of it, as their "family" (Ozorak 1996, 25).

Women and the Medical Community

Women in health care settings are, as Mary Briody Mahowald refers to them, the "unequal majority" (1993). More women than men interact with the medical community. One simple reason is that women live longer than men. They are also the ones who are most apt to interact with medical professionals on behalf of their children and elderly relatives. Over the past few decades, women have become increasingly dependent on medical interventions and treatments at each stage of their life cycle. They interact with the medical community for birth control prescriptions, pregnancy, childbirth, premenopausal, menopausal, and postmenopausal conditions.

Despite women making up the majority of patients, several feminist bioethicists have convincingly argued that the health care system assumes and is biased in favor of male patients. Women are at moral risk in health care settings. They are at risk of being perceived as less worthy of such tangibles as expensive treatments and research dollars and such intangibles as full consideration and respect. Feminists point out, for example, that women are less likely to receive organ transplants or aggressive heart disease treatments than are men with equivalent health difficulties (Nelson and Nelson 1996, Sherwin 1992). Feminists have also stressed the special risks that women have for being treated paternalistically. In her book entitled *No Longer Patient,* Susan Sherwin summarizes this concern:

> In a sexist society where women are regularly denied the status of competent reasoners, where patients are typically women, and where physicians are mostly men, that physicians experience patients as lacking reason does not constitute reliable evidence that patients really are incapable of the reasoning that is required to arrive at reliable decisions. (1992, 142)

The point to be made here is that women's values and perspectives, regardless of whether they are secular or religious, are at special risk of being ignored or discounted in medical settings.[4]

Religious Women in Medical Settings

There are a variety of conditions under which a woman might wish to have her religious beliefs or values taken into account while in a health care setting. Much will depend on her role in the medical setting and her particular relgous beliefs and values. In the patient role, some women may wish to refuse medical treatment for religious reasons (e.g., those who are Christian Scientists or Jehovah's Witnesses). Others may wish to bring their beliefs to bear on treatment decisions, especially reproductive and end-of-life treatments. In the employee or volunteer role, some religious women at health care institutions (e.g., nuns, chaplains, nurses, physicians) may wish to participate in case consultations or serve on ethics committees.

There are, however, special moral risks associated with a woman's holding and attempting to assert religious-based values in a health care setting. As mentioned above, older women are even more vulnerable to these risks than younger women simply because more older women than younger are religious. I will provide two illustrations from my own experience. The first illustration comes from my observations while serving as a medical ethicist on an ethics committee at a Catholic-affiliated urban hospital. The second illustration comes from my research on Christian Science refusal cases.[5]

Religious Women on Hospital Ethics Committees

In order to be accredited, hospitals must show that they have a mechanism for addressing ethical issues. Most have chosen to set up ethics committees as this mechanism. The makeup of these committees includes such hospital employees as physicians, nurses, chaplains, social workers, lawyers, risk managers, and administrators. Some committees also include such "outsiders" as medical ethicists from nearby universities and representative community members. These committees are charged with educating themselves and the hospital staff on medical ethics, determining ethics-related policies and procedures, and consulting on particular cases involving difficult ethical issues.

I have served as a philosopher/medical ethicist on several hospital ethics committees, including an ethics committee at a Catholic-affiliated hospital. As a medical ethicist who researches the ways that secular and religious values conflict, I was especially interested in observing how the ethics committee at the Catholic hospital addressed and resolved such conflicts. This particular committee was co-chaired by a physician with no apparent religious commitments and a nun who directed the hospital volunteers. The committee also included a Catholic priest (chaplain), two additional Catholic nuns (chaplain and social worker), a Protestant minister (chaplain), a deeply committed Catholic woman who served as an administrator at a nearby Catholic long-term care facility, and the usual array of physicians, nurses, social workers, and so on—some of whom were Catholic and some of whom were not. Unsurprisingly, the nuns serving on this committee were older than many members of the committee.

Despite there being so many religiously committed individuals on this committee and despite the fact that the committee served a religiously affiliated hospital, I was surprised to discover that the perspectives brought to bear on the ethical deliberations of this committee were primarily secular. Rarely, if ever, did the nuns directly challenge secular assumptions that conflicted with their religious values or perspective. I recall one particular pain management discussion, for example, in which the physician leading the discussion simply assumed that pain should be avoided at all costs. This physician, like many other physicians and secular medical ethicists, held the view that such costs could include a patient becoming mentally fogged or a terminal patient's hastened death. The nuns remained silent during the meeting, but one of them mentioned to me later that she had been very disturbed by this discussion—that from her perspective not all suffering can or should be avoided. Nonetheless, she felt that it was inappropriate to bring up this religious outlook during committee deliberations.

Women's religious perspectives also exist and are also silenced on ethics committees at secular hospitals. For example, I facilitated a day-long retreat for the ethics committee of a large nonsectarian urban hospital. At the committee chair's request, most of the retreat was devoted to determining the goals and objectives of the committee for the coming year and to discussion of the latest trends in the field of bioethics. However, as a final exercise, the members of the committee were asked to share how they *actually* make difficult ethical decisions in their own lives. Almost every woman on the committee and many of the men reported their church to be their primary source of moral values and prayer to be their primary means to resolving ethical issues. Many also mentioned for the first time that day how confusing it is to have personal, religiously based values and approaches to ethics that often conflict with the secular values and approaches of the committee. Nevertheless, like the nuns discussed above, they too were reticent to bring religious perspectives to bear on ethics committee deliberations.

Religious Women Who Refuse Medical Treatment

Just as more women than men are religious, it is also the case that more women than men are likely to choose spiritual or religious alternatives to medical treatments for both themselves and their children. Such women are at high risk for being treated paternalistically within the medical community. Because physicians base their practices on the medical model of disease, choosing a healing system that directly challenges and conflicts with this medical model may well be perceived by physicians as an irrational choice. Physicians are, for the most part, well intentioned, but find it very difficult to perceive the patient's good as anything other than the good as defined from a medical perspective.

Both medical ethicists and the courts appear at first glance to eschew medical paternalism in favor of patients, both male and female, making informed, autonomous choices for themselves and their children. But a closer look at recent literature on informed consent in medical settings gives us a different and rather alarming picture. In fact, as can be seen from recent court decisions, little is expected of physicians. In his discerning comments on *Canterbury v. Spence,* Jay Katz does not exaggerate when he notes that "the law of informed consent is substantially mythic and fairy tale-like" (Katz 1994, 148). Those familiar with this court ruling know that it sanctions physicians communicating information in such a way that patients will "consent" to the treatments the physician deems best for the patient. In summary, it is considered legally and ethically acceptable for a physician to withhold or present information in a biased way under a wide variety of circumstances, including whenever the physician deems such withholding or presenting to be of therapeutic benefit.

In her discussions of paternalism, Susan Sherwin provides a number of reasons why women as a group have been and still are especially vulnerable to being treated paternalistically in medical contexts. Among these reasons, she notes that medicine has adopted the ideology of science and is fully committed to technological health care solutions in contradistinction to many women who offer "unscientific" perspectives and reports on their own health. I agree with Sherwin's analysis and simply wish further to stress that religiously oriented women with approaches to health and healing that directly challenge "scientific" and technological approaches will be most vulnerable to being overridden in medical settings.

Christian Scientists are a prime example. The Christian Science Church was founded by Mary Baker Eddy in the late 1800s, and the preponderance of Christian Scientists today are women, many of them older women. Although the total number of Christian Scientists in the United States is comparatively small, most major cities have at least one active church with members of the congregation who are well established in their respective communities. One major difference between a Christian Scientist's approach to healing and that taken by members of more mainstream denominations is that Christian Scientists rely exclusively on prayer and do not attempt to "mix" prayer with a medical approach. They view the two approaches—prayer and medicine—as incompatible. Thus, Christian Scientists will usually refuse medical treatment for themselves and their children.

Nonetheless, Christian Science women find themselves in medical settings for a variety of reasons. Most states require that there be an attending physician during childbirth, and many types of birth control, including such "nonmedical" methods as the diaphram, require a prescription. Christian Science mothers must take their children to physicians because school systems usually require physical examinations and vaccinations. Although a few Christian Science nursing facilities exist, many older Christian Science women requiring care are unable to avail themselves of these facilities. And of course, anyone, Christian Science or otherwise, can unexpectedly find herself in an emergency room without having requested to be taken there.

Christian Science women who have talked with me describe both subtle and overt ways that physicians discount and disregard their wishes. They are seldom believed when they report having experienced healings of "medical" conditions in the past. In cases where their children are diagnosed as having a serious condition, some physicians have attempted to obtain court orders to keep their children at the hospital. Many Christian Science women are scared or intimidated into obtaining medical treatment for themselves or their children because physicians "scold" them, exaggerate the risks associated with no treatment, or fail entirely to tell them their rights to refuse treatments. Because physicians assume that choosing a Christian Science approach to healing is tantamount to doing nothing at all, they feel professionally compelled to strongly urge if not actually compel the use of medical means for healing.

Obviously, Christian Scientists are not the only ones choosing alternative approaches to healing. But those who choose to *supplement* a medical approach with alternative spiritual approaches are less likely to have their decisions overridden. Most physicians do not view supplemental prayer as harmful to a patient, and may even acknowledge prayer's usefulness for maintaining an optimistic attitude. It is those women who *reject* a medical approach in favor of a religious approach that are most at risk for excessive medical paternalism. When interacting with such women, physicians are apt to view themselves as objective and scientifically rational decision makers and to view their female religious patients as subjective and unscientifically irrational decision makers and thus as patients who do not know what is "best" for them.

Creating Moral Space for Religious Women in Medical Settings

Unfortunately, many biomedical ethicists continue to believe that ethical expertise consists of mastering and then correctly applying bioethical principles. These bioethicists are, in turn, responsible for training the health care professionals who serve on ethics committees. New trends in bioethics are emerging, however. In a recent piece on health care ethics, Margaret Walker offers a way to conceive of ethics consulting that is, on my view, more responsive than traditional approaches to the moral concerns of religious women in medical settings. Walker proposes that those serving on ethics committees conceive of themselves as "architects of moral space" and as "mediators in the conversations taking place within that space" rather than as experts in "codelike theories and lawlike principles" (Walker 1993, 33).

As ethics consulting becomes less about attempting to apply (impose) "universal" secular principles, as it becomes more responsive to divergent worldviews and value systems, there will be a place within medical settings for religious perspectives. As evidenced by the examples cited above, however, both health care professionals and patients need facilitation and training in how best to express religious perspectives in settings where these views are not necessarily shared by others. Ethics committees, too, need this facilitation and training.

There are any number of reasons why those with religious leanings are reticent to discuss their religious views, even when such views are morally relevant. Some feel that bringing their religious beliefs into a discussion is tantamount to imposing these beliefs on others. Some feel that their religious commitments are intensely personal and private. Others do not wish to defend, or feel incapable of defending, their views to a skeptical and hostile group of individuals. Still others worry that they will lose ethical or professional credibility by appearing to be biased.

Nonetheless, there are some relatively simple techniques for bringing religious perspectives of moral relevance into ethics discussions. One is simply to preface what is said by making it clear that this is just one perspective out of many possible perspectives. Another is to make ample use of hypothetical statements, such as "If one takes the Catholic perspective, one might view the role of suffering as follows" or "If a patient believes that there is an afterlife, then that patient may view death not as an end but as a transition." An alternative approach is simply to note when secular assumptions are being made that may not be held by those with religious perspectives. For example, it can be pointed out when "health" is being conceived of in purely medical terms and that those with religious commitments would view health as incorporating both physical and spiritual well-being.

The first step, then, toward respecting and accommodating medically relevant views of older religious women is to recognize the importance of openly discussing these religious views and perspectives. Once this step has been taken, the discussants will need patience as they attempt to translate religious and secular terminologies, question what others take as givens, and publicly articulate what has previously been behind the scenes and private. This is not to say that they should ignore secular approaches to ethics. Rather, discussions of professional codes of ethics, philosophical ethical theories, and legal precedents should be supplemented with both feminist and religious approaches to ethical decision making.

Notes

Special thanks to Margaret Walker and Robert Richardson for reading and commenting on earlier drafts of this chapter.

1. See, for example, Walker 1998, Held 1993, Bartky 1990, and Ruddick 1989.

2. One exception to this has been some discussion of whether religious "right-wing" women should be held morally accountable for promoting sexist values and advocating traditional subservient roles for women (see, for example, Superson 1995).

3. The *Hastings Center Report Special Supplement* (1990) contains one of the few discussions of the relationship between religion and bioethics. See, for example, Callahan 1990, Campbell 1990, Verhey 1990, and Wind 1990.

4. See Susan Wendell's chapter 8 in this volume on other aspects of women's lower cognitive authority in the eyes of medical professionals.

5. For more on the ethical issues that can arise when Christian Scientists interact with medical professionals see DesAutels, Battin, and May 1999.

Bibliography

Argyle, Michael, and B. Beit-Hallahmi. *The Social Psychology of Religion.* Boston: Routledge and Kegan Paul, 1975.

Bartky, Sandra. *Femininity and Domination: Studies in the Phenomenology of Oppression.* New York: Routledge, 1990.

Callahan, Daniel. "Religion and the Secularization of Bioethics." *Hastings Center Report Special Supplement* 20 (July–August 1990): 2–4.

Campbell, Courtney S. "Religion and Moral Meaning in Bioethics." *Hastings Center Report Special Supplement* 20 (July–August 1990): 5–10.

DesAutels, Peggy, Margaret Pabst Battin, and Larry May. *Praying for a Cure: When Medical and Religious Practices Conflict.* Lanham, Md.: Rowman & Littlefield, 1999.

De Vaus, David, and Ian McAllister. "Gender Differences in Religion: A Test of the Structural Location Theory." *American Sociological Review* 52 (August 1987): 472–81.

Feltey, Kathryn M., and Margaret M. Poloma. "From Sex Differences to Gender Role Beliefs: Exploring Effects on Six Dimensions of Religiosity." *Sex Roles* 25, nos. 3, 4 (March–April 1991): 181–93.

Held, Virginia. *Feminist Morality: Transforming Culture, Society, and Politics.* Chicago: University of Chicago Press, 1993.

Katz, Jay. "Physicians and Patients: A History of Silence," in *Contemporary Issues in Bioethics,* 4th ed., ed. Tom L. Beauchamp and LeRoy Walters. Belmont, Calif.: Wadsworth, 1994.

Lindsey, Linda L. *Gender Roles: A Sociological Perspective.* Englewood Cliffs, N.J.: Prentice Hall, 1990.

Mahowald, Mary Briody. *Women and Children in Health Care: An Unequal Majority.* New York: Oxford University Press, 1993.

Nelson, Hilde Lindemann, and James Lindemann Nelson. "Justice in the Allocation of Health Care Resources: A Feminist Account," in *Feminism and Bioethics: Beyond Reproduction,* ed. Susan M. Wolf. New York: Oxford University Press, 1996.

Ozorak, Elizabeth Weiss. "The Power, But Not the Glory: How Women Empower Themselves Through Religion." *Journal for the Scientific Study of Religion* 35, no. 1 (March 1996): 17–29.

Poloma, Margaret M., and Brian F. Pendleton. *Exploring Neglected Dimensions of Religion in Quality of Life Research.* New York: Edwin Mellen Press, 1991.

Ruddick, Sara. *Maternal Thinking: Toward a Politics of Peace.* New York: Ballantine Books, 1989.

Sapiro, V. *Women in American Society.* Mountain View, Calif.: Mayfield, 1990.

Sherwin, Susan. *No Longer Patient: Feminist Ethics and Health Care*. Philadelphia: Temple University, 1992.

Statistical Abstract of the United States: 1997, 117th ed. U.S. Bureau of the Census. Washington, D.C.: U.S. Government Printing Office, 1997.

Superson, Anita M. "Right-Wing Women: Causes, Choices, and Blaming the Victim," in *"Nagging" Questions: Feminist Ethics in Everyday Life,* ed. Dana E. Bushnell. Lanham, Md.: Rowman & Littlefield, 1995.

Verhey, Allen D. "Talking of God—But with Whom?" *Hastings Center Report Special Supplement* 20 (July–August 1990): 21–24.

Walker, Margaret Urban. "Keeping Moral Space Open: New Images of Ethics Consulting." *Hastings Center Report* 23, no. 2 (March–April 1993): 33–40.

———. *Moral Understandings: A Feminist Study in Ethics*. New York: Routledge, 1998.

Wind, James P. "What Can Religion Offer Bioethics?" *Hastings Center Report Special Supplement* 20 (July–August 1990): 18–20.

· 11 ·

Age, Sex, and Resource Allocation

Daniel Callahan

$\mathcal{T}$here is every reasonable expectation that, around the year 2010, the Medicare program of health care for the elderly will begin encountering a severe financing crisis. Only a number of recent changes in the program—notably because of the Balanced Budget Act of 1997—have been able to hold off the year of reckoning; and it is surely possible that other short-term measures could help for a few years more beyond 2010.[1] Sooner or later, however, the expected impact of baby boomer retirements will begin to overwhelm the present system of financing Medicare.[2] No serious analyst denies this. And that's not all: as if the demographic projections alone were not enough to generate anxiety, it is only prudent to expect—based on recent history—that between now and 2010 there will continue to be a steady stream of beneficial, but usually expensive, new technologies to treat the diseases and disabilities of the elderly.

The combination of demographic and technological change almost certainly points to the likely need to one way or another ration Medicare benefits in the future. The question I want to pose here is whether it will be possible to ration those benefits in a way that is fair to various deprived groups in the American population. Unless the rationing is organized in some sophisticated fashion, there is every reason to expect that it could just perpetuate present disparities, perhaps making the worst-off even worse off. The case study I will work with is that of health care for elderly women. Not only does this group make up the largest portion of the elderly, but their health problems are also in great part one of the characteristic consequences of recent medical progress: the longer the life (for the most part) the worse the health, particularly for those with a history of unhealthy lifestyles. If we can find a way to solve the special health problems of older women, and find ways to ameliorate the baneful effects of longer lives (which affect men and women alike), and do so in the context of rationing, that would be a tremendously important development. While difficult to accomplish, it is not impossible; and, indeed, it might just be the prospect of serious rationing that could push policy in that fruitful direction.

The main difficulty in even imagining that kind of outcome is a familiar one: the unwillingness of the American population in general, and their elected leaders in particular, to willingly accept rationing. By "rationing" I mean the denial or limitation of forms of health care that would be both desired by individuals and beneficial to them. There are other, milder meanings of the word that are sometimes used, for instance, resource allocation or priority-setting, but it is in the harder sense that I will use the term "rationing." It is that sense—denying people something they need or seriously want—that generates the most negative reaction.

Why will rationing be necessary? At some point, in this country and every other, governments reach a political limit on available resources. There is no natural or inevitable economic point at which this happens, and it varies from country to country, but that limit is effectively reached when citizens are unwilling or unable to pay higher taxes for health care. At present about 1.5 percent of everyone's payroll taxes goes to support the Medicare program (with about 6 percent going to Social Security). The projected deficits after 2010 have been estimated to gradually rise to the range of $300 billion to $500 billion a year, far higher than the entire federal budget deficits of recent years. To meet such costs, the estimates are that the payroll contribution would have to go from 1.5 percent to 20–40 percent, an unthinkable tax burden for a single federal program. I have no idea what the public might be willing to tolerate as an upper limit, but it surely will get nowhere near that point.

It is noteworthy moreover that the present congressional debate on the future of Medicare does not openly encompass a discussion of a tax increase or any admission of the likelihood of rationing either. The policy options ordinarily discussed come down to four: an increase in taxation to pay for the expected rise in costs (which seems to have the least support and elicit the least discussion); greater out-of-pocket payments by beneficiaries; reduced payments to providers, whether physicians, hospitals, or clinics; and cuts in reimbursable services.[3] There have also been efforts of late to induce more Medicare beneficiaries to switch to managed care programs, as well as proposals for medical savings accounts, allowing those financially able to set aside money for their health care later in life.

With the exception of the increased taxation option, and the possible exception of the savings account idea (mainly of benefit for the affluent and, in fact, just another way of increasing out-of-pocket costs), all of the debated options tacitly encompass rationing. It is surely possible of course that there will be a change of heart among the public and a renewed willingness to accept a tax increase. But the staggering magnitude of the projected Medicare deficits suggests a political limit to that possibility; and at some point an excessive tax burden on the young to pay for the health care of the elderly—even if they were willing to pay it—would create its own unpleasant set of problems. In the end, then, the most feasible options will be those mentioned: increased out-of-pocket medical expenses, reduction of provider payments, and reduction in services. If those options remain minor in their scope, they could avoid the rationing possibility. But once they become serious and extensive options, they will be nothing less than modes of rationing—though modes that will almost certainly not be labeled as "rationing," a term that legislators and managers will no doubt avoid using in the future as much as at present. But rationing by any other name is still rationing.

Considering the Options

Think about the options I briefly listed. Out-of-pocket health care expenses already average 20 percent of the annual income of the elderly, and 35 percent of the annual income of the poor, an excessive burden by any measure. Since pharmaceuticals, eyeglasses, and many other expenses are not covered by Medicare, it is already the case that the elderly frequently self-ration those items for lack of ability to pay for them. A reduction in payments to health care providers is still another route to rationing, guaranteeing that providers will have strong incentives to pass along their reduced income to their patients in the form of fewer or less-intensive services. This happens already, though perhaps not often with critically important services. But if the economic pressure is strong enough, the temptation will be there to curtail that which is necessary and beneficial for patients. Finally, an open reduction in services—whether through a limitation on Medicare reimbursements for a specified list of conditions or treatments, or through skimpy reimbursements to managed care organizations that have taken on the elderly as clients—would clearly count as rationing.

Now, in pointing out the unpleasant implications of these three methods of controlling costs, I am by no means denying the eventual necessity of rationing or suggesting it cannot be justified. But it is useful to underscore why the costs of health care for the elderly will become such a burden: the added costs of technological progress in caring for the elderly. It will principally be medical progress that will be rationed, as is already the case, albeit in a milder form. If medicine remained, say, at the level of 1980s services and technologies, there would be no problem in 2010. But because of the relentless drive for progress and innovation, the medicine of 2010 will be a more expensive medicine than the medicine of the late 1990s. This likely fact is important for understanding the choices before us, and for framing the special problems of elderly women.

The question that I now pose is twofold: how can women be fairly and well treated within the rationed health care system for the elderly that surely lies ahead? With that question in mind, how might we best think about the medical progress that is likely both to offer benefits to women while at the same time, because of its price, intensifying the pressure to ration?

My general argument in response to those questions can be laid out in three contentions: First, even if elderly women received comparatively poorer care under the present Medicare system than men (which no one has alleged), it would in any event be neither practically possible nor fair to reform the system only to correct for injustices done to women; minorities and some portion of ill-fated white men would surely have the same problem. Second, the reforms most needed to help women should no less help men with equivalent problems, lest one injustice be substituted for another. Third, the most beneficial kinds of health care for elderly men and women would focus on the socioeconomic conditions necessary for good health—and on health for the entire population—placing the burden of the inevitable rationing on expensive technologies more of benefit to individuals than to the elderly as a group.

The Health Status of Elderly Women

I will work my way toward these three contentions by first summarizing what is at present known about the health care given elderly women and about their health status. Since there is a large and well-known literature on this topic, I can be brief. The most striking fact is that women live on average six to seven years longer than men, for reasons not altogether clear. This turns out to be a mixed blessing, for it is no less striking that women pay for those additional years with significantly increased chronic illness and disability. At the same time that they are trying to cope with those burdens, they are more likely than males to be poor, to live alone, and to require institutionalization for their diseases and disabilities.[4]

In 1987, I published a book, *Setting Limits: Medical Goals in an Aging Society*, arguing that an age-based limit on expensive medical technologies would probably be required by the time the baby boomers retired as a way of controlling Medicare costs.[5] By "age-based" I meant the open and explicit use of chronological age as a way of setting a cutoff point for various forms of care, for example, eighty years of age as the limit for some form of expensive, life-extending, high-technology, acute care medicine. Without such a cutoff point, a younger generation would be heavily and unfairly burdened with the cost of paying for that expensive elderly care. With the ratio of tax-paying workers to retired elderly expected to move from 4:1 at present to 2.5:1 by 2020 or so, there is good reason to worry about those burdens.

The idea of age-based rationing was not a proposal accepted with enthusiasm, suggesting to many a thinly veiled ageism along with assorted other moral and policy failings. I had expected most of the criticisms, but there was one effect of an age-based rationing policy that had not occurred to me: potential discrimination against elderly women.[6] Why? For the simple reason that, since women live longer than men, the burden of any age-based policy must of necessity fall more heavily upon women. You can't ration health care for dead men, only for living women. But, if so, then this seems to be an unfair disparity.

Yet what gradually seemed even more apparent to me was the nature of the problems women face by virtue of their longer life. These are not on the whole the kinds of problems that high-technology, acute care medicine can effectively deal with anyway. The great need of elderly women is not for more open heart surgery, kidney dialysis, or expensive life-extending drugs. Although those will surely help some women, the great need *most* elderly women have is for decent primary care, preventive medicine, rehabilitation, and nursing and other forms of assistance for chronic disease and disability—and, above all, decent economic and social support. Actually, my original argument in *Setting Limits* was that while limits would be necessary on high-technology, acute care medicine, that loss should be compensated for by improved caring and welfare resources, aiming to enhance the quality of life rather than seeking to extend its length. While I did not take account of the potential discriminatory effect on women of the limits to be set on high-technology medicine, my alternative plan would, as it turns out, give women what I believe would in the end be most helpful to them.

Before spelling out just what kind of a policy might be most beneficial for elderly women, I need to confront the charge that a limit on high-technology medicine would affect women much more than men, and thus be discriminatory. At the least, such a policy would have a differential impact. But there are different ways we might interpret the meaning of that fact. One way is to limit our inspection strictly to the services women would not get, the high-technology medicine. But in that circumstance women would fail to get what dead males already fail to get as well; it is thus not as if women are being denied a benefit that men get. Men would fail to gain the benefit by virtue of dying before needing it, women by virtue of rationing. Those men who managed to live as long as women would be denied the same high-technology benefit as the surviving women. It is, then, under this interpretation, hard to see where women would be victims of discrimination.

Another possible interpretation would ask whether, over a lifetime, women denied high-technology treatment in their later years would end by receiving less health care than men. If so, that would clearly be discriminatory. But there is no reason to believe this would be the case if, up to the time of the age limit on high-technology treatment, men and women were eligible for, and generally got, the same amount of treatment. If not, then it would be necessary to reform health care to see that they got care at the *earlier* time of life when they needed it—not in the compensatory form of being excused from age limits later in life. In short, if the test is whether men and women receive the same amount of health care over a lifetime, then women who live longer than men would receive more, not less, care, hardly a discriminatory result. Only if women receive less health care than men prior to the age cutoff point, and then are subject to that cutoff point, could it be said they have been discriminated against. But, again, the solution to that problem is to bring them up to parity before the cutoff point. If that were done, then any care women received after the cutoff point beyond that which dead males receive—none—would give them a lifetime advantage over men.

Still another interpretation is possible. Perhaps because women live longer on average, their need for high-technology medicine will come later in life than the needs of men. Men, so to speak, avoid age-based rationing by dying earlier, but—just by virtue of dying earlier—they get the technology that will be denied to women. That surely would be an unfair outcome. But what is the proper response to such a possible outcome? Seemingly, the self-evident response would be to impose no age limit for women, thus balancing the books.

This, however, is a troubling solution. To be really fair it would also have to include a similar provision for those men who live longer than the average and who, like women, will have their acute care needs deferred to a later time in their (longer) life cycle. Yet by the time this policy move has been made, age-based rationing would have effectively been nullified as a possible way to ration health care: it would apply to no one. But could there not be a way out here? Why not simply set a later age cutoff date for women, compensating for their longer lives? That would surely be fairer, but there is a troubling hitch. That strategy could mean an overall worsening of the Medicare crisis, particularly if the costs of setting a later cutoff date for women added significantly to health care costs. Since it is the young who will pay these added costs, not the elderly women themselves, then one unfairness (the excessive burden on the young, including, of course, young tax-paying women) would be created to relieve another (the discrimination against elderly women).

I find myself a bit stymied at this point, unclear in my own mind whether (a) age-based rationing would be discriminatory against women (yes, possibly), and (b) whether it would be unreasonably and offensively discriminatory (no, not necessarily). Fortunately, we probably have at least another decade to debate the matter. No politician in the next few years will propose age-based rationing, much less rationing with even a hint of possible discrimination against women. The more important question is this: If care must be rationed, what is the most important kind of care that women need?

One way of answering that question would be to let women make their own choice, putting the limited Medicare resources into acute care medicine if death was their greatest fear, or into forms of care that would provide benefits focused on the quality of life rather than its length if that is what they most wanted. A project that attempted to discern how people (men and women) would respond to that kind of choice—labeled "Medichoice" by its originators—unfortunately failed because of the difficulty of evaluating the meaning of hypothetical choices.[7] Only a real-life experiment would, it was determined, work to discern the truth and that was not possible to carry out. In any event, I surmise that elderly women are far more concerned about those conditions of old age that affect the quality of that old age than they are about the length of life (even though there is a bit of intriguing evidence to the contrary).

Providing the Needed Benefits

What I would like to lay out here is a cluster of health care benefits to be provided to both men and women, the net effect of which would be to improve the overall health prospects of women (and men too) while allow-ing for, if not an age limit per se, a limitation on expensive, high-technol-ogy, acute care innovations. This proposal is meant to compensate for just those features of the present health and welfare system that seem most harmful to women. The cluster of benefits I propose has four elements: a closer link between health and welfare benefits; greater support for home care and long-term institutional care; greater support for chronic disease and disability; and an effort to create what I call a "sustainable medicine."

Health and Welfare Benefits

Poverty or near-poverty is a serious problem for elderly women, and even those comparatively well off can be impoverished by lengthy longev-ity increases; and even if they are lucky and manage to hold on to their resources, fear of losing them can itself be a source of misery. The only real solution to this problem is both an increased Social Security income for all the elderly and a more generous set of Medicare reimbursements to reduce the need for out-of-pocket expenditures on otherwise expensive illnesses. The earlier-mentioned figure showing that elderly people who live in pov-erty spend on average 35 percent of their income on health care tells a dreadful story. Even those who begin their old age comparatively well off can find their resources depleted by their mid-eighties, a time when health care costs can rise rapidly. The well-known positive correlation between income and good health points directly to the potential health benefits of higher Social Security payments, and the gains to be had from better Medi-care reimbursement for all but acute care medicine are self-evident.

Greater Support for Long-Term and Home Care

The fact that large numbers of women end their lives living alone or dependent upon the help of family members or friends underscores the need for decent long-term and home care. All things being equal, elderly women prefer to remain independent, in their own homes. But to do this as long as possible can require assistance, particularly after age 85. Depen-dence upon unpaid family assistance, usually provided by females, can be a burden not only on the recipient of care but also on the person providing the care, who is well aware that a significant sacrifice may be necessary to provide the care—if not in money, then in time and emotional commit-ment. And sometimes, even under the best circumstances, long-term insti-tutional care is needed. That can now only be obtained by out-of-pocket expenditures of a most expensive kind, or by spending down one's assets to qualify for Medicaid assistance, itself often a humiliating experience. More money, then, is needed to allow the hiring of non-family members to provide necessary care at home, and to help avoid full-scale poverty as a route to institutional care.

IMPROVED CHRONIC DISEASE AND DISABILITY CARE

Chronic disease and disability will be the fate of the overwhelming majority of older women, much more so than men who live to a comparable age. By the age of 85, for instance, 50 percent of women will need assistance for what are called "activities of daily living," for example, bathing, walking, shopping, and the like. By the age of 75 nearly every elderly woman will have at least one, and on average two, disabilities or chronic conditions. But good disability and chronic disease care requires considerable medical patience—for cure is ordinarily not possible—and most of all one simple benefit: time to talk, to help patients cope with their situation and to help them move through a health care system poorly organized to integrate the range of care required by chronic disease. A persistent criticism of managed care, toward which the elderly are being pushed, has been its inept, disorganized response to chronic illness. In theory, managed care should be ideal to meet the multiple needs of the chronically ill, but in practice it has not worked out that way. Rehabilitation is another important need of elderly women, who are subject to a wide range of disabilities, many of which can be relieved by good rehabilitation programs. Such programs can be expensive and are not always conveniently available—an obvious area for reform and improvement.

SUSTAINABLE MEDICINE

All of the reforms I have so far proposed have two features in common: they would increase the costs of health care and they focus on improving the quality of life of elderly women rather than lengthening that life or aiming to cure the diseases of old age. As matters now stand, that combination flies in the face of the present priorities in health care for the elderly, where the emphasis is on cutting costs or holding down cost increases, on the one hand, and giving priority to acute, life-extending medicine, on the other. Since it is most unlikely in the decades ahead that there will be much impetus to increase spending beyond the rate of general inflation, the most imperative need is to shift resources from the acute care sector and put it into the areas I have noted. Since rationing of something will be necessary, I believe it must and can only come from a diminishment of high-technology medicine. We need what I have elsewhere called a "sustainable medicine," by which I mean a medicine that presses toward a steady-state use of technology, an emphasis upon population rather than individual health, and a medicine that is equitably available to all.[8] A medicine that aims for constant and unlimited medical progress and unlimited technological innovation cannot serve the needs of the elderly in the future, men or women, but especially women.

Prevention and Population Health

I contended at the outset of this chapter that it would not be easily possible or fair to take steps that would aim to improve the health outcomes of elderly women only. While there is no doubt that elderly women have in general greater disabilities than men, many men—those who survive as long as women—can have an equally great burden of illness. Hence, to benefit one sex unilaterally while ignoring another unilaterally would surely result in unjust results in many cases. Moreover, if both sexes could be helped by the same policy—of a kind I am proposing here—that would surely seem a more satisfactory outcome.

The problem for both sexes in this country is that we are buying improved health at too high a general price. The Medicare emphasis on acute care medicine drives up the cost of health care, produces a comparatively poor outcome per dollar spent, and ends by limiting social and health care resources to those who have remained alive into old age—those women for whom the triumphs of medicine may have kept alive long enough to spend more time living with the sickness that longer life brings them. The only way out of this trap is by taking two related steps. The first is to have a health care system that emphasizes public health, and health promotion and disease prevention, from the beginning of life (limiting acute care medicine if necessary to establish that priority) right through old age. The second is to limit acute care benefits in order that the released money be spent on caring for the socioeconomic as well as the chronic illness and disability burdens of women in old age. A policy of this sort could decrease the disparity in life expectancy between men and women (improving it for men while not decreasing it for women), possibly increase the average life expectancy of both sexes, and help those who reach old age live to experience a lessened burden of disability and chronic disease. The evidence is overwhelming that it is not the availability of medical care that makes the most difference in health status (though it surely makes some difference) but rather the combination of socioeconomic benefits and of public health benefits. That is true for both women and men.[9]

Notes

1. Marilyn Moon, Barbara Gage, and Alison Evans, *An Examination of Key Medicare Provisions in the Balanced Budget Act of 1997* (New York: Commonwealth Fund, 1997).

2. *Bipartisan Commission on Entitlement and Tax Reform* (Washington, D.C.: U.S. Government Printing Office, 1995); Committee on Ways and Means, U.S. House of Representatives, *Medicare and Health Care Chartbook* (Washington, D.C.: U.S. Government Printing Office, 1997).

3. Marcia Angell, "Fixing Medicare," *New England Journal of Medicine* 337, no. 3 (July 17, 1997): 192–94; Stuart H. Altman, Uwe Reinhardt, and David Schactman, eds., *Policy Options for Reforming the Medicare Program* (Princeton: Robert Wood Johnson Foundation, July 1997).

4. J. C. Henrad, "Cultural Problems of Aging Especially Regarding Gender and Intergenerational Equity," *Social Science and Medicine* 43, no. 5 (1996); Jacqueline A. Horton, ed., *The Women's Health Data Book* (Washington, D.C.: Jacobs Institute of Women's Health [Elsevier], 1995), especially 129–51; Sara Arber and Jay Ginn, *Gender and Later Life: A Sociological Analysis of Resources and Constraints* (London: Sage, 1991), 107–28.

5. Daniel Callahan, *Setting Limits: Medical Goals in an Aging Society* (New York: Simon & Schuster, 1987).

6. See especially Nancy S. Jecker, "Age-Based Rationing and Women," *Journal of the American Medical Association* 226, no. 21 (December 4, 1991): 3012–15.

7. Joanne Lynn, personal communication, 1995; see also Marion Danis et al., "Older Medicare Enrollees' Choices for Insured Services," *Journal of the American Geriatric Society* 45, no. 6 (June 1997): 688–94.

8. Daniel Callahan, *False Hopes: Why America's Quest for Perfect Health Is a Recipe for Failure* (New York: Simon & Schuster, 1998).

9. Robert G. Evans, Morris L. Bauer, and Theodore R. Marmor, eds., *Why Are Some People Healthy and Others Not?* (New York: Aldine DeGruyter, 1995).

· *Part Four* ·

Living Arrangements

· *12* ·

Aging Fairly: Feminist and Disability Perspectives on Intergenerational Justice

Anita Silvers

From the *San Francisco Chronicle*: As the world's population grows steadily older, leading specialists in aging predicted here this month that science will find ways to mitigate the ravages of age in time to help today's graying Baby Boomers.[1]

From the *New York Times*: When Herman and Annette Adelson moved to [a] retirement community 20 years ago, they were happy to pay extra for a condominium on the second floor. . . . There were no elevators, but who needed elevators? . . . But that was another life, when the Adelsons were in their 60's. Today those same stairs—14 concrete steps—loom as an insurmountable obstacle. Now Mrs. Adelson, who is 83, has severe rheumatism [and] can negotiate the stairs only painfully, going down backward with the help of her 85-year-old husband. And she does so only once a week. . . . [The secretary of the Florida Department of Elderly Affairs] said: "There is no money for elevators. What do you do? Do you . . . call out the National Guard to move these people up and down the steps? We didn't think ahead."[2]

How to delay the deterioration of biological functioning usually is thought to be the central problem associated with aging. An equally important matter, but one that has attracted considerably less notice, is how to alter the environment to allow people to retain social function and thereby to flourish, even after their biological functioning has declined. Making the environment more hospitable to people whose physical or cognitive performing has diminished is a less explored approach to mitigating the ravages of age. To explore this alternative to resolving what makes growing old so problematic in our culture, I will examine, and extrapolate from, the proposal that biological decline plays much less of a role than is commonly imagined in the marginalization of old people.

Prominent in the theoretical framework needed to further this discussion are strands of thinking drawn from the emancipatory analyses promoted in contemporary feminist and disability studies. The demographics of the elderly call out for insights developed in these fields. For, first of all, it is well known that the proportion of women to men increases in older populations. Moreover, the noninstitutionalized population over 65 contains three times as many people with disabilities as the population of younger adults.[3] These facts suggest that perspectives drawn from contemporary gender and disability theory may benefit our thinking about becoming elderly.

From these perspectives, the conversation advances by considering how our usual way of thinking about being elderly shapes our moral responses to the oldest old. Characterizing the elderly as a weak class is a familiar feature of social welfare policy, but this social construction has an historical association with oppressiveness. Perceiving individuals as members of a weak class validates the social practices that constrict their opportunities for connectedness. These practices are informed by the belief that the physical, sensory, and cognitive differences attendant on aging signal biological inferiority. Thus, such practices create an environment of social disregard for elderly adults. It is an environment hostile to anyone for whom climbing stairs, reading small print, hearing announcements, or remembering names has become quite difficult.

Such discriminatory and debilitating practices contribute to an environment in which intergenerational reciprocity becomes hard to sustain. In the absence of reciprocity, elderly and young people do not relate as partners in a mutually experienced moral space. (Hilde Lindemann Nelson offers a different, but compatible, account of the construction of moral space in chapter 5 in this volume.) Instead, they become like partisans in an intergenerational conflict between the interests of the debilitated elderly who are in the declining years of their life span, and those of dynamic young people who are at an ascending stage of their life career. At best, the usual way of conceptualizing how old age relates to youth makes the achievement of intergenerational justice appear very arduous.

Though too brief to explore the issue with appropriate thoroughness, my discussion in this chapter questions the common assumption that social justice authorizes disparate treatment of people who are at different stages of the life span.[4] Granted that moral responsiveness must respect differences of situation and context, I nevertheless am suspicious of approaches that attribute enormous difference to, and consequently focus moral relevance on, an individual's being in the latter stages of her life's career. My hesitation here draws upon Joan Tronto's thoughtful caution that focusing on the contextuality imposed by our familiar ways of relating to one another can impede "critical reflection on whether those relationships are good, healthy, or worthy of preservation."[5] As will become evident, my concern acknowledges the differences between being elderly and being young, but is impelled by the conviction that adopting the "life's stages" model does not facilitate aging fairly. (See Margaret Walker's chapter 6 in this volume for a different, and very illuminating, analysis of the drawbacks of the "life as a career" model.) This model impedes our reshaping social practice so as to cultivate the kind of reciprocity intergenerational justice requires young and old to share.

I. Socially Constructed Weakness

Women as a group; people with physical, sensory, and cognitive impairments, taken collectively; and people who are classified as elderly all experience marginalization because their physical and cognitive styles of performance differ from those of the socially dominant group, namely, youngish males. The story of how women's physical and cognitive differences were constructed as deficits is familiar. It is worth retelling, however, because it demonstrates how we rationalize the imposition of social limitation when we construe such differences as signifying weaknesses and thus as occasioning special needs.

During the nineteenth century, the social participation of women was systematically constricted. Such limitations were justified by characterizing women as belonging to a group of persons whom nature made too weak and intellectually deficient, too physically and morally frail, to head households reliably and execute business successfully. Women were assigned a group identity that placed them on the defensive because it marked group members as incompetent. Regardless of their personal capabilities, women were disabled from voting, owning property, and obtaining custody of their children because they belonged to a class that had been constructed as being weak. (People with certain kinds of physical and cognitive impairments were similarly disabled: for instance, deaf people also could not own property, and, to this day, being deaf increases parents' risk that the state will remove their children from their home.)

Susan Sherwin describes how medicalizing their differences contributed to women's disabilities.

The mid-nineteenth century brought . . . a new medical interest . . . to establish menstruation as disability that demands rest and withdrawal from ordinary activities. . . . By the end of the century physicians were in the forefront of the campaign to . . . restrict women's participation . . . the prevailing . . . attitude was that menstruation created invalids out of women and made them particularly unfit . . . no thought was given . . . to adapting the demands of the universities or the workplace to these supposed special needs of women.[6]

Women as a group thus were disabled as the outcome of a social process, one in which their being characterized as belonging to a physically and intellectually inferior class figured prominently in rationalizing their unfavorable legal treatment. Among the earliest targets of organized women's protests during the nineteenth century were laws specifying that to be a woman was to have disabilities, namely, to be unable to exercise the full rights of community membership. Indeed, the Women's Disabilities Bill, debated in Parliament in the 1870s, addressed women's legal status rather than their physical or cognitive condition.

In general, Victorian social theory constricted the social participation of groups characterized as "weak" classes, those whose differences were assessed as originating in their inferior biology. Their roles were narrowly circumscribed, purportedly to protect them from social demands they could not satisfy and to protect society from their failures. Of the "weak" classes thus constructed, women constituted the largest, and the one whose members' activities had the most far-reaching effect on the fabric of everyday social life:

[Herbert] Spencer was not the only man of his time to fear that the price of rescuing women from their "natural" ignorance would be "a puny, enfeebled and sickly race." . . . Women's imputed physical and mental frailty thus became the grounds for refusing her any civil or legal rights, indeed any change from the "state of nature" in which she dwelt.[7]

The Victorian-era idea that certain groups of people are biologically frail and, consequently, that it is in their nature to be dependent remains influential today. It is preserved in rationales implicit in our welfare and social service systems. This idea is explicitly embedded in contemporary Swedish law, which counts the disabled, as well as children, the elderly, and immigrants, as "weak" groups with whose special protection local governments are charged.[8] Furthermore, public policy in many other nations, including the United States, implicitly theorizes "weak" classes to justify special policies and provisions whereby exemptions from responsibility and entitlement to benefits are offered putatively to compensate certain groups for their exclusions from the workplace and the public square.[9]

Initially, we might imagine the theorizing of "weak" classes to be an instrument of beneficent and protective public policy. But on reflection we will see that simply by being associated with a "weak" class, individuals are made out to be too vulnerable and fragile to be participating, contributing community members, regardless of their personal capabilities and competence. Individuals who are perceived as belonging to "weak" classes are expected to need greater than "normal" shares of resources, or to be burdensome in other ways, or to seek exemption from the usual rules and responsibilities because of their weaknesses. All these expectations easily become rationalizations for avoiding, excluding, and even for preventing or terminating the existence of such individuals.[10] As Joan Tronto remarks about our tendency to favor familiar ways of relating, "It is from such unreflective tastes . . . that hatred of differences can grow."[11]

To illustrate, both Sweden and the Netherlands, which provided officially designated weak classes with generous government benefits dating from the era directly following World War II, sterilized women who had physical anomalies (or family histories suggesting that they might give birth to anomalous children) well into the 1970s. Sterilization policies were thought to have the effect of reducing the number of individuals who otherwise would be eligible to have resources transferred to them because they were supposed to be too weak to be productive. Earlier, in the late 1930s, the Nazi regime appointed Dr. Karl Brandt to diagnose people with disabilities as incurable and to euthanize them. Brandt explained at Nuremberg that his actions were informed by "pity for the victim and out of a desire to free the family and loved ones from a lifetime of needless sacrifice."[12] For similar reasons, cultures that practice the termination of female fetuses or neonates rationalize doing so because women's lives are limited and insignificant in virtue of their being a "weak" class. These practices of preventing or terminating certain sorts of lives show vividly how dangerous it can be to belong to a group identified as especially needy and potentially burdensome.

During the present century, women have progressively liberated themselves from their former identification as members of a "weak" class. Nevertheless, having to conduct their lives in physical and social environments arranged to favor the physical and social preferences of youthfully vigorous men still disadvantages women, as it does people with physical, sensory, or cognitive impairments, and elderly people as well. Iris Young cites this source of oppression when she attributes limitations in women's physical activity to the coercion of a patriarchal social structure that cannot abide having women manifest full proficiency: "Women in sexist society are physically handicapped. Insofar as we learn to live out our existence in accordance with the definition that patriarchal culture assigns to us, we are physically inhibited, confined, positioned and objectified."[13]

Nor has our workplace practice fully advanced beyond imagining pregnancy—an element of the life plans of many women but of no men—to be a disability. For some employers, the prospect of a pregnant worker still induces the fears more familiarly evoked if ill or impaired employees are in question. Such a pretext for exclusion—namely, that an individual's fleshly functioning is disruptive because divergent from what is typical in the workplace—also is routinely invoked against people with physical or cognitive impairments, whose personal, civic, and commercial flourishing is chronically compromised by others' regarding their presence as unsuitable, inconvenient, and awkward. One of the most persuasive proponents of such practice is philosopher Allen Buchanan, who maintains that while some compromises with efficiency are required in the name of equal opportunity, those who flourish under our current system have a reasonable interest in promoting the most productive practices in which they themselves can participate effectively.[14]

Until relatively recently, a similar rationale—namely, the declining capability imagined to accompany the biological changes associated with old age—mandated the exclusion of older individuals from the workplace. In the not very distant past, women and old people were relegated to the space circumscribed by home and hearth, the former to the kitchen, the latter to the rocking chair. Social policy has identified "homemakers" and the "elderly" (along with children) as "non-wage-earning" populations, while serious impairment functions as a "discrete categorical workforce exemption for groups otherwise expected to participate in the labor market."[15]

Thus feminine gender and old age traditionally have been categorizations that disqualified individuals from workplace roles in order to confine them to homeplace roles. But contemporary feminist critique has left social philosophy conflicted about the personal value of workplace participation, with some writers assuming that productivity is a beneficial goal that should be equally achievable by women and men, and others repudiating it for being an exclusionary and burdensome male value. Suffused with ambivalence about how to value access to workplace roles, social philosophers have given little attention to the similarities of the social mechanisms for excluding people from the workplace on account of their gender, of their age, and of their being physically or cognitively impaired.

The practices that prevented women from working outside the home emphasized that their role was to devote their labor to their families. In contrast, being classified as being too impaired to remain in the workplace simply renders those so categorized as roleless. They are designated non-contributers. Our contemporary approach to aging prolongs this difference by bifurcating the ways of aging, contrasting the maintenance of vigor with withdrawal and decline. Elderly people who preserve productive family or community roles when they retire from the workplace are considered to be aging successfully, while being relegated to the rolelessness imposed by institutionalization is equated with failure. Jae Kennedy and Meredith Minkler observe that "a problematic consequence of this sort of dichotomy involves the potential for further stigmatization of older people with disabilities."[16]

II. Making People Vulnerable

Far from protecting vulnerable individuals, social systems that assign types of people to "weak" classes do so to keep them from the center of community interaction. The policies and programs that promote their dependence simultaneously preclude their compromising productivity or otherwise impeding the activities of the dominant majority. When interpreted as rendering them weak and needy, women's differences in physical and cognitive performance style were used to justify a system that limited their social participation. Disability studies scholars make similar points about how being cast in the "sick" role, or as a "weak" class, isolates people with physical, sensory, or cognitive impairments. Disability studies scholars Brian Lamb and Susan Layzell comment:

> Disabled people's . . . needs are rarely included in any . . . representation in everyday life. . . . This reinforces the public's attitudes and expectations toward disabled people as seeing them as "sick and sexless" rather than as participating in full sexual and family relationships.[17]

The result of consigning people with physical, sensory, or cognitive impairments to rolelessness is, as disability studies scholar Harlan Hahn describes it, to place their lives at the margin of social participation:

one of the most unpleasant features of the lifestyles of . . . disabled individuals . . . is the pervasive sense of physical and social isolation produced not only by the restrictions of the built environment but also by the aversive reactions of the nondisabled that often consign them to the role of distant friends or even mascots rather than to a more intimate status as peers, competitors, or mates.[18] . . . Few nondisabled individuals would tolerate the curtailments of individual options that become part of the daily experience of people with disabilities.[19]

In fact, however, there is an unmistakable resemblance in how women were condescended to a century ago, and how people with physical or cognitive impairments, whether or not they are elderly, are condescended to today. Victorian women experienced a comparable restriction of opportunity, and their social interaction was circumscribed in similar ways. Victorian men emphasized how both women and children were dependent on adult males for guidance and support. Writing about his blindness, British theologian John Hull describes a similar phenomenon, namely, how both good friends and strangers treat him as a child. Hull's physician friend, also impaired, is described as being similarly diminished by others' behavior to him: "when people see him in the wheelchair, they tend to speak to him in a gentle, slow and compassionate sort of voice. It is a kindly, condescending voice, the way some people speak to children. It is also the voice of uncertainty, people not knowing quite how to react in meeting an adult who has been 'cut down to size.' "[20] The paternalistic voice Hull and his physician friend reproach is also the voice we adopt to communicate with old people who have drifted from the center to the periphery of our customary forms of social engagement. To illustrate, in her memoir "Keeping Mother Going," Mary Anne Montgomery admonishes her mother as a parent might correct a child for carelessness:

> "Mother, your feet are dragging." . . . That foot-dragging dialogue had been played and replayed countless times. I began to feel like a nag. But the shuffling got on my nerves somehow—it seemed so lazy, and it made Mother seem even older than her eighty years.[21]

Of connections like that between Montgomery and her mother, Barbara Silverstone, coauthor of a family guide to dealing with the problems of aging parents,[22] observes:

> The reciprocal relationship between adult children and their adult parents has, unfortunately, been dubbed by some as a form of role reversal, par-

ticularly if the older person is very dependent on his or her children. This notion . . . is not only inaccurate but harmful to both generations. The . . . handicaps that sometimes accompany old age should not be confused with the behavior of a child. If aging parents are regarded as childlike, they can easily be treated as children, in turn, increasing their dependency and possibly undermining their self-esteem.[23]

Why some adults, the dominant ones, are permitted to treat other adults as if they are children is insufficiently well understood. Hull's account of how he is marginalized suggests that this problem may originate in a mismatch between the performance styles of individuals whose physical or cognitive functions are anomalous and the performance expectations embedded in common social practice:

> When I was sighted . . . I would seldom be alone for long. . . . When I had sight, of ten conversations . . . seven or eight would have been initiated by me. . . . All this has changed. I have to wait until someone approaches me, or I have to recognize the voice of someone I know. . . . These days, I often go into the bar, stand there . . . wondering whether anyone will speak to me. Often nobody does. The strange thing is that, as I am leaving . . . I am suddenly approached by all manner of people . . . concerned voices ask if I am all right. . . . The irony of it is that . . . I am besieged with offers of help which I don't need, while previously, when any offer of social converse would have been gladly accepted, I was left to myself.[24]

Roles marked by isolation, lack of social support and social networks, low social esteem, and concomitant feelings of powerlessness or purposelessness are the kind social scientists warn against perpetuating because the individuals assigned to them are highly exposed to psychosocial risk. Whoever has to live this way is liable to suffer adverse psychosocial effects that sooner or later debilitate them. Until they themselves grow old enough to encounter difficulty in commonplace social performances, few nondisabled people fully comprehend the degree to which the insecurity, social invisibility, and abandonment Hahn and Hull describe pervade the everyday lives of people with disabilities at all stages of life and regardless of their achievements.

Does aging per se invite assignment to a similar socially marginalized role? Carola Warren describes how people who become elderly are relegated to devalued roles:

> The social place of the individual alters with the passage of time—the stages of aging and with it the social self. At the center of this process is the body and its betrayals: the graying, wrinkling, sagging, weakening, and their . . . meanings. . . . Old age is biomedicalized, its symptoms treated . . . by physicians and nursing home attendants. . . . To ignore the long history of aging as change and decay, the betrayal of the body . . . is to fly in the face of the wisdom of generations past and those to come.[25]

It is important to recognize that neither growing years nor decreasing competence drives the social process Warren describes. For young, healthy, capable individuals are also subject to it, just in case their bodies meet with changes analogous to those Warren lists. Here is the story of a twenty-one-year-old who is similarly devalued:

> From the *New York Times*, August 1, 1996: Faruk Sabanovic, age 21, who was felled by a sniper on a street in central Sarajevo last year, must now use a wheelchair. "It's strange," said Mr. Sabanovic, a paraplegic who slaloms along the rutted sidewalks or down the streets, going about his business in his Quickie, a state-of-the-art, lightweight wheelchair. "I was walking normally like anybody else. A few days after I was wounded, I was meeting the same people, and they treated me differently. There's something in people's minds that makes them think because we are in wheelchairs we are weird."[26]

When elderly people become physically or cognitively impaired, those who know them best may be the individuals least prepared to adjust to altered modes of interaction. Thus, "Sarah" writes about her eighty-six-year-old mother:

> Mother did not want to live with us. . . . She had friends, she said, and she was not lonely. But the doctor was firm; she could not live alone. . . . This same lady who told me a year ago she was never lonely cannot bear to have me out of her sight, ever. She does not want to be alone. . . . This morning . . . my mother came into the room and announced that she was lonely and just wanted to sit with me. I am constantly interrupted. . . .[27]

Sarah's friends can resolve the problem because they continue to perceive her mother as a social participant:

> My friends said that Mother needed to get out, have some fun, go out to lunch once a week . . . a simple idea but one that had not occurred to

me. . . . Mother now has her hair shampooed and set every week. . . . She is . . . beginning to go to church again. . . . Mother loves [the adult day care program] and tells me about the picnic she had and about the trip.[28]

Kennedy and Minkler comment on our inclination to suppose that old age presents us with two options: successful, because healthy, aging that avoids functional limitation through exercise, diet, and appropriate medical care, or the more usual unsuccessful aging.[29] The Victorian-era notion that a "good and healthy/nondisabled old age" signifies having lived a righteous life has been transformed, as they note, into our contemporary decline-and-loss paradigm.[30] However, when gerontologists object to associating old age with disability by stressing "healthy" aging, "they wittingly or unwittingly help transfer fears about aging to disability."[31]

Older people themselves have come to believe that with the onset of impairment, "hope . . . about full participation in family and society must be abandoned so that all energy can be directed toward the ultimate defeat, which is not death but institutionalization."[32] In most circumstances, to be institutionalized is to lose one's capacity for self-determination and to become an object for other people, those whose profession is to administer care. To become such an object for others disrupts one's life and, as Kennedy and Minkler observe, "the sense of control we now know to be an important component of well-being across the life course."[33] Thus, our contemporary response to impairment is to reassign those who are in noticeable physical or intellectual deficit to an inferior social role that inherently weakens their claims on equality.

In this regard, Lawrence Becker notes that inequality distorts the norm of reciprocity so that its operation "systematically entrenches and deepens differentials of power."[34] And Hull argues in the same vein, observing that the fear of being made into a commodity—being an object for others to manipulate rather than a subject who engages with them on an equal footing—is an important source of the "immense despiritualization of contemporary life." I would add that disquiet about how we expect to experience old age contributes to the cultural malaise Hull describes. Hull thinks that social renewal will be possible only if we come to grips with "the great historic divisions of humanity into the weak and the strong, those in wealth and those in poverty, those in sickness and those in health."[35] Because such divisions embed significant inequalities in the fabric of social practice, they corrupt the processes whereby moral connectedness is furthered and moral community achieved. In what follows, I will invoke a disability perspective to identify practices constitutive of a social environment inherently unfair, and thereby hostile, to the oldest old.

III. A Disability Perspective on Decline

Central to having a disability perspective is the recognition that the division of humanity into strong and weak classes invites the building and organizing of environments hostile to people whose physical, sensory, or cognitive states are different from those of the dominant class. From a disability perspective, defective physical and social environments that are hostile to physical and cognitive difference produce disablement. In contrast, personal deficits are indeterminate in respect to disablement, for whether a person can perform basic activities of daily living such as toileting, bathing, dressing, and traveling has more to do with whether appropriately designed bathrooms, clothing, and transportation are available than with whether the person's physical movement is impaired. Disability studies scholar Liz Crow expresses this disability perspective when she writes:

> the social model of disability . . . gave me an understanding of my life . . . what I had always known, deep down, was confirmed. . . . It wasn't my body that was responsible for all my difficulties, it was external factors, the barriers constructed by the society in which I live.[36]

In *Declining to Decline: Cultural Combat and the Politics of Midlife*, Margaret Morganroth Gullette remarks that "the idea that we might escape being aged by culture is breathtaking."[37] But far from being trailblazing, this is simply a variation of the emancipatory idea of discarding traditions that relegate to the various "weak" classes individuals whose bodies differ too greatly from the standard young male body. Feminist theory has pioneered this account. The social model of disability, which frames American disability discrimination law, is similarly inspired by the idea that inequality is a manifestation of hostile social arrangements, not of inferior bodies or minds.

As a consequence, the 1990 Americans with Disabilities Act is thoroughly grounded in the belief that disability is socially constructed. American disability discrimination law presumes that a significant portion of the social limitation experienced by people with physical, sensory, or cognitive differences is attributable to the pervasive influence of false and biased theories about their competence and talent, theories instrumental in rationalizing social environments hostile to whoever is viewed as being impaired. Because it attributes the dysfunctions of individuals with physical, sensory, and cognitive impairments mainly to their being situated in hostilely built and organized environments, the social model of disability construes the isolation of people with disabilities (and by implication of elderly people as well) as the correctable product of how such individuals interact with stigmatizing social values and debilitating social arrangements rather than as the unavoidable outcome of their impairments.

Analyzing disability this way occurred as a result of crossovers from radical philosophy to the disability movement in Britain. Subsequently, American disability activists adopted the model because it both illuminated how they experienced their restrictions and gave a direction to social reform. In "The Politics of Disability," Joseph Stubbins writes: "The essence of disability is the social and economic consequences of being different from the majority."[38] To paraphrase Carola Warren, aging, and the associated potential for becoming seriously enough impaired to be identified as disabled, "belongs to all, not some of us."[39] Consequently, all of us have an interest in being especially energetic in resolving what Warren[40] describes, accurately in my opinion, as the "enduring cultural and personal ambivalence" toward "aging as change and decay, the betrayal of the body." Equally, we have a common interest in reforming whatever social practice we find to be contaminated by assumptions that an individual's impairment, whether associated with aging or introduced earlier in the person's life narrative, constitutes not a contrived but a natural reason for ignoring, rejecting, or discarding that person, or otherwise subjecting her to less favorable treatment.

With this in view, we may ask whether a cultural tradition that correlates reduced social opportunity with lesser levels of performances in activities like walking, viewing, listening, or remembering, a political tradition that tolerates such limitation, and the resultant isolation and fear, are not mainly accountable for the reduction of flexibility and hopefulness Sandra Bartky supposes, in chapter 4 in this volume, to be a concomitant of becoming aged. Considered in this light, it is evident that proposals rationalizing either exceedingly generous or markedly depleted allocation of resources based on impairment or on advanced age call for very careful scrutiny of their intergenerational fairness. For expanding social inclusiveness to embrace people with immensely diverse modes of physical and intellectual functioning calls first for greater thoughtfulness in our personal practice. Aggrandized allocation of funding for elderly people in our collective practice is no substitute for reforming individual practice because such programmatic growth does nothing to encourage reciprocity or improve intergenerational connectedness. As a society, we are just beginning to explore the degree to which the lowered quality of life associated, in our current circumstances, with aging and with disability is remediable by reforms in interpersonal practice—that is, in how we relate to one another individually rather than collectively.

There is great latitude for improvement here, according to the social model of disability. If our social practices exhibited a greater degree of fairness by equitably accommodating much greater variations in corporeal and cognitive performance than now is the case, people would not be forestalled from participating in reciprocal social interactions and thus would not find themselves roleless as they age, or so readily grow progressively or become precipitously dysfunctional. The neediness of disabled and elderly people is as much an artifact of social arrangements that ignore them as of intrinsic deficits that weaken them.

Deborah Stone believes that in our current social service system classes rather than individuals have a claim on social aid. This is because we have institutionalized caring so as to conceptualize it as the transfer of beneficial resources from stronger to weaker groups; categorizing these groups creates a boundary between the work system and the social service system.[41] Kennedy and Minkler argue that, although a compassionate agenda intended to create pensions and other entitlements for older people informs the decline-and-loss paradigm of old age, framing aging this way has meant that "the elderly were systematically devalued."[42]

To some extent, then, their opportunity to flourish is limited by interactive practices such as those decried by Hull and Hahn, practices that "other" whoever is regarded as physically, sensorily, or cognitively impaired. It is precisely the unreflective acquiescence in such practices that accounts for the way in which the two daughters quoted previously distance their mothers when they speak about them or to them. Social expectations that disregard the physical and cognitive performance styles of elderly people are inequitable. Special support programs do not compensate them for the undeserved loss of social recognition. Furthermore, if old and/or impaired individuals were better able to maintain their connectedness to other people and retain their participation in the central, and thereby centering, practices of community life, there would be considerably less occasion for them to consider themselves justified in claiming either exemptions from public responsibilities or compensation drawn from public resources. Parenthetically, acknowledging the injustice visited by a hostile social environment on people whose physical or cognitive performance differs from those of privileged, vigorous youth indicates that we must revisit proposals to ration health care and other goods inversely in relation to people's age. The usual defense of such proposals is that, having enjoyed a "full life" and their fair share of opportunity, older community members should defer to younger individuals who have not yet received as much. (See Daniel Callahan's chapter 11 in this volume.) Notice, however, how this argument premises that older people have experienced their previous lives under a fair social system with a level playing field. But suppose they have not?

Suppose that earlier social arrangements wrongly constricted their previous opportunities, as is likely to have been the case for older women, older people of color, and older people with disabilities. On the "fair life's share" argument, older persons who have been wronged as a result of their membership in groups misperceived as weak and incompetent now should be offered more opportunity than members of present and past dominant classes. For example, as women belong to a class disadvantaged by being considered, until very recently, to be incapable and dependent, and thereby to be unsuitable recipients of the full range of competitive opportunities, the "fair life's share" argument suggests that aged women be compensated by receiving greater support for actualizing their opportunities to flourish than is afforded to both young and old men. This curious corollary of the "fair life's share" argument occurs because the argument wrongly supposes human flourishing to be the product of distributive justice, that is, of the fair allocation of resources. From a disability perspective, however, it is less important to reallocate resources from supposedly stronger to theoretically weaker classes, and thereby to compensate marginalized elderly people with exemptions and entitlements, than to promote the equality and thereby the reciprocal connectedness of members of these classes by reshaping social practice.

IV. Interconnectedness, Interdependence, Injustice

So far, I have set the scene for remodeling social practice to better accommodate the changes age brings in physical and cognitive performance. I discussed an important ground on which traditional political morality has excluded people from full social participation because they are women, because they are disabled, and because they are old. What do these sad histories have in common? In each case, the marginalized group's difference has been medicalized. As a result, the inferior treatment each group endures has been defended as being the natural outcome of the biological inferiority that is wrongly imagined to characterize the group.

To advance the conversation, I reviewed how feminists condemn the medicalization of women's difference, and how disability studies scholars likewise reject the medical model of disability. Similar considerations suggest that we are misled when we think of aging primarily as a condition of deteriorating biology. A more useful way of conceptualizing aging is as a progressive mismatch between individuals and our social expectations of them.

Biological and social models problematize aging very differently. The biological framework presumes that the process of aging naturally disqualifies people from fully engaging in social participation and contributing to their communities. How to cope with older people's neediness seems to be the most pressing policy issue when aging is thought about in this way.

In contrast, the social model's framework portrays exclusion due to aging as the artificial result of arrangements that advantage youth over age. When policy is viewed from such a perspective, there is no presumption that aging creates any special needs. There are, however, policy issues about whether prevailing social practice is equitably responsive to aging people's ordinary needs. Consequently, it makes sense to ask which idealizations of social participation facilitate older persons' flourishing, and which, instead, exacerbate the mismatch between older individuals and the socially constructed environment?

To pursue this question, I now consider whether certain influential models of moral connectedness are helpful in addressing gender- and disability-related inequities that are aggravated by aging. In particular, I explore whether ideals that celebrate interdependence cohere with, or instead challenge, ideals that elevate autonomy, and whether the conduct these values promote is fairly responsive to aging women.

Because caregivers and recipients are interdependent, Susan Wendell rightly argues, their interactions should be supported by a reciprocity that is a morally important guide or ideal.[43] Kennedy and Minkler echo this view: "Of at least equal importance is movement toward a moral economy of interdependence, which moves beyond narrow conceptualizations of needs, rights, and entitlements, to focus instead on a broad vision of reciprocity."[44] But how people with physical, sensory, or cognitive impairments can reciprocally relate to "normal" people, that is, to the dominant social group, is a crucial part of the puzzle in respect to their attaining the "connectedness" characteristic of moral bonding.

Lawrence Becker warns that "reciprocal exchanges between unequals tend to increase . . . inequality and to drive the disadvantaged toward forms of reciprocation that involve subservience."[45] However, Wendell seems unconcerned about (in)equality. Maintaining reciprocating connectedness does not depend on all parties contributing equally to the relationship, she observes.

Reciprocity is the practice of returning like for like, although what is given and returned need not be material or emotional support. For reciprocity may be secured by being accepting of, reliant on, and empathetic with each other. Similarly, Annette Baier considers reciprocal feeling for one another to be the mutuality of exposure to risk—for instance, the sharing of shame if one fails the other, or the mutual loss of independent judgment and decrease in self-reliant conduct—the giving of one's self as a virtual hostage to the other.[46] For Baier, inequality—manifested as dependence—promotes rather than impedes reciprocal feeling. On views like Wendell's and Baier's, reciprocity is achieved by giving up self-control in order to share the feeling of mutually experienced dependence.

But standardizing what persons should feel not only for, but with, one another excludes, for example, people with autism and people with certain cognitive deficits such as those characteristic of certain forms of senile dementia. These are individuals whose impairment lies in their being unable to empathize, trust, and thereby rely on others. Furthermore, we must consider the larger number of persons with impairments who, being subjected to a social environment hostile to, unreliable for, or dismissive of individuals like themselves, are forestalled from enjoying reciprocal personal or social relations of the character that establishes participants as interdependent persons.

Interdependence is an integral part of human life. But if magnified into a regulatory social ideal, interdependence elevates heteronomy over autonomy. Imagining that they speak on behalf of the powerless and disabled, some commentators approve this shift. They are persuaded, for instance, that serious impairment precludes autonomy. If this were so, social arrangements governed by the ideals of self-determination and personal control would disadvantage people with disabilities and aged people just because, more than most people, the elderly and the disabled seem to need others' help. So, for instance, in chapter 6 in this volume Margaret Walker proposes that "the career self was never an option for many people whose lives did not offer substantial promise of successful self-control . . . [such as the] seriously disabled."[47]

But impairment does not preclude autonomy, any more than impairment prevents productivity. There are individuals with impairments who flourish in careers one would think impossible in view of their impairments: deafness does not bar the performance of classical music, as the percussionist Evelyn Glennie demonstrates, nor does blindness forestall an outstanding scientific career, as shown by the paleontologist Gerrit Vermaaj, nor did being a wheelchair user prevent journalist John Hockenberry from reporting from the battlefields of war. These self-reliant individuals are sometimes supposed by the nondisabled world to be models to whose achievements all similarly impaired individuals should also aspire. Consequently, many disability activists reject them as aberrations. So it is important to emphasize that their careers should not be thought prototypical of people with impairments. Rather, their examples demonstrate the contingency of the ties between having a normal or prototypical American life and achieving self-control.

Because examples like these magnify the attractiveness of self-reliance over interdependence, Wendell fears that their influence will be the deprecation and dismissal of whoever needs help from other people.[48] This is also an exaggeration, I think. Even the most unsociable among us relies unhesitatingly on the products or the good offices, if not the charity, of others. We are so dependent on others for the transactions of ordinary life that it would be unrealistic to dismiss interdependence. Nor, in approving of self-reliance, does our culture celebrate solitariness.

Far from it. We are such devoted admirers of connectedness that we pity the aged and the disabled just because of their isolation. Acknowledging the premium we place on connectedness returns us to the question of how to reform social arrangements hostile to people whose corporeal or cognitive functioning is impaired so as to facilitate their mutuality with other people. To do so, we need to be much clearer about what values would impel such a change.

V. Refashioning Reciprocity

Kant writes, in *The Metaphysics of Morals: Metaphysical First Principles of the Doctrine of Virtue*, that "one cannot, by any repayment of a kindness received, rid oneself of the obligation for it, since the recipient can never win away from the benefactor his priority of merit, namely having been the first in benevolence." To forbear from placing others in an inferior position, Kant therefore advises the benefactor to "show that he is himself put under the obligation by the other's acceptance or honored by it."[49]

Kant's observation reminds us that drawing individuals into a mutual moral space requires engaging in social practices that maintain reciprocity between them regardless of how needy one is for assistance by the other. But, as feminist disability studies scholar Jenny Morris notes in assessing current social arrangements:

> it is the loss of reciprocity which brings about inequality within a relationship—and disabled and older people are very vulnerable within the unequal relationships which they commonly experience with the non-disabled world. . . . Very little attention has been paid to disabled and older people's experience of physical and emotional abuse within caring relationships.[50]

To comprehend the importance of reciprocity for moral connectedness, we should notice how broad a role it plays in our techniques for structuring relationships in which very dissimilar people can be mutually and comparably engaged. Social spaces that partition humanity into the weak and the strong—those who can't lift one hundred pounds and those who can, those who can't climb stairs and those who can, those who don't see faces or hear voices clearly and those who do—are not congruent with moral spaces that maintain reciprocity between people who are physically or cognitively less dexterous than is common and those who perform in the fashion common to the dominant group. This observation returns us to the problem with which we began: how to refashion our social environment so as to allow people to retain social function although some aspects of their biological function have declined. We have seen that an important dimension of the problem originates from assigning such people to membership in a "weak" social class, which attenuates their claims on social participation. It now is time to consider the result of distancing the individuals so classified: namely, embracing interactive practices unsuited to their styles and levels of performance in the erroneous belief that these ways of relating to each other are natural, optimally efficient, or otherwise justified.

To illustrate, John Hull analyzes the isolation his blindness occasions by explaining that "the main point about (sighted people's relationship to the blind) is its lack of reciprocity."[51] For a sighted person, others in a room are co-present in the visual field; a blind person hears them serially and must "make a mental note of who is at a meeting, and a conscious effort of memory all the time."[52] The occasions for connectedness "become meager," Hull says, because:

> a common deterioration of mutuality takes place when a blind . . . person believes . . . they are in a face-to-face situation but in fact you, the sighted one, are looking out of the window.[53]

Furthermore, the convention that interlocutors communicate through body language as well as speech curbs the connectedness seeing and non-seeing colleagues can achieve with one another. Hull explains:

> There is . . . an anticipation, a sort of witness beforehand, which greatly enriches the mutuality of the experiences of sighted friends. The failure of the blind and the sighted to live in the same process of time becomes clear if we realize that this mirroring, this mutual witnessing, is diminished . . . the mere fact that blind and sighted people cannot watch things together . . . deprives them of a major field of togetherness.[54]

As Hull points out, practices that place individuals under different constraints within a relationship, so that one may be in the presence of the other but not attend to the other, impede recognition of the mutuality of our positions and devastate reciprocity. "It is thus more difficult to establish that blind and sighted people really share the same social and emotional time and space," he comments.[55]

More generally, in the absence of an equitable interpersonal environment, one facilitated by conventions that embrace rather than ignore considerable diversity in physical, sensory, and cognitive performance, it becomes problematic for people with and without impairments to fashion a common moral space within which to connect with one another. To understand this point gives pause to the uncritical acceptance of dialogical accounts of democratic morality, which make communicating with one another the crucial moral activity and the central component of human flourishing. We should not ignore the steep practical and personal prices that must be paid whenever interpersonal conventions intrinsic to establishing moral community are predicated on performances not all community members can execute and therefore are exclusionary.

For to condition moral participation (and the acknowledgment of accountability that pertains to it) on participants' being able to communicate in the manner commonly adopted by unimpaired individuals in mid-life span (that is, by those neither immature nor elderly) is to abstract from the particularities of real people to a privileging ideal. For instance, the fashion of organizing verbal communication by catching each other's eye disadvantages those whose sight is dimmed. Nor is this mode of regulating conversation natural, for by no means is it practiced universally across cultures. Nor would it be a hardship to discipline ourselves so as conventionally to supplement visual conversational cues by adding verbal ones (and to adopt more replete and direct conventional visual cues for those whose hearing is becoming less acute).

But why be impelled to refashion conversational convention (and other basic practices)? As Harry Moody argues in *Ethics in an Aging Society*, justice across generations requires intergenerational solidarity. But relationships between people of superior and inferior status can never secure the connectedness we require to thrive, however well intended the former take themselves to be to the latter. This means that proximate generations must cultivate the ability "to know one another directly . . . to influence one another, and, perhaps most important, to feel themselves part of a common world or way of life . . . that leads them to share common burdens and benefits and to preserve a common historical way of life."[56]

To enhance the personal connectedness of mothers and daughters as they both age and, as well, to maintain the intergenerational links that are a foundational component of social welfare policy, we would be well advised to review and reform the conventions that affect achieving intergenerational mutuality of experience. In this chapter, I have proposed that we reshape the physical environment and refashion interpersonal practice so as to facilitate mutuality in the capability of people with vastly different abilities to execute physical, sensory, and cognitive activities. Aging fairly, and avoiding decline, turns out to be as much a matter of altering our surroundings, our expectations, and our understandings at the present moment as of arresting or overcoming biological deterioration when our years are greatly advanced.

Notes

1. Richard Knox, "Science May Soon Take the Ache Out of Aging, Experts Say," *San Francisco Chronicle* (December 19, 1997), A1.

2. Sara Rimer, "New Needs for Retirement Complexes' Oldest: New Needs for Retirement Communities in Trying to Serve the 'Oldest Old,'" *New York Times* (March 23, 1998), A1, A14.

3. Jae Kennedy and Meredith Minkler, "Disability Theory and Public Policy: Implications for Critical Gerontology," in *Critical Gerontology: Perspectives from Political and Moral Economy*, ed. Meredith Minkler and Carroll L. Estes (Amityville, N.Y.: Baywood, 1998): 91–108, 91.

4. For a very good account of how this model affects discussions of intergenerational justice, see Harry Moody, *Ethics in an Aging Society* (Baltimore: Johns Hopkins University Press, 1992): 187–250. Moody identifies Norman Daniels, Daniel Callahan, Margaret Battin, Dan Brock, and Robert Veatch as bioethicists who assume this model and consequently agree that scarce resources should be withheld on the basis of age. Moody himself attempts—unsuccessfully, I think—to preserve the model but downplay this conclusion.

5. Joan Tronto, "Beyond Gender Difference," *Signs* 12, no. 4 (Summer 1987): 644–61, 660.

6. Susan Sherwin, *No Longer Patient* (Philadelphia: Temple University Press, 1992), 182.

7. Rosalind Miles, *A Woman's History of the World* (London: Michael Joseph, 1988), 187.

8. Gerben DeJong, *Independent Living & Disability Policy in the Netherlands: Three Models of Residential Care & Independent Living* (New York: World Rehabilitation Fund, 1984).

9. Anita Silvers, "Disability Rights," in *The Encyclopedia of Applied Ethics*, vol. I, ed. Ruth Chadwick (San Diego: Academic Press, 1997): 781–96. Also, Deborah Stone, *The Disabled State* (Philadelphia: Temple University Press, 1984); and Leo Aarts, Richard Burkhauser, and Philip DeJong, *Curing the Dutch Disease: An International Perspective on Disability Policy Reform* (Aldershot: Avebury, 1996). See also Nancy Fraser, *Unruly Practice: Power, Discourse, and Gender in Contemporary Social Theory* (Minneapolis: University of Minnesota Press, 1989), 149, for a similar analysis of contemporary social mechanisms of workforce exclusion.

10. To illustrate the pervasiveness of the consequences of being considered a weak class, consider why physicians have little information about the appropriate dosage of cancer medications for the elderly. It is because the elderly typically are omitted from clinical drug trials (as women have been omitted from trials of medications and surgical procedures for heart disease). A newspaper article on the subject states: "doctors are generally reluctant to recommend patients for cancer trials, which are perceived as too demanding for older people." That is, because they are perceived as a weak class, the elderly are "protected" from enduring the rigors that are necessary to gain promising cures. Lawrence K. Altman, "Treating Elderly's Cancers Is Frustrating Many Experts," *New York Times* (May 20, 1998), A1, A12.

11. Tronto, "Beyond Gender Difference," 660.

12. Jenny Morris, "Tyrannies of Perfection," *The New Internationalist* (July 1, 1992): 16–17.

13. Iris Marion Young, *Throwing Like a Girl and Other Essays in Feminist Philosophy and Social Theory* (Bloomington: Indiana University Press, 1990), 153.

14. Allen Buchanan, "Choosing Who Will Be Disabled: Genetic Intervention and the Morality of Inclusion," *Social Philosophy and Policy* 13, no. 2 (Summer 1996): 42.

15. Kennedy and Minkler, "Disability Theory and Public Policy," 91.

16. Kennedy and Minkler, "Disability Theory and Public Policy," 91.

17. Brian Lamb and Susan Layzell, *Disabled in Britain: A World Apart* (London: SCOPE, 1994), 21.

18. Harlan Hahn, "Civil Rights for Disabled Americans," in *Images of the Disabled, Disabling Images*, ed. Alan Gartner and Tom Joe (New York: Praeger, 1987), 181–204, 198.

19. Hahn, "Civil Rights for Disabled Americans," 193.

20. John Hull, *On Sight and Insight: A Journey into the World of Blindness* (Oxford: One World Publications, 1997), 95–96.

21. Mary Anne Montgomery, "Keeping Mother Going," in *Daughters of the Elderly*, ed. Jane Norris (Bloomington: Indiana University Press, 1988), 51–64, 51.

22. Barbara Silverstone and Helen Kandel Hyman, *You and Your Aging Parent: The Modern Family's Guide to Emotional, Physical, and Financial Problems* (New York: Pantheon, 1982).

23. Barbara Silverstone, in *Daughters of the Elderly*, ed. Norris, 104–9.

24. Hull, *On Sight and Insight*, 138–39.

25. Carola Warren, "Aging and Identity in Premodern Times," *Research on Aging* 20, no. 1 (January 1998): 11–35, 31–32.

26. Jane Perlez, "Bitter Burden on Sarajevo: Invalids of War: A City with a Legacy of Tolerance Finds It Hard to Help the War Wounded," *New York Times* (August 1, 1996), A5.

27. "Sarah, A New Crisis," in *Daughters of the Elderly*, ed. Norris, 3–9, 7.

28. "Sarah, New Crisis," in *Daughters of the Elderly*, ed. Norris, 8.

29. Kennedy and Minkler, "Disability Theory and Public Policy," 91.

30. Kennedy and Minkler, "Disability Theory and Public Policy," 102. See also W. Achenbaum, *Images of Old Age in America: 1770 to the Present* (Ann Arbor/Detroit: Institute of Gerontology, University of Michigan/Wayne State University, 1978).

31. Kennedy and Minkler, "Disability Theory and Public Policy," 101.

32. E. Cohen, "The Elderly Mystique: Constraints on the Autonomy of the Elderly with Disabilities," *Gerontologist* 28 (1988): 24–31, 25.

33. Kennedy and Minkler, "Disability Theory and Public Policy," 103.

34. Lawrence Becker, "Reciprocity," in *The Encyclopedia of Ethics*, ed. Lawrence Becker (New York: Garland, 1992): 1075–78, 1076.

35. Hull, *On Sight and Insight*, 233–34.

36. Liz Crow, "Including All Our Lives: Renewing the Social Model of Disability," in *Exploring the Divide: Illness and Disability*, ed. Colin Barnes and Geoff Mercer (Leeds: Disability Press, 1996), 55.

37. Margaret Morganroth Gullette, *Declining to Decline: Cultural Combat and the Politics of Midlife* (Charlotteville: University Press of Virginia, 1997), 18.

38. Joseph Stubbins, "The Politics of Disability," in *Attitudes toward Persons with Disabilities*, ed. Harold Yuker (New York: Springer, 1988), 22–32, 24.

39. Warren, "Aging and Identity," 32.

40. Warren, "Aging and Identity," 31–32.

41. Stone, *Disabled State*, passim.

42. Kennedy and Minkler, "Disability Theory and Public Policy," 102.

43. Susan Wendell, *The Rejected Body: Feminist Philosophical Reflections on Disability* (London: Routledge, 1996).

44. Kennedy and Minkler, "Disability Theory and Public Policy," 105.

45. Becker, "Reciprocity," 1075.

46. Cf. Annette Baier, *Moral Prejudices* (Cambridge: Harvard University Press, 1994), 34.

47. See chapter 6, this volume.

48. Susan Wendell, "Toward a Feminist Theory of Disability," *Hypatia* 4, no. 2 (Summer 1989).

49. Cf. Baier, *Moral Prejudices*, 190–91. See Immanuel Kant *The Metaphysics of Morals: Metaphysical First Principles of the Doctrine of Virtue*, tr. Mary Gregor (New York: Cambridge University Press, 1991), part 2, The Doctrine of Virtue, sec. 32 and sec. 31.

50. Jenny Morris, *Pride against Prejudice* (Philadelphia: New Society, 1991), 163–64.

51. Hull, *On Sight and Insight*, 107.

52. Hull, *On Sight and Insight*, 107.

53. Hull, *On Sight and Insight*, 107.

54. Hull, *On Sight and Insight*, 108.

55. Hull, *On Sight and Insight*, 107.

56. Harry Moody, *Ethics in an Aging Society* (Baltimore: Johns Hopkins Press, 1992), 231.

Home Care, Women, and Aging: A Case Study of Injustice

Martha Holstein

$\mathcal{H}$ome care provides a lens through which to view complex relationships between cultural assumptions, public policy, and private lives. These interactions result in practices that raise questions about care, justice, and welfare rights, the relationship of women (and other "informal" carers) to the state, complex meanings of autonomy, especially in conditions of dependency, and the gendered nature of work. Home care illuminates the gender and class injustices that are historically endemic to American social welfare policy.

Women who provide care to elderly people at home are profoundly affected by policy choices, with their generally unarticulated normative assumptions, and by cultural factors. Family caregivers, paid and unpaid, are overwhelmingly female. Wives, daughters, and daughters-in-law, who assume major responsibility for caregiving in the home, are rarely able to relinquish tasks they find onerous; they do not have the resources to purchase help while publicly funded benefits have strict—and low—income ceilings.[1] Paid aides, who are most often themselves economically and socially disadvantaged, generally earn minimum wages and rarely receive benefits; yet few have alternative opportunities to earn a livelihood. Predictably, the shortage of home care workers in many parts of the country will make it a ripe placement for "welfare-to-work" women. Thus, caregiving, rendered with or without pay, falls most heavily on lower-income women who often care for other low-income women. Caregiving's strong gender and class biases (which often map onto race) are rooted in the political and moral economy and the cultural values that have prevailed in American life.

Yet women who provide such care are also subjects of their own lives and so interpret and negotiate external claims in different ways. For this reason, understanding relationships among policy, culture, ideology, and personal biography can suggest how change might evolve. To see how and why certain patterns of responsibility have come to dominate thinking and action, while identifying locations for change, is a contribution that feminist work can make toward healing the world. By examining how structural and cultural forces occasion the inequalities that are so evident in home care, scholars and activists can challenge the status quo created by the dominant social, economic, and political system. We can ask if the often unexamined presuppositions of the system are anti-ethical.[2]

In this chapter, I will both describe and explain the path to the present—why and how women, especially low-income women, were placed in the situation of having to meet seemingly unlimited caregiving demands. The political and moral economy of aging provides the overarching conceptual framework while contemporary moral values, including the emphasis on autonomy, rights, independence, family, and privacy play vital supporting roles. I will suggest ways to think about caregiving that mitigate the disadvantages and isolation of younger and older women who already are often marginal in terms of income and social location. To do so, however, will require cultural, social, and policy shifts. It will require recognizing that caregiving, whether paid or unpaid, is not primarily the responsibility of women; reconceptualizing notions of dependence, independence, autonomy, and related terms; challenging current relationships among family, government, and the labor market that affect the social construction of caregiving;[3] redefining cultural norms; and dissociating caregiving from "social norms and power relations that contribute to women's subordinate status."[4]

Home As a "Site" of Care

Caregiving is essential if older people with mental or physical disabilities are to remain at home, where they clearly want to be, especially given the options available. Visit any nursing home and you will find that even patients seriously affected by dementing illnesses plead for home. Home has powerful emotional and symbolic meanings. It connotes family, security, comfort, treasured memories, and even "independence." If one is home, then one is not fully "sick."[5] Implicit norms about independence, autonomy, and productivity reinforce the lure of home. Infused with these values, older people resist encroaching dependencies that arise from chronic illness. Threats to biographical continuity, to dignity, and to a sense of worthiness and competence as adult men and women, become particularly difficult to remedy when popular cultural norms do not speak to dignity or autonomy within the context of dependency.

The operative language of "formal" home care elevates client autonomy, self-determination, and independence as central tenets and features of a powerful belief system. In this milieu, however, these words have a highly individualistic tone that makes it difficult to account for the relational aspects of autonomy that are writ graphically in conditions of dependency. Achieving autonomy or self-determination in common home care situations is inherently a social process—a fact that the language, articulated values, and practices of home care conceal. If autonomy's social and relational character is not accounted for in home care situations, then preserving the elder's autonomy, when he or she cannot manage alone, can negate the very same possibility for the caregiver. Important value conflicts and threats to the identity of both the giver and the receiver of care may emerge. Since respecting an elder's self-determined wish to stay at home may require many extra hands, often at a considerable cost, and since it is unlikely that public spending will increase, the one expandable component of that cost is the "informal" care provided by family members, especially women. Yet, what women do is not counted as a cost.

Staying at "home" may mean staying in someone else's home—one's daughter's or daughter-in-law's—where there are established routines with which the elder is unfamiliar and that he or she may interrupt. And the home, instead of being a place of security and privacy, becomes a "new healthcare marketplace that depends on self care and women's domestic work."[6] So the emotional connotations of home often exist in the realm of ideology or imagination rather than in the experienced world of the older person and her caregiver. In this way, home is often a site of contestation; a recent book by Arlie Hochschild suggests that people often work for long hours not because they must but rather because work is more pleasant, more fun than the demands of home.[7] Despite that common reality, older people find home to be a good place; it is where most of us seek comfort, refuge, and safety. The task, as I see it, is to discover how to support the sacred meanings of home in ways that neither harm nor trump all other social values. It may mean alternatives to home that we have not yet even imagined. When I return to this theme in the conclusion, I will suggest that we picture autonomy, but also responsibility and sacrifice, for care receivers and care givers, stereoscopically, so that their similar but not identical needs are within sight simultaneously.

Who Are the Caregivers?

The most common caregivers are spouses, but gender-neutral language masks an important gender distinction. Demography may not be destiny, but the longer lives of women and the relatively older ages of men at marriage mean that men have spouses to care for them while women are likely to be widows. Most seemingly objectivist accounts of home care lose sight of this particular genderized quality, that access to spouses as carers almost invariably depends on marital status. Most people who receive care at home from *nonspouses* are women.

Three-quarters of unpaid caregivers live with the care recipient, and the majority give care for an average of four hours a day. For some caregivers, their responsibilities at home equal that of a full-time job.[8] Such caregiving often lasts for years. Women represent 70 percent of all caregivers[9] and 77 percent of children giving care. Almost one-third of all caregivers of frail elderly persons are adult daughters; while sons also provide care, they generally assume instrumental and time-flexible tasks like paying bills or mowing the lawn. Daughters shoulder tasks that keep them on call 24 hours a day, with little or no assistance, while sons typically get help from their wives. Paid services may also be distributed unequally—men caring for elderly spouses or parents seem to obtain more paid in-home services than their female counterparts.[10] "The daughters of working-class elderly people are bearing the brunt of informal care in the community."[11] In practice, daughters reduce work, while men reduce caregiving, and as a result, daughters are more likely than sons to perceive caregiving as stressful. As I shall discuss below, other important consequences, particularly economic ones, flow from caregiving responsibilities, and these consequences also affect men and women unequally.

This picture belies the oft-quoted assumption that families abandon their elders. Families take care of their elders, often at great cost to themselves. Older people see their children or other relatives frequently, and that contact generally translates into assistance during times of crises.[12] As important, because the vast majority of older people manage quite well on their own, many also provide personal help and financial support to their children and grandchildren. In the occasionally rancorous and politicized debate about "intergenerational equity" it is easy to lose sight of the two-way nature of support. The invisibility of elder-to-younger care, once again, has to do with the distinction between public and private. Social Security and Medicare are visible intergenerational transfers of public resources; grandparents paying for the grandchildren's summer camp or providing regular child care are private and hence unseen. This fact suggests the dangers of forcing a false division between public and private. When the media and other commentators blame the old for their putative greed, they are ignoring their very real contributions, albeit in the private sphere.

In yet another way, it is easy to forget how elders, even those with seriously disabling conditions, try not to burden their children or grandchildren, often endangering themselves in the process. Translating cultural messages about independence into their own lives, older women are often reluctant to ask for the help they might need. Older women, for example, seek to "conform to the cultural injunction . . . that they do not impose burdens on their children . . . [they] wish to behave in accordance with norms of self-reliance and individualism."[13]

Making Connections: The Public, Private, Political, and Personal

Public policy seeks to "balance the responsibility of individuals, families, and the state" in meeting human needs.[14] While it rests on normative assumptions—how society should be ordered, what values ought to be enhanced, who owes what to whom—these are seldom articulated. But even if stated, these assumptions rarely move beyond platitudes—quite a contrast to their powerfully felt effects. For most of American history, what has become late-twentieth-century rhetoric was reality—government was small and provided few services to anyone. Necessarily, the balance of responsibility rested with individuals and families; this balance made home the taken-for-granted site of care for the ill, the frail, and the dying, but also for those just coming into the world. With few alternatives, women, often joined in unspoken bonds of mutual assistance, were central participants in these fundamental dramas of human life.[15]

Today, despite the exponential growth in medical and even social services, women still perform home care services. Considered as essentially domestic labor, the reality of hands-on, long-term homemaker services matches neither the postacute model that Medicare supports nor the strong ethos of self-care and familism that historically has interpreted public charity as both demoralizing and a largely mythical excuse for families to relinquish their responsibilities. To the legislators and administrators who designed Medicare (enacted in 1965), social services for a dependent population seemed a luxury. Who, some legislators asked, would not like to have his bed made or his meals prepared?[16] Ironically, one suspects that these skeptical legislators neither made their own beds nor prepared their own meals. The invisible work that contributes to and creates the conditions of privilege is largely ignored, unexamined, and undervalued. The norm supporting such a policy choice seems quite clear—someone will (should) be available to cook, clean, and so on, for people unable to do it for themselves, and therefore such caregiving responsibilities, with few exceptions, are not a public responsibility.

Hands-on supportive services were thus left to the residual "welfare," or needs-based, sector of the welfare state. As such they carried the historical baggage associated with notions of deservingness, as defined by the culturally elite, and paternalism. Rarely asking potential or current beneficiaries to define their needs,[17] the designers of welfare programs assume that need is fundamentally apolitical, objective, and easily ascertainable through responses to questions on a standard needs-assessment form or through simple analysis of what interventions would benefit a client. Foucault, in contrast, calls attention to need as a "political instrument, meticulously prepared, calculated, and used."[18] Whoever gets to define some condition as a need also defines the remedy proposed. This permits the enclaving of certain needs so that they never enter the political sphere. The late philosopher Judith Shklar put it boldly: If one is not asked about how one feels about the arrangements that control one's life, one is reduced to a zero.[19] Taking this welfare state mentality to task, Michael Ignatieff, in his elegant and moving meditation on human need, reminds us that "it is because money cannot buy the human gestures which confer respect, nor rights guarantee them as entitlements, that any decent society requires a public discourse about the needs of the human person."[20]

Welfare benefits also lack the seemingly invincible status (at least until recently) of a program like Social Security, an "earned" benefit closely linked to "productive" employment, that is, a worthy activity in the public sphere. In the moral economy, services provided at home—presumably unskilled and domesticated in nature—are not something that society "owes" to its oldest members and their families as we "owe" retirement benefits, via Social Security, to those who contributed to the nation's economic productivity. Reassurance that one will be cared for so as not to burden one's children too greatly and that one's dignity will be honored despite dependencies is not, in the contemporary moral economy, a social obligation, that is, a burden that the prevailing market economy ought to assume. The moral limits on a market economy, historically envisioned as a constraint to exploitation and oppression, are today quite narrow. This parsimony translates into a long-term care policy grounded in free care provided by women. The generally marginal social and economic status of older women in our society compounds the problem. They rarely have the power to speak authoritatively about the issues that affect their lives. It is in this arena that public home care has had to carve out its acceptable place.

Operationally, this approach to long-term care policy disadvantages women economically both in the short and long term. Spouses providing care often must use up accumulated savings and other resources at a time in their own lives when they have little or no ability to recoup; yet the government does not calculate the actual out-of-pocket costs of such caregiving when it calculates overall costs. Caregiving also harms women's economic future. The work–retirement system currently in place rests on male models. Many older women do not have the consecutive work histories or jobs that offer retirement benefits, conditions that make the system work for men. Caregiving women either reduce the hours they work for pay, rearrange their work schedules, take time off without pay (the option available to them under the Family and Maternal Leave Act of 1993), or quit their jobs to resolve conflicts between work and caregiving. "Women who take early retirement or otherwise modify their employment to provide care not only lose wages and wage-related benefits, but also jeopardize their own sources of income for their later years."[21] Social Security benefits, private pensions, and the opportunity to accrue retirement savings, for example, are negatively affected by the "drop-out" years when women earn no income and receive no Social Security credits. The work that women do at home, whether for children, spouses, or elderly family members, is a public good, often supportive of economic growth. But rather than also bringing her economic benefits, it has a negative affect. This factor rarely receives attention outside of feminist circles. Productivity, long associated with a paycheck, ignores the productive roles that women, including elderly women, play in supporting the publicly valued productivity of others.[22]

In the last quarter century, hospital cost-containment efforts, supported by renewed ideological commitments to traditional gender roles and a vigorous preference for private rather than public provision of services, accelerated demands on unpaid women caregivers.[23] Since the introduction of Diagnostic Related Groups (DRGs) in the mid-1980s, for example, women increased by twenty-one million days the amount of care they provided. "The sandwich generation of women of all ages are being asked to make great sacrifices of their own time, employment, income, and health to achieve . . . *cost savings* for the government."[24] For policymakers, whose primary interest was cutting government expenditures, caregiving by families was a bonanza—it simultaneously saved money and supported traditional "family values." The women who would provide the bulk of care to patients discharged from hospitals in the subacute phase of an illness had few advocates with power to shape public action, a graphic example of how the distribution of power betokens the actual distribution of resources.

In the 1990s, legislative action in the area of home care increased. Initially Medicaid waiver programs gave states new options. Some states responded with their own community care programs for poor elders who cannot bathe, or dress, or cook, or shop. While the primary goal was cost containment, the language of choice and the humanitarian end of keeping people out of nursing homes supported program development. As a result, many states now screen patients before admitting them to nursing homes and offer an array of services to allow them to stay at home. As with other publicly funded programs, these community care options are struggling to provide as much care as possible to as many people as possible with limited resources. Agencies are thus grappling with timeless questions—breadth versus depth of services and how to use the informal caregiver.

In some states and in some situations, consumer-directed care allows lower-income older adults to hire family members as their caregivers. While not relieving the intensity of the caregiving experience, this option eases somewhat the financial hardships that often result when women leave the workforce to provide care. The low pay attached to home care services, however, hardly remedies the loss of income from most other jobs. Paying relatives for home care also keeps the state at arm's distance from the caregiving situation; state officials then express concern about the adequacy and quality of the care rendered, which can become problematic (conversation with Jean Blaser, Illinois Department on Aging, February 17, 1998). Once public dollars enter the equation, issues of quality assume a different dimension than when families provided the care for free. The most dramatic examples, of course, are indications of abuse or neglect, a particularly problematic concern when older adults do not want to implicate their relatives and would rather risk abuse than be placed in a nursing home (which they see as their only alternative).

Caregiving by women has thus become the unarticulated cornerstone of American long-term care policy, a vivid example of historian Linda Gordon's observation that the effects of policy are determined as much by what it omits as what it addresses.[25] American social welfare policy assumes a residual function in caring for people with mental or physical disabilities; public services meet some needs that families cannot. Families come first, and life in families is private, outside the scope of government. Such primacy and privacy are taken to be normative; therefore, government is justified in staying away. As a result, there has been little incentive to examine—with intent to modify—the ideological and structural conditions that exacerbate the difficulties implicit in the caregiving experience. With few important exceptions,[26] recent attention to caregiving "burden," while unmasking the extent of caring practices, has tended to focus on individual remedies (support groups, education, more "help" for the caregiver, and recently, pay for such caregiving), which renders invisible this burden's structural and cultural roots and obscures the profound economic and other consequences that many women experience.

In sum, policy and its omissions can explain why home care has become primarily a family responsibility. The gendered nature of the labor market offers some suggestion as to why "family" most often means women. Cultural values and assumptions, even ideologies, also support women's primary responsibility for caregiving. These values and assumptions enter into conventional moral understandings about accountabilities and responsibilities.[27] Because they are often internalized and taken as given, they are rarely exposed to analysis. Women's moral perceptions and judgments—what they demand of themselves, how they define their "oughts," what they expect of others—are so shaped by these cultural forces that insight into the situation is often elusive. Both the care giver and the care receiver, in different ways, experience the pressures of cultural norms and ideals that encourage them to live "up to certain standards that define what it means to be a person of worth."[28] They, and in this case lower-income women in particular, do this at considerable cost to themselves and with few opportunities to define those conditions. The pressure is compounded by the sheer weight of responsibility and sorrow that many daughters and sons, no matter their income status, feel as they watch their parents become increasingly disabled.

Patterns of Caregiving: Who Is Responsible for Whom and Why?

Several factors profoundly direct the gendered nature of caregiving. Most salient are the inner experiences and intentionality of women, the ideology of familism and the way this ideology has historically rendered invisible intrafamily oppression and injustice, the assigning of men and women to separate spheres (the public and the private) for much of American history, and the configuration of the labor market. That women tend to be clustered in low-wage occupations, for example, makes it a matter of simple logic—natural and necessary—that if someone needs to leave work to provide care it will be the woman. The consequences are not innocuous; one result, as noted above, is a lifetime loss of earnings that can significantly affect her own late-life possibilities.

Since women have historically been defined as wives and mothers their role as caregivers for elderly family members seems fully naturalized; what is "natural" does not require examination.[29] Familism's prescriptive assumptions about the "natural" and "right" position of women constrains women's actions and results in economic gender-based inequities across the life span.[30] It also creates, in many families, gender injustices without sources of remedy, since locating such caregiving in the protected private realm guarantees, by virtue of invisibility, noninterference. Only in cases of reported elder abuse (or child abuse) do caregiving activities within the family come under public scrutiny. And because women's work in the home has often been hidden, a taken-for-granted aspect of daily life, the added responsibilities that come from caregiving for the elderly are also obscured by their seemingly commonplace nature. If our proverbial legislator did not notice that his meals appeared with no apparent effort on his part, then why would he notice that many women prepared meals for their immediate family and then rushed over to the mother's home to make sure that she was properly fed? He would have few ways of understanding the moral value of that act, its implications for gender inequality across the life course, or her anger at this inequality, because he would not have noticed it in the first place. If he sees her at all, perhaps it is as a person *choosing* to act in this way since his range of moral concepts leaves no space for encumbrances that women rarely see as choices. As Diana Meyers so tellingly points out, "insofar as a culture's rules of moral salience occlude dependency, many moral concerns will be denigrated, and the needs of dependents marginalized."[31] Just recently, the *New York Times* quoted a case worker describing a reluctant welfare-to-work client as someone who just stayed home all day and did nothing (except, that is, take care of her three small children).

Women themselves commonly accept these responsibilities with their physical, emotional, and financial costs as "just the way it is," and because resistance has too high a price. They may also experience them as desirable. Personal experience and public ideology become entangled for both care giver and care receiver. To not provide care is to render oneself vulnerable to negative judgment not only by others but by one's own internalized acceptance of cultural norms. Many older women, recognizing their socially devalued status within the family and in society, are reluctant to ask for what they need.[32] Even older women and their caregivers, who have some resources, are often unwilling to buy services. Internalizing the ideology of familism, women see families as the proper givers of care and as closed systems in which outsiders have no place;[33] to seek outside help also means acknowledging that these women cannot cope. Thus, older women simultaneously "take comfort" in having daughters and recall their own sense of obligation to their mothers in the past, while worrying about the burden they place on these same daughters and feeling shame that they do not exemplify cultural ideals of independence and self-sufficiency.

Familism, reborn in the new rhetoric of family values, not only assumes that family care is naturally superior to other forms of care but it also assumes that someone—most probably the woman—not only *is* at home but *ought to be* there with enough free time to provide a full panoply of services to the person needing them. This picture fails to take into account the decline in the birth rate, the delay in the age of parenthood (so that women are likely to have children at home while they are providing eldercare), the increase in divorce, and the creation of blended families. Perhaps most important, the picture ignores women's increased labor force participation, an increase so dramatic since the onset of World War II that it has become one of the defining features of twentieth-century America.[34] That this picture has little connection to reality has not significantly modified the value structure that supports it.

As a result of the apparent naturalness of the caregiving role, families develop patterns of caregiving over time in which expectations are established, and reputations imputed.[35] Families adopt these commitments in different ways. In some cases, the negotiating terms are tacit; everyone expects that one or more individuals will undertake certain responsibilities; once it occurs, they rarely revisit that expectation and since commitments build up over time, individuals cannot easily withdraw or renegotiate moral boundaries. Even when they try, situational factors make it more difficult for some people than others to redraw boundaries; for example, women and people within a parent-child relationship have a more difficult time than men having their excuses for not providing care accepted. Men, with the "excuse" of their "own" family, for example, are often relieved of the commitments that women assume. Work outside the home also provides an excuse for men that is unavailable to women who do not work outside the home; yet even women who hold jobs can rarely use the excuse of work. For a reason to be acceptable, others must see it as morally praiseworthy. The way it has evolved, women have fewer morally acceptable excuses for not providing care than men and so become the obvious carers *without* need for discussion.[36] "These shared assumptions about families, obligations and gender can be understood as the key ingredients in the ideological context in which women find themselves."[37] Mothers and daughters each play out culturally validated rules for morally praiseworthy behavior, often at a serious price to themselves, but with few options. Women know that "pride" derives from exemplifying in their own lives normative expectations.[38] Women—especially daughters—have difficulties establishing limits for the care they provide.

A woman friend, arriving home after a frantic day at work, described an agitated phone call she received from her mother moments later. Her mother wanted her to drive thirty miles to move her car for her. "She was never good to me; yet, now I feel guilty whenever I set limits to the demands I let her place on me. She's not a very nice person, but I keep hoping that she'll change so that before she dies we can have the relationship we never had" (conversation, September 1990). This middle-aged lawyer's internal landscape resembles a battlefield where rage, reluctant love, and dreams of the mythic mother-daughter relationship war with each other. The wisdom of friends—to remember you are doing the best that you can—the advice she would give if she were in their shoes, registers but moderates the turmoil only momentarily. She describes the anxiety she feels when her mother does not answer the phone. Has she fallen and broken a hip? Had a heart attack? Is she lying on the kitchen floor unattended for hours? In seeking to set limits, women's own wishes and aspirations take second place to husbands or children or work as alternative commitments.[39] Setting limits is especially difficult for women who do not work outside the home or who are single and childless.

While the reasons that woman offer for giving care, especially to parents, vary considerably (filial responsibility and reciprocity are not necessarily the dominant themes), a feature of almost all caregivers is the inexorable feeling of necessity—if not me, then who? Their experiences, while stressful psychologically, cannot be singularly captured in the language of stress. Nor can they be reduced to specific tasks. Rather the experiences of caregiving translate into generalized ways of being, of fairly constant anxiety, relentless tiredness, and an urgent need to protect the parent's dignity and maintain his or her sense of self. Caregivers describe feeling powerless because they can change little or nothing, an encompassing sense of responsibility for their parents' lives, and a deep need not to alter previously established relationships. They wish to preserve a sense of maternal omnipotence, and so hide the care they are giving because they do not want to demean their mothers, yet still want to receive praise for what they are doing. While one external observer is often quick to proclaim the woman as a "saint" (conversation, May 1996), thereby relieving society of responsibility to change her situation, another is as likely to wonder why she does that sort of activity.

> A society that extols the virtues of independence, views old people with dread, and seeks to distance itself from fundamental life events will disparage as unhealthy women who devote themselves to nursing sick and dying elderly people. A major problem for women is that they are simultaneously encouraged to provide care and condemned for doing so. . . . Caregivers, like mothers, are simultaneously sentimentalized and devalued.[40]

The downside of such treasured values as family, independence, and privacy becomes patently obvious in the context of home care. The perceived obligation to care, one of the unchosen obligations that Annette Baier and other feminist writers describe, clearly places these values in conflict and challenges a rationally self-interested chooser model of moral agency.[41] Many women are emotionally and ideologically attuned to accepting the caregiving role; they find the tasks of caregiving deeply satisfying. The work they do is personal, often demanding, repetitive, mundane, and laden with emotion. Yet it allows them to honor the often inchoate and unspoken sense that this is something that they must do and that others expect of them.[42] More communal values that recognize dependencies and mutual vulnerabilities better articulate what is morally necessary for care at home. A critical sociocultural task is to uncover and create sources of assistance to sustain women so that they are less alone and less at risk economically. The adage "the personal is the political" can be a point of departure for women trying to understand their conflicting feelings, their needs and wants for taking care and being free, for being cared for, secure, but also valued and dignified.

Conclusion

Care giving and receiving can reflect unspoken patterns of love and affection that importantly affect, even transform, each participant. In the best caregiving situations, care givers and care receivers affirm each other as persons of worth while care receivers come to recognize that the care giver is reliable and accountable. For all the tales of elder abuse, there are also stories of the dying mother surprising her caregiving daughter with a birthday party, stories where that same mother develops dubious errands so her daughter can get out of the house for a little while, where she continues her vital involvement with caregiving friends by offering pointed advice, political commentary, and reflections on the afterlife.[43]

The moral worlds of care giver and care receiver, in these situations of excellence, transcend tasks—cleaning and dressing, for example—and open up opportunities for growth, forgiveness, and friendship, all morally noteworthy. Psychologist Tom Kitwood once sagely observed, "A psychology of morality will be very much concerned with what people do to one another in the minutiae of everyday life, often without explicit awareness, and almost always without involving conscious moral dilemmas."[44] One task, as we think about the mutualities that inhere in care giving and care receiving is to imagine more caregiving situations that have the opportunity to be exemplary. Instead what one often encounters is frayed nerves and rather grim physical conditions.

Margaret Urban Walker reminds us that while morality is fundamentally interpersonal, it is constrained and made intelligible by background understandings about what people are supposed to do, expect, and understand.[45] In home care, especially in its most quotidian aspects, we see how people make sense of responsibility in terms of identities, relationships, and values; home care also shows how the phenomenological world is molded by more impersonal forces like race, class, and gender that the political economy explicates. To generate a different world of home care would then call for transformations in the background conditions and in the policy arena. Based on interviews with thirty-two women between the ages of 35 and 85, Jane Aronson notes that if

> the broad social context were one that valued older people, communicated entitlement to needed supports and provided for individual and collective sharing of their provision, Mrs. E. S.'s low spirits and sense of jeopardy might have been much less. If straightforward statements of need were easily speakable, she would not have had to fend off shame, and Mrs. A. C. and her mother would not have had to preserve pride at the cost of denying real need. Mrs. P. S. would have struggled less if prevailing ideologies made possible a wider sharing of responsibility for the care of others, instead of singling her out as an unmarried daughter and pressing her into a caregiving position.[46]

Older women and their female caregivers are particularly vulnerable to cultural messages that might not grip men with equal power. To return to our proverbial legislator, while incontinence and other physical losses may embarrass him, he is not a stranger to receiving care that his privilege has always brought him. The fear of being a burden might be a less familiar emotion to him than to his wife, although some men experience great satisfaction in caring for their spouse—in a sense it offers them a way to "pay back" for the caring they have received.

Much of the material on the stress and burden of caregiving that dominates the gerontological literature focuses on documentation and recommendations for alleviating stress on a personal level through education and counseling and perhaps through additional formal supports. Caregiver support groups can certainly play an important role in helping caregivers cope with their emotions, but they are an unlikely path to resistance unless they begin to unravel the structural and cultural sources of the difficulty and help caregivers renegotiate their response to these external forces. But even that is not enough; serious work on cultural transformation must accompany political work to alter policies. The professional social work and the ethics and aging literatures emphasize elder self-determination and autonomy. Yet, until and unless elders and their caregivers are viewed simultaneously in a relational context, it will be impossible to generate more responsive ways to give care to those who need it without creating patterns of self-sacrifice that neither the older nor younger women deem desirable.

So much of what occurs in caregiving relationships is tacit. Caregivers accept responsibilities because it is what they expect of themselves and it seems to be what others expect of them. These patterns of responsibility and accountability, in Margaret Urban Walker's terms, are not developed collaboratively; instead they reflect how women internalize but also resist cultural impositions, ideological suppositions about family and gender, and impoverished policy responses in the context of their own lives. Jane Aronson says "motivated to reduce feelings of guilt and shame, women implicitly suppress assertion of their own needs, so that the broad pattern of care of old people goes unchallenged—rather it is sustained and reproduced."[47] Encouraging heterodox moral perceptions to flourish as the foundation for identifying wrongful treatment is a good starting place for women, both old and young.[48]

Simultaneously, researchers, scholars, practitioners, and others can ask different questions about caregiving. They can ask not only how to provide support to informal caregivers or protect the self-determined wishes of older clients (which are necessarily influenced by how they perceive their deservingness as older women) but also how to modify those cultural constraints that serve as mechanisms of social control, and how to enrich the options for secure care that policy and economic change can offer. They could ask what it would take to dissociate care from the social norms and power relationships that contribute to women's subordination.[49]

A new language of needs and the creation of proper forums for discussion of needs from the perspective of recipients and care providers are starting places; they can open possibilities previously unnoticed. These public conversations can generate a new language that can situate notions like dignity, self-respect, and cultural inclusion within the context of relationships of dependency. "Without the light of language," Michael Ignatieff observed, "we risk becoming strangers to our better selves."[50] We need to find a way for "positive" heterodox emotions, like compassion, to reenter our public conversation.[51] Such reentry can evoke a commitment to action by opening us to the suffering of others and accepting that our reactions to such suffering are fundamentally moral. Alertness to how the normative assumptions that support politics and policy and the power of ideology and culture become manifest in "ordinary" lives can become the foundation for a sustained ethical analysis of how background conditions mediate life's possibilities and reinforce conditions of inequality.

Notes

1. Emily Abel, *Who Cares for the Elderly? Public Policy and the Experience of Adult Daughters* (Philadelphia: Temple University Press, 1991).

2. Mario Fabri dos Anjos, "Bioethics in a Liberationist Key," in *A Matter of Principle? Ferment in U.S. Bioethics*, ed. Edwin Dubose, Ron Hamel, and Laurence O'Connell (Valley Forge, Pa.: Trinity Press International, 1994).

3. Nancy Hooyman and Judith Gonyea, *Feminist Perspectives on Family Care: Policies for Gender Justice* (Thousand Oaks, Calif.: Sage, 1995).

4. Emily Abel, "Representations of Caregiving by Margaret Forster, Mary Gordon, and Doris Lessing," *Research on Aging* 17, no. 1 (1995): 63.

5. Baila Miller, Role of the Family in Homecare, unpublished manuscript.

6. Nona Glazer, "The Home As Workshop: Women and Amateur Nurses and Medical Care Providers," *Gender and Society* 4 (1990): 479–99.

7. Arlie Hochschild, *The Time Bind: When Work Becomes Home and Home Becomes Work* (New York: Holt, 1997).

8. C. Feldblum, "Home Health Care for the Elderly: Programs, Problems, and Potentials," *Harvard Journal of Legislation* 22 (1985): 194–254. Cited in Terry Arendell and Carroll L. Estes, "Older Women in the Post-Reagan Era," in *Critical Perspectives on Aging: The Political and Moral Economy of Growing Old*, ed. Meredith Minkler and Carroll L. Estes (Amityville, N.Y.: Baywood, 1991), 209–26.

9. Robyn Stone, G. L. Cafferata, and J. Sangl, "Caregivers of the Frail Elderly: A National Profile," *The Gerontologist* 27 (1987): 616–26.

10. Abel, *Who Cares for the Elderly?*

11. Alan Walker, "Care for Elderly People: A Conflict between Women and the State," in *A Labour of Love: Women, Work and Caring*, ed. Janet Finch and D. Groves (London: Routledge and Kegan Paul, 1983), 124.

12. Abel, *Who Cares for the Elderly?*

13. Jane Aronson, "Women's Perspectives on Informal Care of the Elderly: Public Ideology and Personal Experience of Giving and Receiving Care," *Ageing and Society* 10 (1990): 61–84.

14. Philip Clark, "Public Policy in the United States and Canada: Individuals, Familial Obligation, and Collective Responsibility in the Care of the Elderly," in *The Remainder of Their Days: Domestic Policy and Older Families in the United States and Canada*, ed. Jon Hendricks and Carolyn Rosenthal (New York: Garland, 1993), 13.

15. Abel, *Who Cares for the Elderly?*

16. Joanna Weinberg, "Caregiving, Age, and Class in the Skeleton of the Welfare State: And Jill Came Tumbling After," in *Critical Gerontology: Perspectives from Moral and Political Economy*, ed. Meredith Minkler and Carroll L. Estes (Amityville, N.Y.: Baywood, 1998); Nona Glazer, "The Home as Workshop: Women as amateur Nurses and Medical Care Providers," *Gender and Society* 4 (1990): 479–99.

17. See Nancy Fraser's *Unruly Practices* (New York: Routledge, 1989) for an interesting and important discussion of needs negotiation.

18. Michel Foucault, *Discipline and Punish: The Birth of the Prison*, tr. Alan Sheridan (New York: Random House 1979), 26.

19. Judith Shklar, *The Faces of Injustice* (New Haven: Yale University Press, 1990).

20. Michael Ignatieff, *The Needs of Strangers: An Essay on Privacy, Solidarity, and the Politics of Being Human* (New York: Penguin Books, 1984), 13.

21. Arendell and Estes, "Older Women in the Post-Reagan Era."

22. Walker, "Care for Elderly People," 124.

23. Arendell and Estes, "Older Women in the Post-Reagan Era."

24. Carroll L. Estes and Elizabeth A. Binney, "Toward a Transformation of Health and Aging Policy," *International Journal of Health Services* 18, no. 1 (1988): 69–82.

25. Linda Gordon, "The New Feminist Scholarship on the Welfare State," in *Women, the State, and Welfare*, ed. Linda Gordon (Madison: University of Wisconsin Press, 1990), 9–35.

26. Two fine examples of attending to the structural origins of caregiver burden are Suzanne England, Sharon Keigher, Baila Miller, and Nathan Linsk, "Community Care Policies and Gender Justice," in *Critical Perspectives on Aging*; Nancy Hooyman and Judith Gonyea, *Feminist Perspectives on Family Care: Policies for Gender Justice* (Thousand Oaks, Calif.: Sage, 1995).

27. Margaret Urban Walker, *Moral Understandings: A Feminist Study in Ethics* (New York: Routledge, 1998).

28. Donald Moon, "The Moral Basis of the Democratic Welfare State," in *Democracy and the Welfare State*, ed. Amy Gutmann (Princeton: Princeton University Press, 1988), 32.

29. See Janet Finch and Jennifer Mason, *Negotiating Family Responsibilities* (London: Routledge, 1993), for a careful analysis, based on interviews, of how women internalize these cultural values.

30. Hooyman and Gonyea, *Feminist Perspectives on Family Care*, 112; Susan Moller Okin, *Justice, Gender, and the Family* (New York: Basic Books, 1989).

31. Diana Tietjens Meyers, "Emotion and Heterodox Moral Perception: An Essay in Moral Social Psychology," in *Feminists Rethink the Self*, ed. Diana Tietjens Meyers (Boulder: Westview, 1997), 200.

32. Aronson, "Women's Perspectives on Informal Care of the Elderly."

33. Miller, Role of the Family in Home Care.

34. Walker, "Care for Elderly People."

35. Finch and Mason, *Negotiating Family Responsibilities*.

36. Finch and Mason, *Negotiating Family Responsibilities*.

37. Walker, "Care for Elderly People," 67.

38. Aronson, "Women's Perspectives on Informal Care of the Elderly."

39. Aronson, "Women's Perspectives on Informal Care of the Elderly."

40. Abel, "Representations of Caregiving," 62; Abel, *Who Cares for the Elderly?* 8.

41. Annette Baier, *Postures of the Mind: Essays on Mind and Morals* (Minneapolis: University of Minnesota Press, 1985); see Meyers, ed., *Feminists Rethink the Self*, for a number of thoughtful essays that touch upon the theme of women's experiences that include many of such relational obligations.

42. Finch and Mason, *Negotiating Family Responsibilities*.

43. I speak here of Laurie Shields, the cofounder (with Tish Sommers) of the Older Women's League and one of my heroines. It was to me that she offered a very wise guidance, in the form of a novel she gave me as a Christmas present shortly before she died.

44. Tom Kitwood, "The Dialectics of Dementia: With Particular Reference to Alzheimer's Disease," *Ageing and Society* 10 (1990): 177–96.

45. Walker, *Moral Understandings*.

46. Aronson, "Women's Perspectives on Informal Care of the Elderly," 77.

47. Aronson, "Women's Perspectives on Informal Care of the Elderly."

48. Meyers, "Emotion and Heterodox Moral Perception."

49. Abel, "Representations of Caregiving."

50. Ignatieff, *The Needs of Strangers*, 142.

51. Meyers, "Emotion and Heterodox Moral Perception."

· *14* ·

Caring for Ourselves: Peer Care in Autonomous Aging

Robin N. Fiore

$\mathcal{O}$ne of the major challenges of women's aging is securing appropriate supportive care without surrendering dignity. Maintaining dignity and self-respect is reckoned in terms of maintaining autonomy and independence. Newly published research suggests that the sheer determination to remain in charge of their lives actually helps older people live longer and remain healthier.[1]

The old, in virtue of poverty, frailty, disability, and so forth, are especially vulnerable to assaults on their autonomy. Women are at greater risk of diminished autonomy with age because of their comparative disadvantage in key resources that influence the ability to live independently. The most significant factors contributing to autonomous aging are material and financial resources, health and functional ability, and access to caring resources.[2]

Access to informal caring resources depends in large part on marital status and personal relationships. More than 25 percent of U.S. households consist of only one person; the proportion among the elderly is higher, with elderly women 2.5 times more likely to be alone than elderly men.[3] Twice as many elderly women as elderly men need supportive care to live independently; 14 percent of elderly women are severely disabled—they cannot climb stairs, walk down the road, bathe completely—compared to 7 percent of elderly men.[4] The majority of severely disabled men can rely on care provided by their spouses; in contrast, half of severely disabled women—compared to one-quarter of severely disabled men—live alone.[5] Among the elderly with very severe disability the gender differences are even greater.

It has been estimated that between 70 percent and 80 percent of care to elderly persons is rendered by family members, typically younger female relatives within co-resident families. However, the traditional mode of caring for the elderly is increasingly untenable given pervasive demographic changes in family life such as delayed childbearing, high female employment, and increased parental longevity. The acceptability of nontraditional lifestyles and the availability of social options add to the numbers of women who will enter old age without the traditional support of children or partners. Moreover, the data indicate that a majority of the elderly themselves does not share the ideological preference for family care; minimizing dependency on adult children is a prominently expressed concern.[6] Thus, we can expect that care of the aged will become more institutionally based in the future.

The shift from private care by family members to public, institutionally based care intensifies ethical concerns about maintaining autonomy and personal integrity as we age. Institutional models of care, including home nursing care, objectify the old and undermine autonomy. Care services are designed in response to a constructed and imposed set of needs rather than in response to particular individuals in need. *Care* is commodified, translated into discrete measurable services organized in terms of bureaucratic convenience and efficiency. The trend toward for-profit management of institutions of care, and control of whole segments of the human services economy by a few corporate giants, further exacerbates concerns about the moral risks of becoming dependent on institutional caregivers.

Many elderly people struggle alone, refusing much needed assistance and living lower-quality lives because the terms of accepting care are morally and personally objectionable to them. The medico-gerontological industry pathologizes refusal as irrational self-endangerment because of willful noncompliance or cognitive incapacity. For example, the standard view in gerontological ethics is that the elderly individual's interest in personal autonomy is to be "balanced against the collaborating or competing interests of [affected] family, friends and others . . . [as well as] balanced against the autonomy of formal caregivers and care-giving agencies."[7] On this view, an agent's essential interest in the maintenance of personal integrity is rendered as on par with other agents' interests in acting without constraint for convenience and profit. More importantly, characterizing the concern as a matter of justice completely obscures the central ethical issue: those with the power to determine what counts as the appropriate compromise operate under financial incentives to provide care in forms that undermine the care recipient's autonomy, and ultimately her health and well-being.

The issue that motivates this chapter is the necessity of finding ways to be less dependent on bureaucratic care without unnecessarily sacrificing quality of life in old age. One overlooked possibility is caring for ourselves. Traditional stereotypes of the old as frail and dependent focus on their needs for care and fail to take account of the caring labor of the elderly themselves. Although fewer than 5 percent of those aged 65 or more and 10 percent of those 75 or more are disabled to the extent of requiring nursing home confinement, the representative elderly person who is the subject of gerontology is comprehensively incapacitated. Thus it is hardly surprising that long-term care policy discussions ignore the fact that the elderly are significant caregivers as well as recipients of care—caring for grandchildren, disabled adult children, and other elderly people. The importance of developing the potential of peer care is underscored by studies showing that the elderly themselves prefer care by peers to care received from adult children or professionals.

In this chapter, I want to consider the idea of peer care as a defense against totalizing dependence on forms of care that undermine autonomy. I start by introducing the ethical concept of care and discussing two specialized practices of care—nursing and friendship—in terms of their implications for autonomy. I argue that institutional forms of care (including home care) endanger autonomy and are antithetical to fully ethical notions of care. Next, I propose that aging and aged women defend autonomy by networking to develop cooperative means of care that they both construct and manage. I conclude by offering examples of a specific context of peer care—cooperative living arrangements—in which the old and the very old maintain dignity and independence by sharing tasks, providing moral support, and monitoring and aiding each other.

Autonomy and Dependency

Since the chapters in this volume are written for a mixed audience—philosophers and social scientists, health care practitioners, caregivers and laypersons of varying backgrounds—let me start by briefly describing my use of the terms *autonomy* and *dependency*.

In moral theory, autonomy is predominantly understood as a psychological capacity for reflective self-determination. It refers to the internal process by which a moral agent comes to have the values and purposes that define her as a person—a self. Critics of strictly internal interpretations of autonomy have argued that actually being autonomous requires more than a free will. In addition to procedural independence, a certain amount of control over the external circumstances of one's existence is necessary for practical or effective autonomy. The autonomous agent must in fact be able to direct her life according to independently chosen values; that is, she must be able to pursue actions that importantly affirm her self-concept without unduly burdensome social cost.[8]

As I use the term autonomy here, I mean some version of effective autonomy, that is, freedom from external coercion, availability of meaningful choices, and not unduly constrained by social or material circumstances. On this view, autonomy can be importantly diminished by personal relations or social institutions and by negative cultural attitudes that undermine values and images central to one's self-concept and personality.

Autonomy is commonly contrasted with dependence. To be dependent is to be subject to the control of others in matters that affect values and purposes constitutive of one's personality. As such, one is unable to act independently, to be self-determining; one's will is subordinate. Dependence in this sense may arise from cognitive incapacity, or an agent's laziness or submissiveness, or another's deliberate interference, fraud, or manipulation. In the present context, excessive or inappropriate care, no matter how benignly motivated, constitutes a similar moral hazard. While autonomy is not *necessarily* compromised by dependence on others for provision of care needs, as a practical matter, physical frailty and disability jeopardize the effective exercise of autonomy even when there is no cognitive impairment. Caregivers are powerfully placed to disregard care recipients' choices and preferences and may intentionally or unintentionally exact autonomy surrenders in return for servicing care needs.

Care Ethics and Caring Practices

According to Nel Noddings, "To care is to act not by fixed rule but by affection and regard."[9] Respect for others as moral equals requires "seeing the other's reality as a possibility for oneself."[10] To care is not to identify with another's situation or circumstances but to recognize the other's unique particularity. In contrast to empathy, care involves apprehending the world from the other's reality and acting on the basis of the other's understanding of herself and her needs.

Initial theoretical work in care ethics took mothering as the paradigmatic form of care. Feminists have fruitfully extended the ethics of care to practices such as friendship, citizenship, and of course, nursing. However, care means different things in different concrete contexts. As Lawrence Blum puts it, specialized practices of care may require distinct "moral competencies." For example, the specific sensitivities and virtues appropriate to mothering include *responsibility for* the child's good. In contrast, reciprocity and mutuality are the virtues characteristic of friendship care.[11]

Differences in caring practices are shaped by more than the distinctive needs of particular person-to-person relations. Even though various caring practices are nominally grounded in care and share similar form, similar terms, and even a common ethical starting point, they are also embedded in and shaped by larger social practices in which different ethical orientations dominate. In what follows, I maintain that nursing care, embedded as it is in the organization and worldview of medicine, inclines toward annulling rather than aiding autonomous aging. I propose friendship care or peer care as a counterstrategy.

Joan Tronto's nuanced analysis of care is particularly useful for contrasting friendship care and nursing care because it severs the conceptual link between affective tasks (emotional support, fostering dignity, visiting, reminiscing) and instrumental tasks (bathing, feeding, dressing).[12] Tronto distinguishes between *caring about, taking care of,* and *caring for. Caring about* involves feelings of affection and affinity but it is person oriented rather than action oriented. In Tronto's scheme, *caring about* has no specific implication for action or motivation.[13] *Taking care of* encompasses taking responsibility for initiating and maintaining caring activities. *Caring for* includes the concrete, hands-on tasks associated with directly servicing needs.

It is important to emphasize that these aspects of care are not necessarily related; caring about does not entail caring labor (taking care of or caring for), and taking care of and caring for may or may not include caring about. The provision of care need not be motivated by affinity or affection but may be based on other forms of obligation—for example payment or generalized commitments to compassion or humanitarian service, to norms of kinship responsibility, or to requirements of social roles, as in "mother" or "teacher."

Blum describes specialized practices of care such as nurse, doctor, teacher, and so forth, as *vocational carings.*[14] Vocational caring includes concern for a person's overall good, but only because it has implications for the specific aspect of that person's good—health, athletic performance, education, and so forth—that is the focus of care. In contrast, caring in what I call the fully ethical sense is a recognition of and attention to the particularity of the one cared "in her totality."[15]

Tronto's distinction between *care* and *protection* offers another way to understand the different ethical possibilities of nursing and friendship. Whereas care attends to subjectivity, in contrast, protection is a response to objective threats of harm. My view is that medical care—and practices such as nursing that are embedded in it—are properly understood as a species of protection rather than caring. Medical forms of knowledge are analytical, distanced, rather than engaged; its characteristic forms of concern involve transforming human subjects into objects of care.

Friendship care, in my view, exemplifies fully ethical caring. Unlike motherhood and nursing, friendship "present[s] the possibility of caring relationships that are connected with actively chosen sharing and reciprocity."[16] The essential element of this mode of responsiveness is mutuality, specifically, "mutual well-wishing"—a shared giving and receiving of concern. Friendship care is instrumentally valuable, as a source of practical aid, as well as intrinsically valuable in realizing personal identity.

The ethical possibilities of friendship exceed those of other forms of care because of its unregulated character. Relative to the conventionally designated obligations of kin relationships and public practices of care, the negotiated responsibilities of friendships allow us to escape thorough social regulation.[17] In other words, friendship provides the condition for the possibility of freedom in an age of comprehensive social regulation.

I expand on the possibilities of friendship care in the final section of this chapter. Let me turn now to the current organization of care for the elderly and its implications for autonomy.

Aging in Place: The Continuum of Care

The idea of care in gerontology is represented as a continuum of need. In housing, it is a series of arrangements that are responsive to increasing needs for medical and support services. Typically, the older individual is seen as progressing from either single or multifamily community-based housing through a variety of congregate housing alternatives, ultimately to long-term care or a nursing facility when the focus of care is primarily medical.

In the past decade, the continuum-of-care approach has given rise to so-called "life care" residential communities that offer various levels of care—assisted living, intermediate assistance and nursing care—in the same vicinity. Most of these are operated as for-profit enterprises and are beyond the means of those with moderate and low incomes. Nevertheless, the life-care community model has come to be regarded as the paradigm of older living.

Life care communities appeal to fears about being able to obtain needed care, fear of becoming dependent, disabled, a burden, fear of having no "place." Place, as I use it here, refers to the vital personal relationships that sustain our identity.[18] In addition to losses of functioning, the old suffer significant losses of these vital others. The nightmare of old age for many is that they will find themselves having no one they *care about* and no one who *cares about* them.

The lure of these communities is primarily the guarantee of being allowed to stay in one's "place," if not one's actual residence, should frailty or ill-health befall. In *The Fountain of Age*, Betty Friedan exposes the hollowness of this guarantee.[19] She lays bare the denial of aging that undergirds the organization of many such communities and results in rules that isolate less robust residents. For example, there are usually rules that prohibit wheelchairs in the dining room; the special nursing care facilities tend to be at a remove from the rest of the community, so not easily accessible to former friends and acquaintances. In my own experience, it is increasingly common that nursing care beds are contracted for with a local nursing facility that is not even part of the actual community or premises, forsaking entirely the pledge of remaining in place.

Another disturbing aspect of life care communities is the necessity of joining well before the need for care presents itself. Most have initial health and mobility requirements and maximum ages for entrance. Friedan and others worry that the aging are needlessly trading robust current life years for the security of final nursing care, care that statistically very few actually need. The price of that security is comprehensive regimentation and supervision.

It is widely recognized that nursing homes often unintentionally damage the health and attitudes of those in their care in a number of ways. Both staff and family members encourage cooperativeness, passivity, and risk aversiveness; physical safety and health care are ranked higher than other values such as autonomy and privacy.[20] Group-oriented activities and congregate meals subject residents to unavoidable and sometimes unwanted social interactions; bureaucratically derived routines deny residents control over the organization and use of their time.[21] Limits on personalizing spaces effectively diminish self-identity and awareness.

From the point of view of autonomy, the key issue in evaluating care arrangements is the impact of the environment on an elderly person's self-concept. To what extent "are the past activities, current identifications and commitments and envisioned enterprises respected and encouraged or ignored and demeaned?"[22] Recently, I had the opportunity to personally assess life care communities in an area that caters to retirees. With the exception of very high-end resort communities for the affluent, most were oppressively institutional and harbored the same types of moral risks noted for nursing homes. Let me mention some of the more common surrenders.

For individuals who are deeply attached to companion animals, institutional living can be considered only as a last resort. Despite the acknowledged therapeutic benefits of pets, animals are out of the question in most facilities for reasons of insurance, asthma and allergies, hygiene, and potential burdens on staff. Even in communities that do permit dogs, designated dog-walking areas are distantly and inconveniently located.

One resident with whom I spoke was depressed because she had to give up all her "beloved" houseplants—she had nothing to care for. Plants are not allowed, even in the individual apartments, because clutter makes things more difficult for the cleaning service. Some of the more modest communities discourage "excessive" knickknacks and prohibit more than token personalization of living space, placing limits on the number and value of personal items. While these surrenders might seem reasonable in the abstract, personal artifacts link present and past and are known to contribute to the maintenance of our sense of identity, a common concern of age.

Typically, all residents must report to the dining room for all meals whether they are eating or not; seating is usually assigned at breakfast and dinner. This makes it easy for the staff to make sure that no one has wandered off. Residents complained about contentious meals and desperately wished they could dine with their preferred companions. The more modest the facility, the higher the percentage of residents who were suffering from dementia. The physically frail who were not cognitively impaired complained that they were treated by staff as if they too were demented, and they complained of boredom.

Personal automobiles are often prohibited for insurance reasons; group transportation to churches, doctors, and shopping is regularly scheduled but the cost of taxis for personal trips is prohibitive. Individuals become isolated from remaining friends and suffer the loss of other connections—church, favorite grocery, and so forth. Even those who remain in the same locale find that their doctors represent the main source of social continuity.

Another alternative being championed is community-based care or home care. Community-based care initiatives such as the *Medicaid Community Attendant Services Act* (HB 2020)[23] are one of several types of proposals for "keeping the elderly in their own homes" by providing trained assistance with activities of daily living (bathing, dressing, toileting, and so forth). However, the driving motivation is to save the Medicaid bottom line. The additional costs of providing so-called nontechnical assistance to elderly Medicaid-eligible persons in their homes are justified only to the extent that such costs are less than what would otherwise be reimbursable—specifically nursing home care for the same limited population subgroup. Since no more than 5 percent of those aged 65 and older reside in nursing homes (10 percent aged 75 and older) and only a portion of those are eligible for Medicaid, the impact of such proposals on rates of institutionalization would be negligible. Nor is it likely that the eligible population will be expanded since that would increase rather than decrease absolute program costs, given the projected increases in the number of elderly living to old, old age. In fact, Medicare coverage for home health care assistance has been drastically cut back because of dramatic increases in utilization by elders who need modest help to remain at home but who are not eligible for Medicaid. The benefit cutbacks were officially characterized as a response to "abuse."

There are powerful economic and social justifications for deinstitutionalizing a broad range of health and human services, from surgery to mental health care to nursing home care. However, in the current "age of bureaucratic parsimony," outpatient and home-based forms of care are indiscriminately and often inappropriately mandated. Managed care efforts to reduce costs ignore the fact that individuals differ in their access to the supplemental private, informal sources of support that are often crucial to a complete care plan—for example, transportation to and from care sites, practical nursing services such as wound care, assistance with hygiene and medication, and preparation of special diets.

The combination of stringent eligibility rules for professional home health services and health plan coverage limitations shifts significant amounts of care—and the costs of such care—to private caregivers who are assumed to be both available and able. These outdated assumptions about the availability of assistance from family members resist revision in the profit-driven human services economy where the mission of reducing third-party costs depends on the avoidance of expensive care. Nothing is cheaper than kin care.

Setting aside the issue of cost, we must be wary of equating the provision of certain types of home assistance with maintaining elderly independence and social integration. Merely keeping the elderly out of nursing homes is no assurance of personal autonomy. While home care may give the appearance of enhancing personal control because the care recipient is not physically residing in an institution, home care is "thick with institutional structures and controls."[24] All aspects of care are strictly under the control of a third party; the services available are, of necessity, quite restrictive and the delivery of care is regimented rather than individualized. Moreover, home care is provided through multilayered arrangements of referral, subcontracting, and interagency agreements that resist accountability. The frail elderly person, now isolated in her own home, is unlikely to be able to effectively negotiate or challenge the fragmented and chaotic "system" that enables her to stay in place; she remains an object of bureaucratic care.

An Argument for Peer Care

Sociologists suggest that it is not physical dependency per se that is detrimental to the autonomy of care recipients, but the inability or lack of opportunity to reciprocate, leading to perceived power imbalances and excessive feelings of obligation.

Studies of successful aging in neighborhood settings have identified informal peer networks as a significant factor in making it possible for frail and disabled elderly to live independently in their own homes. Here the peers are long-time neighbors who cooperatively provide physical assistance and moral support among themselves, including sharing their sources of caring assistance—relatives and friends. Although spontaneously formed and loosely organized, these voluntary, mini-mutual-aid societies resemble "the stability and power of collective family life" in that they permit individual members to maintain independence and remain socially integrated in the larger community into very old age.[25]

Certain conditions are necessary, it is thought, for such networks to develop spontaneously: stability (long-term residence), similarity of need, shrinking social worlds (for example, widowhood, loss of mobility) and common values, particularly independence and security.[26] For many elderly, however, the first condition—remaining in one place—is problematical. Reduced income often necessitates relocation upon retirement or widowhood, and many elderly choose to leave familiar surroundings for other reasons such as climate, health, to be near children, and so forth. Because of job mobility, multiple marriages, and so on, those now entering old age may not have lived in one place for any significant period or acquired a stable local network of friends and peers.

The point of departure for my proposal is that spatial proximity is not necessary for the formation of mutual aid compacts. While mobility detaches us from communities of place, it brings us into contact with many more people. We can nourish relationships as we move around and work toward a future rendezvous. We are used to thinking about future needs largely in terms of finances. It is perfectly acceptable, even obligatory, to make provision for meeting the financial demands of aging and dependency. Reflection on the nature of organized care should prompt us to plan for other anticipated needs as well.

I have tried to show that for autonomy's sake, and the sake of our health and well-being, we should be concerned about utter dependence on corporate and bureaucratically organized care. The peer care strategy I develop below is suggested by the idea that voluntary associations buttress autonomy by redistributing the power associated with the satisfaction of care needs. The possibility of autonomy, of resisting totalizing external control and preventing coercive power from becoming concentrated and comprehensive, lies in the private spaces created by voluntary relations of care.

The idea of peer support is not new, especially for women. Formal peer support groups have arisen and proliferated because of the need to deliberately construct what once we may have been able to take for granted. Radical changes in mobility, work patterns, and neighborhood life have altered the mode of obtaining many kinds of informal social support. I want to consider how the idea of peer support could be useful in assisting aging and aged women to meet needs in a fashion that affirms rather than undermines their autonomy by allowing them to be less dependent on corporate sources of care.

Consider the model of mothers' groups forged in recent years for the purpose of mutual aid, offering play opportunities for isolated children, facilitating the exchange of child-care services and information, and providing a source of emotional support. Group members are usually strangers initially; they become linked as a result of participating in activities—Lamaze class, nursery school projects, PTA, working on local child-related issues, and so forth—which identify them both as individuals with similar interests and as individuals who are willing to address needs cooperatively.

Currently, a variety of experimental cooperative living arrangements for aging and aged women are being developed by social services professionals, and some may prove quite successful. However, the structure and the management of these arrangements remain under the control of professionals. I am suggesting that women prepare their own future "place" by actively seeking out peers who are similarly interested in strategizing for autonomous aging. By nurturing mutually supportive peer relationships that include intentional reflection about cooperative approaches to care as we age, we can decline to become total objects of care.

I will say more later about actual experiments in peer support for aging and older women, but first I want to address some ethical concerns. The notion of overtly planning for and strategizing with respect to personal relationships may strike some as unattractively calculating. Part of the distaste is attributable, I think, to deeply entrenched nonrational ideals of spontaneity—"naturalness"—and serendipity that are fundamental elements of the feminine mystique. In contrast, traditional male norms encourage the pursuit of relationships based on prudence and mutual advantage, for example, strategically choosing activities and associations that allow them to develop mentoring and networking partnerships.

We have seen how feminist demands that intimate relationships embody egalitarian ideals of mutuality and reciprocity have been vilified as selfish and unwomanly. It is not surprising then, given the relational ideals of altruism, self-denial, and self-sacrifice traditionally recommended to women, that the idea of their overtly pursuing relationships for the potential benefits to self might seem alien and ethically dissonant.

The source of apprehension might be that such a proposal appears to value voluntary relations of friendship solely or primarily in terms of their usefulness in achieving one's own personal end(s)—here, assistance with future dependency needs. My response is that there is nothing to suggest that more deliberately developed peer relationships are *inherently* or more likely to be exploitative than more spontaneous or serendipitous relationships. Selfishness is a disposition, a feature of individual personalities, not of relationships; thus the issue of using others unacceptably needs to be addressed separately from questions about the ethical or aesthetic desirability of reflectively choosing peer relationships.

Another worry might be that I am advocating an impoverished account of friendship, a strictly functional personal relationship. As Blum notes, "It is not simply responsiveness to particularity . . . that gives value and meaning to our practices of friendship but the particularity of the relationship itself, the shared attachment and intimacy for its own sake."[27] While a relationship might begin with functionality in view, that is only to establish certain shared concerns and values. The aim is to nurture the relationship to the point where it has a unique, irreplaceable value that precludes it from falling victim to calculations of individual self-interest. Marilyn Friedman succinctly captures the paradox of this ideal: "The flourishing of loved ones promotes my own well-being, yet my motivation to care for them does not require me to compute how their well-being will favor my own interests."[28]

Experiments in Peer Care

Experiments in peer care have shown that independence need not be an all-or-nothing proposition. We can creatively and cooperatively develop alternatives that avoid surrendering autonomy for caregiving. Let me offer just a few creative responses that suggest possibilities for long-range planning for mutual support.

A group of younger adult women who became close friends as a result of participating in a peer counseling support group founded "The Clovers Retirement Community." Several of them who remain in close contact contribute to a retirement fund that is earmarked for purchasing land or a residence for their joint retirement.[29]

The University of Arizona has developed a not-for-profit cooperative housing community for retired academics, Academy Village, that includes various housing options and services, long-term health care and the opportunity for continued academic and professional interaction at the Arizona Senior Academy. Recently, the University of Florida announced similar plans for "Gators"—alumni fans of their athletics teams.

A group of feminists purchased a 150-acre farm, calling it "the Susan B. Anthony Memorial UnRest Home," with the idea of developing a collectively owned land trust with individually owned homes. They envision cottage industries, meeting spaces, and guest facilities as possible revenue producers to allow the community to be self-sufficient.[30]

Although I believe that longtime friendships are most likely to succeed as sources of peer care, it is also possible to form peer care groups at the point of need. One popular approach is communal or co-housing, a form of housing pioneered in Denmark more than twenty-five years ago. Co-housing may consist of individually owned housing units built in clusters around common yards or it may be a multiperson residence with shared kitchen and living areas or an apartment building managed jointly by the tenants. The significant feature of communal housing is that residents design and manage their own residence. There is no staff, and no services are included in the cost of housing; the residents share tasks or jointly purchase needed services. It is typically age-integrated but also may be age-segregated.

Secular and religious not-for-profit organizations are developing communal-housing options for middle- and low-income seniors in a number of states. One example, the Crone's Nest in St. Augustine, Florida, is an intergenerational community-building endeavor that raises funds for intergenerational communal housing. A clearinghouse for co-housing projects estimates that there are thirty American projects already in operation, some twenty-two under construction, and more than one hundred fifty in planning stages.

Conclusion

The attitude that dependency justifies a kind of second-class autonomy seems to pervade the long-term care industry. The literature is filled with recommendations such as "autonomy must be tempered by a recognition of the realities of dependency."[31] Ideally, we should seek to orient care toward maintaining effective autonomy rather than trimming autonomy aspirations to fit the organization of care services. In this less than ideal world, the bottom line dictates the style and delivery of care.

Autonomy is a difficult achievement in societies, like our own, characterized by comprehensive social institutions.[32] We need strategies that enable individuals to define themselves in age, to control their mode of aging as befits their understanding of their needs, and that permit them to resist giving up integrity and autonomy in exchange for care. Additional flexibility in public assistance and support programs does not by itself reduce dependence on autonomy-undermining institutions and practices that present themselves in the guise of care. Peer care is about maintaining a space of self-determination by collectively caring for ourselves.

Notes

    1. *St. Petersburg Times* (January 1, 1998), citing *Journal of Gerontology: Psychological Sciences.*

    2. Sara Arber and Jay Ginn, *Gender and Later Life: A Sociological Analysis of Resources and Constraints* (New York: Sage, 1991).

    3. U.S. Bureau of Census (Washington, D.C.: U.S. Government Printing Office, 1990).

    4. Arber and Ginn, *Gender and Later Life*, 128.

5. Arber and Ginn, *Gender and Later Life*, 145.

6. Arber and Ginn, *Gender and Later Life*, 139.

7. B. Collopy, N. Dubler, et al., "The Ethics of Home Care: Autonomy and Accommodation," *Hastings Center Report* 20, no. 2 (March–April 1990 Special Supplement): 9.

8. See Joseph Raz, *The Morality of Freedom* (Oxford: Clarendon Press, 1986).

9. Nel Noddings, *Caring: A Feminist Approach to Ethics and Moral Education.* (Berkeley: University of California Press, 1984), 2.

10. Noddings, *Caring*, 14.

11. L. A. Blum. "Vocation, Friendship and Community: Limitations of the Personal-Impersonal Framework," in *Moral Perception and Particularity* (Cambridge: Cambridge University Press, 1994), 98–123.

12. J. C. Tronto, *Moral Boundaries: A Political Argument for an Ethic of Care* (New York: Routledge, 1993).

13. B. Fisher and J. Tronto, "Toward a Feminist Theory of Caring," in *Circles of Care: Work and Identity in Women's Lives*, ed. E. K. Abel and M. K. Nelson (Albany: SUNY Press, 1990), 42.

14. Blum, "Vocation, Friendship and Community," 109.

15. Blum, "Vocation, Friendship and Community," 110.

16. P. Bowden, *Caring: Gender-Sensitive Ethics* (London: Routledge, 1997), 61.

17. Bowden, *Caring*, 64.

18. *Place* denotes "an organized world of meaning." Places in which we have lived for a long time become filled with meaning; similarly, personal objects, carried from location to location, turn abstract space into *place*. Yi-Fu Tuan, *Space and Place: The Perspective of Experience* (Minneapolis: University of Minnesota Press, 1997), 179.

19. Betty Friedan, *The Fountain of Age* (New York: Simon & Schuster, 1993).

20. Charles Lidz, Lynn Fischer, and Robert Arnold, *The Erosion of Autonomy in Long Term Care* (New York: Oxford University Press, 1992), quoted in L. Polivka, "Autonomy and Dependency in an Ethics of Care for the Frail Elderly" (Tampa: Florida Policy Exchange Center on Aging, University of South Florida, 1997).

21. G. Agich, *Autonomy and Long-Term Care* (New York: Oxford University Press, 1993).

22. Lidz, Fischer, and Arnold, *The Erosion of Autonomy in Long Term Care.*

23. This bill would amend Title XIX of the Social Security Act-Medicaid to create a new option called "Qualified Community-Based Attendant Services." Anyone eligible for a nursing facility or intermediate care facility would be allowed to stay in their own home (or move out of congregate housing) and receive attendant care to assist in activities of daily living (bathing, dressing, toileting, and so forth).

24. Collopy, Dubler, et al. "The Ethics of Home Care."

25. Barbara Myerhoff, *Number Our Days* (New York: Simon & Schuster, 1978).

26. Natalie Rosel, "Growing Old Together: Communality in a Sarasota Neighborhood," in *What Does It Mean to Grow Old: Reflections from the Humanities,*

ed. Thomas R. Cole and Sally A. Gadow (Durham: Duke University Press, 1986), 231.

27. Blum, quoted in Bowden, *Caring*, 82.

28. M. Friedman, "The Social Self and the Partiality Debates," in *Feminist Ethics*, ed. C. Card (Lawrence: University of Kansas Press, 1991), 164.

29. Paula B. Doress-Worters and Diana Laskin Siegal, *The New Ourselves Growing Older* (New York: Touchstone, 1994), 166.

30. Doress-Worters and Siegal, *The New Ourselves Growing Older*, 167.

31. L. Polivka, "Autonomy and Dependency in an Ethics of Care for the Frail Elderly," v.

32. Karol Edward Soltan, "Institution Building and Human Nature," in *The Constitution of Good Societies*, ed. Karol Edward Soltan and Stephen L. Elkin (University Park: Pennsylvania State University Press, 1996), 91.

· 15 ·

Age-Segregated Housing As a Moral Problem: An Exercise in Rethinking Ethics

Joan C. Tronto

> After all that has been said of the levity and inconstancy of human nature, it appears evidently from experience that a man is of all sorts of luggage the most difficult to be transported.—Adam Smith, *The Wealth of Nations* (1981 [1776], 92–93)

$\mathscr{P}$erhaps nothing shapes the quality of our daily lives so much as the place that we call home. Usually we think of "home" as a matter of taste that reflects nothing more than each person's highly personal choice. Nevertheless, if we think of ethics as the study of how to live a good life, then where we call "home" is not simply a matter of taste but is also a question of great ethical significance. Ethics concerns not only the avoidance of wrongdoing to others, but reflection upon and action toward affecting the conditions that make a good life possible. From such a broader understanding of ethics, then, we need to consider housing in order to think about the ethical lives of older women. This concern is relevant in a discussion of women and aging on the first level because where older women live—in a home that they find pleasing, in a nursing home, in an unsafe neighborhood, near to their family, and so on—will vitally affect how older women can live their lives. Beyond this obvious aspect of this question, though, I will argue that to conceive of the place called "home" in ethical terms requires that we think more collectively about ethics. After all, our "home" is not just about our own individual dwelling, but also about our connections to people with whom we may have daily neighborly contact, even though they are part of our "home" only incidentally. If this is true, then circumstances beyond our control or choice can profoundly affect how we live our lives. In this chapter, I will look closely at one governmental policy to try to show these larger connections. In the end, I will argue that public policies that create age-segregated housing are a concern not only for those who live in such housing, but for everyone. Everyone's life, I will argue, is diminished by living in age-segregated circumstances. I want to suggest, then, that the question of where elderly women might find a place to live is not only about the lives of elderly women, but about everyone's lives.

By law, the United States forbids housing agents from discriminating against families with children or anyone else because of their age. Nevertheless, there is a large exception to this application of the principle of nondiscrimination. Housing for "elders only" was excluded from the original Fair Housing Act, and the exception was broadened by the Housing for Older Persons Act of 1995. Initially, the exception was granted to housing that had "significant facilities and services to meet the physical or social needs of older persons." It was based on the fact that if elders lived in special housing that required special facilities, such as elevators, ramps, medical care locations, and so forth, such housing should be exempted. In 1995, the Department of Housing and Urban Development, supported by the lobbies of real estate agents and the elderly, argued that such a requirement discriminated against the poorer elderly who could not necessarily afford such amenities. As a result, any housing group that states it is "elderly only housing" and has at least one resident age 55 or older in 80 percent of its units is exempted from the Fair Housing Act (Lehman 1996, Albro 1996, Minicucci 1995).

Age-segregated housing violates our national value against all forms of invidious discrimination; that is why Congress passed the Fair Housing Act. As I have searched the scholarly literature for a discussion of the moral justification for this departure, I have found only silence: apparently nothing has been written about this question. Whenever we are willing to make an exception without at least thinking about why we are so willing, such a gap in our moral thinking is probably worth closer inspection. As I began to wonder about this situation, it opened up a much broader question about how we engage in ethical thinking.

In this chapter I will work through what might serve as a traditional justification for age-segregated housing for the elderly. Then I will propose an alternative framework for thinking about moral questions: the feminist care ethics framework. Because care ethics requires a richer account of the moral situation that we face and recognizes the political context as part of the ethical situation, it allows us to explore a thicker version of any ethical situation. When we finish with our investigation of age-segregated housing as a moral problem, then, we will have before us a much richer appreciation of this issue and of how to think about moral problems that confront women and men as they age.

I. Is There Any Justification for Age-Segregated Housing?

Most ethical theorizing involves working out the basic inner logic of or justification for moral rules, not thinking through some exceptional cases. This tendency is unfortunate, for the investigations of exceptions might serve as a source for challenging the ways that we construct moral rules in the first place. In this case, we need to determine that, if age segregation in housing is wrong, then on what grounds can this exception be justified? Why is it acceptable to exempt elderly housing from compliance with the law?

Most of the study of age discrimination in the United States has been about discrimination based on mandatory retirement ages. But in forcing elderly people to retire even if they do not wish to stop working, government requires older people to do something that they do not want to do. Allowing elderly people to live in "elders-only" communities permits them to do something that they do want to do.

Nevertheless, other groups of people are not permitted to discriminate in this way. People who do not wish to live near children, and people who do not wish to live near people of different racial, ethnic, or religious affiliations, are not permitted to create adult-only, or race-, ethnicity-, or faith-based segregated housing. Is there justification, then, for allowing older people to make this choice?

Several justifications come quickly to mind. The first is that although only elderly people benefit from this exception, since everyone has the opportunity later in life to become elderly, in fact the exception does not discriminate against anyone, just against people who are now in a particular, nonelderly stage of their lives. But since they, too, will someday be elderly, the exception is justifiable. Such an argument sounds familiar. It might also serve, for example, to keep young people from voting. But it opens the question of whether elderly people have some special reason for the exemption. Children are usually excluded from voting because they are too young and their rationality and knowledge may be underdeveloped. But are older people in a similar situation, and what is it? If this logic alone were sufficient to justify such discrimination, then all forms of age discrimination might become reasonable. On its face, such an idea is absurd. Simply because everyone will pass through some particular age does not justify imposing extra burdens or providing extra advantages to them: it interferes too much with how we think people live their lives. So too, saying that it does not matter if elderly housing is discriminatory must rest upon some other assumptions that we have yet to uncover. If discrimination is wrong, then it is not a very convincing moral justification to say that everyone will be able to perform this wrong at some point in their lives.

A similar argument might be that elderly people have a right to discriminate against younger people in housing because they have earned this right. Just as elderly people receive Social Security payments for their contribution to the labor market, so too should they receive a benefit from their participation in the life of the nation and be able to ignore the age discrimination housing laws. Our familiar use of the locution "senior citizen" usefully conveys the notion that seniors have been contributing citizens and should receive some benefits from these contributions. Nevertheless, this argument presumes that we should give people the right to do wrongs. Such a justification is too broad: this logic would also justify providing the elderly with the right to discriminate against others on the basis of race, religion, or ethnicity. Yet we do not permit those forms of discrimination. Nor would we want to extend the notion that people who have made special contributions should be able to violate the rights of others: many kinds of mischief would arise from such a general principle. So we cannot argue that the elderly have "earned" the right to discriminate.

The most convincing arguments that are given for positions such as this exception follow an argument advanced by the philosopher Robert Goodin. Goodin advocates exceptional treatment to some on the grounds that it is morally necessary to "protect the vulnerable." Although our philosophical premises suggest that we should not interfere with other people's liberty, when some populations are particularly vulnerable, we may need to make exceptions to our general principles. Goodin describes the elderly as "vulnerable" and worthy of special protection in this way. Following the logic of Goodin's account, because elderly people are more susceptible to having their lives disrupted by younger people, because their senses of personal safety are diminished by being in the presence of young people who may be intentionally or unintentionally unaware of their particular vulnerabilities, there is a sufficient need for elderly people to receive an exception from the policies of nondiscrimination.

This account of the matter presumes that elderly people have different needs and interests than other people. Following Goodin's argument, we might ask, what vulnerabilities of the elderly require their protection from age discrimination laws? The first version of the law required that there be special facilities for the elderly, such as those requiring the presence of medical personnel, which would be important to elderly people and more difficult to provide if they were not living in one location. But the 1995 amendments no longer require any special facilities for the elderly. At the time, proponents of the change made an argument that raised a point about economic equity: those who can afford to live in elders–only communities, who can afford special medical and other facilities, should not receive a benefit that is not extended to all elderly people. They argued that relatively less affluent elderly people should have the same chance to choose to live among elderly people as more affluent ones (Williams 1995). The law now simply requires that a living community enforce its rules and make certain that a sufficient proportion of elderly people live in the elders–only housing. If the elderly want to live among themselves, then such discrimination is permissible.

Many elderly people do live in such housing situations. Further, many elderly women who initially move into such housing arrangements when they are married are left alone in these settings when their husbands pass away. If these choices were not only or primarily the wife's choice in the beginning, by the time she is widowed she is probably left with the situation, regardless of her own choice.

The most usual reason given for such housing is the need for safety. Elderly people are more likely to be physically frail than are other people. As a result, the threats to physical safety that arise from children and others are likely to be greater among the frail elderly (Williams 1995).

Of course, not all elderly are frail. Thus, in order for Goodin's argument to stand as a justification of protecting the vulnerable, it requires a second element: choice. Given that some elderly are vulnerable, if the elderly choose to live in age-segregated housing because of their own senses of vulnerability or other need, then they should be given permission to violate the laws against discrimination.

In fact, many elderly people do choose to live in these situations. Those who do report that they enjoy these living arrangements. Not only is it safer, but what is perhaps more important, when asked about it, elderly people find it very comforting to live with people who share their age-related problems and perspectives. They find that they have much in common with people who have gone through common life experiences. The process of aging in our culture is attached to such changes as the loss of one's life work, the change in family structure, physical decline, changes in the ability to drive, and so forth. To be among others who understand one's life situation is a great comfort (Vesperi 1985).

Nevertheless, the desire of, for example, Protestant white people to share their common life with others is not usually taken as a justification for discrimination based on race and religion. Is there something particular about saying "old people will want to be with other old people" that makes such a form of discrimination automatically acceptable?

One possible account of this situation is that discrimination based on age is somehow not really discrimination because it is based on something "natural." (Of course, racial segregationists also think racial discrimination rests upon something "natural.") We assume the "naturalized" nature of discrimination based on age. Thus, all elderly people can be assumed to share interests and needs, and therefore have special claims to exemptions from discrimination laws.

Goodin's argument is inaccurate when applied to all of the elderly (and it is an important question whether such generalizations should ever suffice for ethical and moral judgments). Beyond that, the argument about protecting the vulnerable contains another serious flaw. It looks at the issue only from the perspective of the elderly themselves. Usually when we think in terms of segregation, we think also of the damage to those who are excluded. The parallel logic would require that we think of the damage done to everyone who is excluded from living in the company of the elderly. We will return to this concern in the conclusion: I will suggest that everyone's life is diminished by living in age-segregated circumstances.

For now, though, we have explored a number of possible justifications to allow elders-only housing to discriminate against people of other ages. We have noted that despite federal laws that permit such discrimination, from the standpoint of the moral rule not to discriminate, the grounds for this exception have never been carefully evaluated and do not seem to rest on any principled position that is defensible. The strongest justification is the Goodin-like argument that it is all right to make exceptions to "protect the vulnerable." But we noted that such an argument rests upon many questionable assumptions. First, it takes for granted the idea that elderly people have "chosen" to live in these communities, but such an account of choice rests upon many other factors that remain obscure because we do not think about how our choices have been shaped fundamentally by a variety of social and political concerns. Second, it presumes that elderly people share a set of common needs that can be simply identified and described by their status as "vulnerable" elderly. Third, it presumes that the elderly, and not everyone else, are the people who are affected by such discrimination.

The question of whether a particular policy is "ethical" can be answered in either a straightforward and narrow way by focusing on the various rights and opportunities that present themselves, or we can change the framework for the moral discussion. In this chapter, I wish to change the framework.

II. An Alternative Framework: The Care Ethic and the Problem of Privileged Irresponsibility

The alternative framework that I will offer here is the framework devised in the feminist ethics of care (Tronto 1993 and 1996, Sevenhuijsen 1998).

Defining Care

The activities that constitute care are crucial for human life. Care can broadly be defined as "a species activity that includes everything that we do to maintain, continue, and repair our 'world' so that we can live in it as well as possible. That world includes our bodies, our selves, and our environment, all of which we seek to interweave in a complex, life-sustaining web" (Fisher and Tronto 1990, 40).

In addition to defining care in broad terms, as a species activity, Berenice Fisher and I also delineated four component phases in the process of caring that provide us with the basis for an analysis of care. There are four component phases: caring about, that is, becoming aware of and paying attention to the need for caring; caring for, that is, assuming responsibility for some caring; care giving, that is, the actual material meeting of the caring need; and care receiving, that is, the reciprocal response of the thing, the person, the group, and so on, that received the caregiving. We argued that any full account of care includes all four of these phases, and that given the complexity of these different phases, they will frequently become fragmented and come into conflict with each other. Indeed, conflict seems inherent in care: because there are more needs for care than can ever be met, because caregivers have needs at the same time that they give care to others, there is inevitably conflict within care. By allowing that care is a complex process with many components, we did not romanticize the care process; care is more likely to be filled with inner contradictions, conflict, and frustration than it is to resemble the idealized interactions of romanticized caring. This realistic and practical concept of care allows us many possibilities in thinking through the relationship of moral and political life. In the first place, some moral virtues seem intrinsic to the process of care itself. Each of the four phases of care brings not only its own distinctive set of resource demands, skills, power relationships, and ideals, but each phase of the process also has a distinctive moral value.

1. Caring about requires the moral virtue of attentiveness. Attentiveness requires that we treat as moral questions such questions as: What care is necessary? Are there basic human needs? What types of care now exist; how adequate are they? Who gets to articulate the nature of needs, and to say which problems should be cared about and how?

2. Caring for, that is, assuming responsibility, obviously requires the moral element of responsibility. We must then ask such questions as: Who should be responsible for meeting the needs for care that exist? How can and should such responsibility be fixed? Why?

3. From the standpoint of caring, competence is a moral virtue associated with the phase of caregiving. Giving care well creates a moral requirement that those who give care do so with competence. These dimensions suggest that in order to understand the moral nature of caring, we need also to know: Who actually *are* the caregivers? How well can/do they do their work? What conflicts exist between them and care receivers? What resources do care givers need in order to care competently?

4. The final phase of care, care receiving, requires that those who receive care and those who are involved in giving care provide an evaluation and judgment about care. This requirement makes responsiveness a moral virtue, and demands that we think about these questions: How do care receivers respond to the care that they are given? How well does the care process, as it exists, meet their needs? If their needs conflict with another's, who resolves these conflicts?

In the second place, care as a moral concept complicates our view of the world. To look at the world in terms of this complex account of care changes our perceptions of what morality requires. The care ethic requires that we go beyond thinking of moral activity in terms of fulfilling specific obligations. From the standpoint of caring (all that we need to do to maintain the world so that we may live in it as well as possible), the range of concerns that are properly moral is very wide.

In the third place, care as a moral concern widens the questions we should consider because it raises the questions about the context within which care will occur. Often our decision about the proper level of analysis for thinking through a moral question determines our judgment. For example, imagine a situation in which caregivers appear uncaring. On a simple analysis, they may seem to have failed in their moral task of providing care competently. Imagine, though, that they are operating with such a shortage of resources that they find it more caring to be brusque than to mislead potential care receivers about the likely outcome of this caring practice. In the broader context, these uncaring workers locate the problem of this care situation at a higher social level. Often, in order to conceive of care as a whole process, many more actors, levels of society, constraints, and opportunities are involved than at first seems the case. Such broader moral stories, in which all of the dimensions of care are examined and their interaction is explored, are thus crucial to using the care ethic appropriately.

This broad framework for the morality of care requires that we think about the alternative justifications for different types of care. Kari Waerness (1990) distinguishes between "personal service," which is care that one could do for oneself but has someone else do (such as hiring someone to clean the house), and necessary care, which is care that one cannot do for oneself (such as the care given by a doctor). In making judgments about how much and what kinds of care to provide, such distinctions are useful.

This broad framework for the morality of care also requires that we think about the ways in which care is unequally distributed in our society. For example, often the market distributes personal service; it may also distribute necessary care. The market provides greater opportunity to those with greater economic resources. Further, in our society caring work is often distributed along gender lines. Caring work is also distributed along class and racial lines in our society, so that often the poorest, least well paid workers are doing caring work for others (Tronto 1993, Omolade 1996).

Care and Privileged Irresponsibility

If we adopt the moral framework of caring, then we will notice many more activities as part of our moral world. Further, care can make us aware of the many ways in which we *ignore* some of the moral requirements of both our daily lives and our lives as citizens. Noting differences in the types of care and in the allocations of the burdens of doing care work, we begin to notice an aspect of social life that has previously been obscured. Some people are required to pay a great deal of attention to the caring dimensions of their lives, while others take care for granted or assume it to be nonproblematic. Those who have bought or presumed themselves free from their caring roles have engaged in a process that I have called *privileged irresponsi-*

bility. Privileges of wealth or status have conferred upon them an opportunity to ignore their caring responsibilities.

Privileged irresponsibility emerges from this analysis as an important form of moral vice. Although it is most closely connected with a failure to carry out the moral task of assuming responsibility, it may also involve a violation of all of the moral elements of care: the harm of inattentiveness, irresponsibility, incompetence, and unresponsiveness. Privileged irresponsibility, I will argue, helps us to think differently about the question of age-segregated housing.

III. Privileged Irresponsibility and Age-Segregated Housing

The caring perspective makes this question more complex by adding new considerations to the question of age-segregated housing.

The Complexity of "Choosing" Housing

"Home" is obviously deeply intertwined with how well any of us are able to live. If we live in a home that is comfortable, where we feel safe and secure, we are better able to live well and to care for ourselves and others than when we live in circumstances that make us uncomfortable, unsafe, or insecure. The care ethic thus requires that we think of the question of where we live as implicated in people's caring lives.

From this perspective, the moral complexity of the issue of elders-only housing becomes more apparent. We need to think of the question of "choosing" to live in such housing in a more complex way.

As people age, most still feel most comfortable living in the homes in which they have lived. Surveys show that if they could, 84 percent of people would remain in their homes as they age. Yet economic need and frailties of old age often make this option less possible (Groves and Wilson, 1992).

Rather than thinking of decisions about housing choice from the standpoint of individuals who choose to live in one place or another, though, let us take another step urged by the care ethic and look more broadly at the context within which such caring decisions are made. Often when elderly people do decide to move to new housing, it is because they have encountered some difficulties in living in their former situation. Many older people move from northern states in the United States to the "Sunbelt" because they find it difficult to continue to negotiate living in harsh winter climates. Many others move because, though they own their houses, they find the expense of paying property tax prohibitive. They move to the Sunbelt in order to avoid such problems and to live well. For themselves, they have taken a caring step.

This analysis of the choice of elders-only housing, though, needs to be put into several broader contexts. In the first place, we need to recognize that there is a serious shortage of adequate low-income housing in the United States: the estimates of the number of people whose housing is inadequate because of the unavailability of affordable housing ranges as high as one-third of the nation (Einbinder 1995, Stone 1993). This lack creates great pressure for the small supplies of low-income housing opportunities that exist, and explains why there were many lawsuits brought by younger people to disqualify housing areas from this exemption under the first version of the original Fair Housing Act.

Indeed, when older people make a "choice" on the basis of "safety" to live among only other elderly people, they are also making that choice based partly on the economic realities of the way housing is provided in the United States. Housing for the poor is also segregated, and poor people are most likely to be the victims of crime. People at higher income levels who live in less densely populated housing, and who can afford private security means, are able to purchase greater levels of safety. Excluding younger people from an elders-only living situation provides safety that more affluent people might be able to purchase.

Another framework that greatly influences people's choices is the strong value in the United States to continue to live in "nuclear family" units. In the United States, there is a strong norm that people will marry and live with their spouses and children. When the children grow up, they will move into their own nuclear family, that is, a normal heterosexual household. This norm is strongest among white Americans; in African American and Latino households, there are many more occurrences of extended families living together. Among gay men and lesbians, who have not conformed to this norm, there are more cases of individuals living alone or in pairs or in communities (Groves and Wilson 1992, Speare and Avery 1992, Warnes 1993). This value constrains choice in two ways. In the first place, it discourages older men and women from contemplating other living arrangements. In the second place, there are not many houses, physically, that can easily accommodate other living arrangements.

Thus, while the "choice" to move or not should be left to elderly people who want to decide for themselves whether to move to elders-only communities, these choices are highly mediated by other social values and conditions. I submit that in allowing these other dimensions of these choices to remain invisible, we as a society are able to engage in a process of privileged irresponsibility. The inadequacy of public transportation, the lack of sufficient low-income housing, the unfairness of using property taxes to fund local government functions such as education, and continuing norms about the "proper" nature of families work to the disadvantage of many people, including older people who are less well off. The result is that we may stand back and say "It is their choice"—at the same time we are unwilling to recognize how society as a whole has constructed a limiting range of choices.

Determining "Needs" and Privileged Irresponsibility

Thus far we have applied the care ethic as if the relevant carers were elderly people themselves. A larger question also emerges, though, if we begin to think about the needs of the elderly in relation to the question of who is attentive to their needs.

In the first place, many elderly people have profound material needs. Although there are fewer elderly people who are poor now than before the creation of Social Security and Medicare, many elderly women still rely primarily on Social Security and are quite poor. Those without families and those with high medical expenses are more needy in physical terms. Class, race, and gender differences are not erased but continue to affect people as they become elderly.

In the second place, many elderly women must provide both necessary care and personal service for their spouses or aging parents. For most people, providing care becomes more difficult with the constraints of aging, yet if those in one's life require care, then women who have provided care throughout their lives will continue to provide it. Women may end up struggling to meet others' needs and ignoring their own needs. Further, there is no place for them to explore how their own needs are being ignored.

In the third place, older people are like all people in having a need for self-respect. The values of our society are not conducive to treating those who are older with respect. As a result, the elderly often must struggle to meet the needs that fulfill their sense of self-respect.

One such problem confronted by the elderly is what the anthropologists label "role loss" (Vesperi 1985).[1] Since industrialization, people are largely conceived of as workers. Once people become older and retire from the workforce, they are no longer "workers." Both men who were members of the workforce and women who were workers or were defined by their relationship to a working spouse suffer role loss. One role that is ostensibly important for women in our society is the role of "mother," but here, too, our conception of the nuclear family and the passage of individuals into maturity means that mothers lose their role when their children are grown. Such role loss means that the elderly find they have much to share with other elderly people, and find it difficult to communicate with younger people. This problem becomes even more serious when elderly people move away from the communities where they have lived.

Another way in which the elderly are not accorded proper respect in our society is that they are not seen as sources of wisdom or knowledge. Our society thrives on "information," but knowledge conceived as accumulating greater amounts of "useful information" is very different from knowledge that comes from long practical experience or from serious reflection on the human condition. People such as Ivan Illich[2] have written about the denatured kind of knowledge that results from the schooling practiced in industrial societies. The substitute of information for knowledge affects everyone, but it has a particular effect on the elderly's senses of importance. Because their practical experience counts for nothing, the lives of older people are less valuable.

All of these various needs—for material resources, caring, and continuing senses of involvement and respect—can be met. As a society, though, we have mainly presumed that once money has been provided through Social Security payments and Medicare, we are absolved of any continued responsibility. The cultural value that the elderly should remain independent reinforces the norm of living in single-family units, the belief that they should look after themselves, and the belief that their problems are their own and of no concern to the rest of us.

Our cultural inattentiveness to the needs of the elderly also begets a vicious circle. When those who are not elderly pay no attention to them, the elderly have more incentives to avoid contact with younger people. Usually, people only know the elderly to whom they are related. As Frida Kerner Furman wrote, "Few of us get to interact in a meaningful way with older people who are unrelated to us . . ." (1997, 2). As older people become more and more isolated, then, they are less likely to be able to engage in a broader public discussion about their needs and about the needs that shape their choices. Under such a circumstance, it becomes even more reasonable for the elderly to choose to live in elders-only housing.

We began with the question of whether it is permissible to allow elderly people to discriminate against others and to live in elders-only housing. By now, it becomes clear that this question is too simple. Although such a policy cannot be justified using the usual moral arguments, something more disturbing actually underpins what is wrong with such housing arrangements. The problem of elders-only housing is that it provides another mechanism by which the needs of the elderly are obscured. By allowing elderly people to place themselves in isolated communities, everyone else is able to presume that they have made a good choice for themselves. It promotes the exercise of privileged irresponsibility.

IV. Toward a Better Future

In a society organized around economic productivity and "usefulness," the elderly represent a challenge to the "model of man" that informs society. Many prescriptions for the lives of the elderly involve making them more productive in one way or another. The goal, however, should be to expand our vision of whose needs should be taken into account.

Whenever a choice seems to turn into a dilemma, we should step back and ask about the needs that are being considered and also ask which ones are being ignored. To ask people to choose between leaving their homes and lives behind and living in a community that has as one of its effects their continued isolation from the rest of society is surely a dilemma.

The solution is to provide many more varied types of housing for everyone, to challenge the notion that only independent living is "normal," and to be more attentive to the needs of those who are less physically able. Imagine living in communities that are integrated by age, race, economic level, and types of family structure. Although conflicts are inherent in life, surely in such a world we would be better able to care for one another. Such solutions will benefit not only the elderly, but everyone. After all, everyone's life is diminished by being unable to learn from the life experiences of many other people. "Interest in learning from all of the contacts of life is the essential moral interest" (Dewey 1929, 418).

Notes

I am especially grateful to Selma Sevenhuijsen and Anamarie Mol, who have discussed this point with me over the years. I also wish to thank Margaret Urban Walker and the other contributors to this volume for their comments and criticisms.

1. This notion of "role loss" is illuminating, but it is also problematic. For the most part, it is a deeply gendered concept, assuming the model for roles are those

of working for males and raising children for women (cf. Walker, ch. 6 in this volume). It portrays people's previous roles inaccurately, then, insofar as it ignores the fact that many women work outside of the home and that some women do not have children. ("Of women born prior to 1915, for example, approximately 20 percent are childless; of women born between 1916 and 1920, about 15 percent are childless, and of women born between 1921 and 1930, slightly more than 10 percent are childless. . . .") Robert Rubenstein, "Childlessness, Legacy and Generativity," *Generations* 20, 3 (September 1996): 58.

More seriously, though, the notion of role loss ignores the fact that caring is the unexamined aspect of life, especially important for women, throughout life. After retirement, women still bear disproportionately the tasks of caring for themselves and others. Patterns of women doing the caring work persist into retirement, with women doing more housework, making new friends, and so forth. Forty-two percent of elderly women lived alone, according to the Census Bureau in 1992, and were thus more responsible for self-care. See Leonard Kaye, *Self-Help Support Groups for Older Women: Rebuilding Elder Networks Through Personal Empowerment* (Washington, D.C.: Taylor and Francis, 1997), ch. 1.

2. "School programs hunger for progressive intake of instruction, but even if the hunger leads to steady absorption, it never yields the joy of knowing something to one's satisfaction. Each subject comes packaged with the instruction to go on consuming one 'offering' after another. . . .

"But growth conceived as open-ended consumption—eternal progress—can never lead to maturity. Commitment to unlimited quantitative increase vitiates the possibility of organic development." Ivan Illich, *Deschooling Society* (New York: Harper and Row, 1971), 42–43.

References

Albro, Walt. "Danger Zone: 55 and Over," *Today's Realtor* 29, no. 4 (April 1996): 26.

Dewey, John. *Democracy and Education*. New York: Macmillan, 1929.

Einbinder, Susan D. "Housing Affordability for Families With Children," *Journal of Interdisciplinary Studies* 7, nos. 1–2 (1995): 83–100.

Fisher, Berenice, and Joan Tronto. "Towards a Feminist Theory of Care," in *Circles of Care*, ed. M. Nelson and E. Abel. Albany: State University of New York Press, 1990, 36–54.

Furman, Frida Kerner. *Facing the Mirror: Older Women and Beauty Shop Culture*. New York: Routledge, 1997.

Goodin, Robert. *Protecting the Vulnerable: A Reanalysis of Our Social Responsibilities*. Chicago: University of Chicago Press, 1985.

Groves, Mark Andrew, and Vicki F. Wilson. "To Move or Not to Move?

Factors Influencing the Housing Choice of Elderly Persons," *Journal of Housing for the Elderly* 10, nos. 1–2 (1992): 33–47.

Gullette, Margaret Morganroth. *Declining to Decline: Cultural Combat and the Politics of the Midlife.* Charlottesville: University Press of Virginia, 1997.

Illich, Ivan. *Deschooling Society.* New York: Harper and Row, 1971.

Kaye, Lenard W. *Self-Help Support Groups for Older Women: Rebuilding Elder Networks Through Personal Empowerment.* Washington, D.C.: Taylor and Francis, 1997.

Lehman, H. Jane. "As Baby Boomers Age, How—and Where—Will They Live?" *Newsday* (April 28, 1990): 5.

———. "Senior Complexes Freer to Exclude Children; New Law Widens Fair Housing Exemption," *Washington Post* (January 6, 1996): E6.

Minicucci, Elena R. "Housing for Older Persons Exemption in the Fair Housing Amendments Act of 1988: Can Mr. Wilson Really Stop Dennis the Menace from Moving Next Door?" *Nova Law Review* 17 (1995): 761–91.

Omolade, Barbara. *The Rising Song of African American Women.* New York: Routledge, 1996.

Rubinstein, Robert L. "Childlessness, Legacy and Generativity." *Generations* 20, no. 3 (September 1996): 58–60.

Sevenhuijsen, Selma. *Citizenship and the Ethics of Care: Feminist Considerations on Justice, Morality and Politics.* London: Routledge, 1998.

Smith, Adam. *An Inquiry into the Nature and Causes of the Wealth of Nations.* Indianapolis: Liberty Press, 1981 [1776].

Speare, Jr., A., and R. Avery. "Changes in Parent-Child Coresidence in Later Life." Washington, D.C.: U. S. Department of Commerce, Bureau of the Census, Survey of Income and Program Participation No. 162, 1992.

Stone, Michael E. *Shelter Poverty: New Ideas on Housing Affordability.* Philadelphia: Temple University Press, 1993.

Tronto, Joan C. *Moral Boundaries: A Political Argument for an Ethic of Care.* New York: Routledge 1993.

———. "Care As a Political Concept," in *Revisioning the Political: Feminist Reconstructions of Traditional Concepts in Western Political Theory,* ed. Nancy Hirschmann and Christine Di Stefano. Boulder: Westview, 1996, 139–56.

Vesperi, Maria. *City of Green Benches: Growing Old in a New Downtown.* Ithaca: Cornell University Press, 1985.

Walker, Margaret Urban. *Moral Understandings: A Feminist Study in Ethics.* New York: Routledge, 1998.

Waerness, Kari. "Informal and Formal Care in Old Age: What Is Wrong with the New Ideology in Scandinavia Today?" in *Gender and Caring: Work and Welfare in Britain and Scandinavia*, ed. C. Ungerson. London: Harvester, Wheatsheaf, 1990, 110–32.

Warnes, Anthony M. "Residential Mobility and Housing Strategies in Later Life," *Ageing and Society* 13 (1993): 97–105.

Williams, Bill. "Testimony of Bill Williams, President of the Federation of Mobile Home Owners of Florida, Inc." Senate Judiciary Committee, August 1, 1995, Federal Document Clearing House.

Index

About the Contributors

Sandra Lee Bartky, professor of philosophy and women's studies at the University of Illinois, Chicago, teaches feminist theory, phenomenology, poststructuralism, and critical theory. She is author of *Femininity and Domination: Essays in the Phenomenology of Oppression.* She is also a founder of *Hypatia: A Journal of Feminist Philosophy* and of the Society for Women in Philosophy, now an international network with chapters in seven countries.

Daniel Callahan, a philosopher by training, is a co-founder of the Hastings Center, Garrison, New York, and now its director of international programs. He is author of *False Hope: Why America's Quest for Perfect Health Is a Recipe for Failure* and *Setting Limits: Medical Goals in an Aging Society.*

Joan C. Callahan is professor of philosophy and director of the women's studies program at the University of Kentucky, Lexington. She has published numerous articles in books, journals, and encyclopedias, and several books, including *Reproduction, Ethics, and the Law: Feminist Perspectives; Menopause: A Midlife Passage*; and *Ethical Issues in Professional Life.* She is co-author of *Preventing Birth: Contemporary Methods and Related Moral Controversies.*

Peggy DesAutels is director of the medical ethics program and assistant professor of philosophy at the Ethics Center, University of South Florida, St. Petersburg. She has published articles on religion and medical ethics, moral perception, and cognitive science. She is lead author of *Praying for a Cure: When Medical and Religious Practices Conflict.*

Robin N. Fiore is assistant professor of philosophy at Florida Atlantic University, Boca Raton. She currently teaches bioethics, feminist ethics, and environmental ethics. Her principal research interests are managed health care, privacy, and women and aging.

Frida Kerner Furman is associate professor of religious studies at DePaul University, Chicago. She is author of *Beyond Yiddishkeit: The Struggle for Jewish Identity at a Reform Synagogue* and *Facing the Mirror: Older Women and Beauty Shop Culture*, which received the 1997 Elli Kongas-Maranda Prize from the American Folklore Society/Women's Section.

Martha Holstein is a research scholar in medical, social, and feminist ethics at the Park Ridge Center for the Study of Health, Faith, and Ethics in Chicago, where she directs the program in aging. She is author of numerous articles and book chapters, co-editor of *A Good Old Age? The Paradox of Setting Limits*, and editor of special journal issues on ethical issues in aging, dementia, and home care.

Diana Tietjens Meyers is professor of philosophy at the University of Connecticut, Storrs. She is author of *Inalienable Rights: A Defense; Self, Society, and Personal Choice*; and *Subjection and Subjectivity*. Editor of *Feminists Rethink the Self* and *Feminist Social Thought: A Reader*, she has also co-edited *Women and Moral Theory* and *Kindred Matters: Rethinking the Philosophy of the Family*.

Hilde Lindemann Nelson is director of the Center for Applied and Professional Ethics at the University of Tennessee, Knoxville. She is co-author of *The Patient in the Family* and *Alzheimer's: Answers to Hard Questions for Families*, co-editor of *Meaning and Medicine: A Reader in the Philosophy of Health Care*, and author of many articles on bioethics and feminist philosophy. She is editor of *Feminism and Families* and *Stories and Their Limits: Narrative Approaches to Bioethics*.

James Lindemann Nelson is professor of philosophy at the University of Tennessee, Knoxville. He has published widely in bioethics and moral theory, and on feminist themes, in journals such as *Hypatia, Theoretical Medicine, The Hastings Center Report*, and *The Kennedy Institute of Ethics Journal*. He is co-author of *The Patient in the Family* and *Alzheimer's: Answers to Hard Questions for Families*, and co-editor of *Meaning and Medicine: A Reader in the Philosophy of Health Care*.

Sara Ruddick teaches philosophy and literature at the New School for Social Research in New York. She is author of *Maternal Thinking: Toward a Politics of Peace* and co-editor of *Mother Troubles: Rethinking Maternal Dilemmas*.

Anita Silvers, professor of philosophy at San Francisco State University, is co-author of *Disability, Difference, Discrimination: Perspectives on Justice in Bioethics and Public Policy* and *Puzzles about Art*. She has co-edited three volumes and authored more than fifty essays about ethics and bioethics, aesthetics, feminism, disability studies, social philosophy, law, and public policy. She was the first recipient, in 1989, of the California Faculty Association's Equal Rights Award.

Joan C. Tronto is professor of political science at Hunter College and the Graduate School, City University of New York. A specialist in political theory and women in American politics, she is author of *Moral Boundaries: A Political Argument for an Ethic of Care* and co-editor of *Women Transforming Politics: An Alternative Reader*.

Margaret Urban Walker is professor of philosophy at Fordham University in New York. She has been Frances Elvidge Fellow and Visiting Senior Scholar at the Ethics Center of the University of South Florida, St. Petersburg. She is author of *Moral Understandings: A Feminist Study in Ethics* and many articles on moral agency, judgment, and responsibility.

Susan Wendell is professor of women's studies at Simon Fraser University, British Columbia. She is author of *The Rejected Body: Feminist Philosophical Reflections on Disability* and of articles on feminist ethics and politics.

DATE DUE

MAR 1 4 2000			
APR 1 0 2000			
12/1/00			
MAR 2 4 2003			
APR 2 2 2003			